The Question
of
Pornography

The Question
of
Pornography

RESEARCH FINDINGS AND POLICY IMPLICATIONS

Edward Donnerstein
Daniel Linz
Steven Penrod

THE FREE PRESS
A Division of Macmillan, Inc.
NEW YORK

Collier Macmillan Publishers
LONDON

Copyright © 1987 by The Free Press
A Division of Macmillan, Inc.

The Free Press
A Division of Macmillan, Inc.
866 Third Avenue, New York, N.Y. 10022

Collier Macmillan Canada, Inc.

Printed in the United States of America

printing number
1 2 3 4 5 6 7 8 9 10

Library of Congress Cataloging-in-Publication Data

Donnerstein, Edward I.
  The question of pornography.

  Bibliography: p.
  1. Pornography — Social aspects — United States.
I. Linz, Daniel. II. Penrod, Steven. III. Title.
HQ471.D66 1987   363.4'7   86-33546
ISBN 0-02-907521-1

To Deborah with love and, of course, to Sarah and Sasha

—E.D.

To Madge and Bruce Lester, two people who had faith in me long before I deserved it

—D.L.

To Joan and Rachel

—S.P.

Contents

Preface

Americans are troubled by pornography. A poll taken for *Time* magazine (Pornography: A Poll, *Time Magazine*, July 21, 1986, p. 22) by Yankelovich, Clancy, and Schulman has found that nearly two-thirds of the respondents are "very" or "fairly concerned" about the pervasiveness of pornography in the United States. Sixty-five percent of the Americans questioned in this poll believe that pornography leads people to be more sexually promiscuous, 61 percent believe that it encourages people to consider women as sex objects, and 57 percent believe that exposure to porn will lead to a breakdown of social morals. Fifty-six percent believe that pornography leads people to commit rape, and 54 percent believe that pornography leads to other forms of sexual violence. When asked whether the selling of magazines with nude pictures in local stores should be outlawed, 67 percent of the women and 49 percent of the men replied Yes.

It is perhaps ironic, but we did not write this book because of our concern about the prevalence of sexually explicit materials in American society. Rather, we were concerned that so much attention was being paid to the possibly damaging consequences of exposure to pornography that more pervasive and more troubling combinations of sex and aggression in the media were being ignored. We contend that the violence against women in some types of R-rated films shown in neighborhood theaters and on cable TV far exceeds that portrayed in even the most graphic pornography.

This book is designed to give the reader the most up-to-date summary of the scientific research on the effects of exposure to sexually explicit images on antisocial attitudes and behaviors.

In Chapter 1 we develop a typology of the stimulus materials used by social scientists interested in the effects of pornography. We also critically examine the limits of social science research, particularly laboratory research on pornography (a methodology we have often embraced): What can we conclude from experiments, and what cannot be safely concluded about the effects of pornography studied from this perspective? We also cite research that may be helpful in informing us as to when media effects will most likely be translated into behavior.

In Chapter 2 research conducted by the 1970 Obscenity and Pornography Commission is reviewed. In the chapter we first ask: What did the commission know about pornography research conducted prior to 1970? We then summarize the research conducted by the commission itself to answer the following questions: Did the American public see pornography as a serious problem? What were the effects of exposure to pornographic materials in the late 1960s? Did exposure to these sexually explicit materials affect attitudes and perceptions about women or sexual relationships? Did exposure to pornography increase aggressive behavior or influence crime and delinquency rates? How were the findings of the commission received by scientists and lay persons? We have included an annotated bibliography of the individual studies conducted by the commission, in an appendix at the end of the book.

In Chapter 3 we turn our attention to more recent laboratory studies of effects of nonviolent pornography on same-sex aggression. After a brief introduction to the way a typical aggression experiment is conducted (Who participates in these studies? What do they think is the study's purpose? How and when are subjects exposed to pornography? What do researchers mean by "aggressive behavior"?), we explore research studies that have examined male-to-male aggression following exposure to pornography. We are interested in finding out when aggression will increase and when it will decrease. Perhaps more important, we also examine research involving nonviolent pornography and men's aggression against women. Here the laboratory research is replete with interesting failures to increase male subjects' aggression against women following exposure to nonviolent materials. Our interpretation of the outcomes of studies in this area is that only when we create labora-

tory conditions quite favorable to the expression of antisocial behavior do we observe an increase in male-to-female aggression. We
then examine research attempting to link pornography and violence against women outside the laboratory: Did changes in laws
regulating pornography increase or decrease crime rates in Denmark? How can we explain the substantial positive correlation reported recently between rapes known to and recorded by the police
and pornographic magazine sales here in the United States?

Chapter 4 is devoted to the fledgling body of research on the
effects of pornography on antisocial attitudes. Of special concern
here is whether long-term exposure to nonviolent but "degrading"
forms of pornography results in less sensitivity toward female victims of sexual assault, less interest in stable intimate relationships,
and decrements in ratings of attractiveness for one's own partner.

Chapter 5 covers the research on violent pornography. We begin
by asking if there really has been an increase in violence in pornography over the last several years. We conclude that, regardless of
whether or not violent materials have increased relative to other
forms of pornography, there are good theoretical reasons to assume
that exposure to violent pornography will increase aggression
against women. Most important, the research has borne out these
assumptions. We describe research which suggests that not only is
violent pornography sexually arousing to men, but it also plays a
part in changing the way men think about women. We end the
chapter with a discussion of research which suggests that sexual
arousal to depictions of rape and antisocial attitudes about women
may be related to sexually violent behavior.

In Chapter 6 we pose the question: Is it the sexual explicitness or
the message about violence against women that drives the negative
changes in attitudes and behavior following exposure to violent
pornography? We suggest that, if males are responding primarily to
the violence in these depictions, there exists a whole genre of mass-
released R-rated films that depict violence against women in ways
that may harm young viewers. We describe recent research into the
effects of prolonged exposure to violence against women on both
male and female viewers. We conclude with a discussion of when
one might expect the desensitization to violence that results from
exposure to these films to lead to aggressive behavior.

Chapter 7 is devoted to a discussion of legal and other regulatory
reactions to contemporary pornography. Here we report on the
response to pornography of some feminists, in the form of advocat-

ing civil rights legislation, as well as discuss traditional obscenity law and the attempts of American film producers to regulate themselves in order to avoid state censorship. Chapter 8 continues this discussion by briefly outlining the changes recommended by the Attorney General's 1986 Commission on Pornography and posing the question: Do these recommendations follow from what we know about the results of research? We end with a discussion of research that suggests an alternative approach to the recommendations of the commission, one that emphasizes programs to educate consumers about the effects of sexual violence in the media.

Acknowledgments

FIRST we wish to acknowledge the National Science Foundation (Grant No. BNS-8216772) and the National Institute of Mental Health (Grant No. 1 R01 MH408894-01A1) for their support of our research over the last five years. We also wish to acknowledge the National Institute of Health for Biomedical Support Grants we have received through the University of Wisconsin, and the U.W. Graduate School for a special financial grant awarded to Edward Donnerstein while a member of the faculty there.

Thanks go to colleagues at Wisconsin including Leonard Berkowitz, John Delamater, Joanne Cantor, Joseph Cappella, Mary Ann Fitzpatrick, and Donald Smith for their constructive criticism of our research over the years. We wish to thank all those investigators who were kind enough to send us copies of their latest reports and articles so that we could be sure that this book represented the very latest word in research on pornography. Among these were Neil Malamuth, James Check, Dolf Zillmann, Joseph Scott, Larry Baron, Murray Straus, Gene Able, Donn Byrne, Kathleen Kelly, Rowell Huesmann, and Leonard Eron.

We are especially grateful for opportunities we have had, while researching the topic of pornography for this book, to meet and talk with law professor Catharine MacKinnon and author Andrea Dworkin. While their perspectives on the effects of exposure to pornography and ours have often differed, we nonetheless owe them a debt of gratitude for the insights they provided us, and we will always stand in admiration of their commitment to their cause.

We would also like to thank Carol Krafka, Margo Chapin, Rebecca Collins, Michael Bross, Robert Ogles, and Cynthia Hoffner, all of whom have helped us in thinking about and undertaking a good deal of the research reported on in this volume.

Free Press senior editor Laura Wolff and editing supervisor Edith Lewis deserve special thanks for their patience (in waiting for our ever promised but often late chapter submissions) and commendation for their skill as editors.

Finally, a very special and heartfelt thanks to James Coward, whose dedication to his word processor and genius for the organization of the day-to-day operations of our research make him every bit as responsible for the success of these products as any of us.

1 | Studying the Effects of Pornography: An Introduction

NEWSPAPER columnist James Kilpatrick once wrote, "Common sense is a better guide than laboratory experiments; and common sense tells us pornography is bound to contribute to sexual crime. . . . It seems ludicrous to argue 'bad' books do not promote bad behavior."[1]

While there are many who would agree with this statement, just as many would disagree. The issue of whether or not pornography has a negative impact on people's behavior and attitudes is not new. What is relatively new, however, is social science research directed at finding an answer to the question: What are the effects of exposure to pornography?

During the last 20 years this research has produced significant advances in our knowledge about the influences of pornography. In the following chapters we will examine what this research has shown about the effects of pornography and sexually violent material on laboratory aggression, attitudes toward women, sexual arousal, rape, and other behaviors.

Unfortunately, the term "pornography" has been loosely applied to many forms of explicit and nonexplicit depictions of human sexual activity. The kinds of depictions encompassed by the term vary widely and depend on the political and religious orientation of those who use it. For some, pornography is defined as depictions that elicit or are intended to elicit sexual arousal in the viewer.[2] Others[3] have suggested that depictions be labeled pornographic only if they include degrading and dehumanizing portrayals of women, not simply if they are sexually arousing.

1

Feminist Gloria Steinem,[4] for example, stresses the idea that the dehumanizing aspect of pornography distinguishes it from material that may be termed "erotic." According to Steinem, the message in pornography "is violence, dominance, and conquest. It is sex being used to reinforce some inequality, or to create one, or to tell us that pain and humiliation . . . are really the same as pleasure."[5] On the other hand, erotica portrays "mutually pleasurable, sexual expression between people who have enough power to be there by positive choice. It may or may not strike a sense-memory in the viewer, or be creative enough to make the unknown seem real; but it doesn't require us to identify with a conqueror or victim."[6]

This book is about the effects of sexually explicit and nonexplicit images of women on the attitudes and behaviors of people exposed to them. The primary purpose is to provide the reader with the most up-to-date understanding of the scientific research on the effects of these images. Many of the studies described involve the images that would be considered "pornographic." To this extent the book is about pornography and its effects on those exposed to it.

But the book is about exposure to other images of women as well. In much of the research described, experimenters have used materials that would not be considered pornographic by most people. When people think of pornography they usually think of explicit portrayals of human sexual activity in magazines and movies. Furthermore, they often assume that the central concern of researchers is with this sexual explicitness, and that this explicitness accounts for the outcomes of many experiments. However, our discussion of the research in the following chapters will emphasize that, for the most part (we will discuss the exceptions in detail), sexually explicit images, per se, do not in the short run facilitate aggressive behavior against women, change attitudes about rape, or influence other forms of antisocial behavior. Instead, the research indicates that it is the violent images fused with sexual images in some forms of pornography, or even the violent images alone, that account for many of the antisocial effects reported by social science researchers.

In Chapter 2 we will discuss the studies undertaken by the 1970 Presidential Commission on Obscenity and Pornography.[7] In Chapter 3 we describe the work undertaken by social psychologists following the commission's inquiries. This work concentrated primarily on the effects of nonviolent pornography either on same-sex aggression or on male aggression against women. In Chapter 4 we also examine the research on nonviolent pornography, but the outcome variable considered there is not aggression but attitudes about women, sexual partners, and sexual relationships rather than aggressive behavior. In Chapter 5 we explore the research on the effects of exposure to violent pornography; these effects include changes in attitudes, aggressive behavior, and sexual arousal. In Chapter 6 we investigate the question of whether the sexually explicit images or the depictions of violence against women account for the antisocial effects observed in experiments on violent pornography. We also consider research on the effects of prolonged exposure to depictions of violence against women that are not sexually explicit but are brutally violent. Chapters 7 and 8 we discuss a range of policy issues, including recent legislative attempts to define pornography as a violation of civil rights, the 1986 Attorney General's Commission on Pornography,[8] and the recommendation that intervention programs rather than legislative action be undertaken to ameliorate the effects of exposure to violence against women in the media.

As an aid in understanding the experimental research on pornography and sexual violence, we have grouped the variety of stimulus materials used by social psychologists in their research into six categories. The first two consist of nonviolent sexually explicit stimuli that are either high or low in their tendency to degrade women. The third and fourth categories include stimuli that portray the myth that women benefit from rape or desire it. The difference between the two categories is the level of sexual explicitness. The fifth and sixth categories include R-rataed films that are not sexually explicit but either juxtapose sex and violence or are portrayals of brutal rape.

1. *Nonviolent, low-degradation sexually explicit stimuli.* This material is most consistent with Steinem's definition of erotica (e.g., nonviolent, noncoercive, and nondegrading, but sexually explicit). These materials are usually X-rated, although in the past (early 1970s) many researchers employed X-rated materials that would carry an R rating by today's standards. These stimuli have been presented to research subjects in the form of depictions of mutually consenting sexual activity, pictures, verbal descriptions, and films.

2. *Nonviolent, high-degradation sexually explicit stimuli.* More recently, researchers have employed materials that, although not expressly violent, are, according to many, demeaning and degrading to women. These materials take two forms: feature-length, X-rated pornographic films; and shorter, less well-produced depictions. An

example of the former would be the popular X-rated film *Debbie Does Dallas*. Examples of the latter would include the 10–12 minute "stag" or "peep show" films once widely available in pornographic bookstores. What both kinds of material have in common is the debasing depiction of women as willing recipients of any male sexual urge (excluding rape) or as oversexed, highly promiscuous individuals with insatiable sexual urges.

3. *Violent pornography.* This material depicts sexual coercion in a sexually explicit context. Usually, a man uses force against a woman in order to obtain sexual gratification (e.g., the materials contain scenes of rape and other forms of violent sexual assault). A common feature of many of these depictions is the tendency to portray "positive victim outcomes." Rape and other forms of sexual assault are depicted as pleasurable, sexually arousing, and beneficial to the female victim. This theme contrasts with other forms of media violence (e.g., most TV violence) in which victims are usually not portrayed as enjoying their victimization. Researchers have presented violent pornographic depictions to subjects via film presentations, audiotapes, and written portrayals.

4. *Nonexplicit sexual aggression against women.* This category includes depictions of sexual violence against women that are similar to violent pornography but are less sexually explicit. While there may be a rape scene, it is often of the kind that would be permissible under television broadcast standards. While the sexual behavior in these materials is far less explicit than in the X-rated materials just described, the idea that women derive positive benefit from sexual abuse is nonetheless a recurring theme.

5. *Sexualized explicit violence against women.* The materials considered here are R-rated because of the lack of explicit portrayals of sex, but are typically much more graphically violent than X-rated aggressive pornography. These materials do not depict positive victim outcomes, and the violence is not sexual violence (rape) but contains images of torture, murder, and mutilation. The victims of this violence are usually women. Furthermore, the unique feature of these films is the sexual context in which the violence against women occurs. As film critic Janet Maslin notes:

The carnage is usually preceded by some sort of erotic prelude: footage of pretty young bodies in the shower, or teens changing into nighties for the slumber party, or anything that otherwise lulls the audience into a mildly sensual mood.[9]

6. *Negative-outcome rape depictions.* These materials depict

graphic and brutal rapes, but unlike most forms of violent pornography there is no indication that the victim enjoys being raped. The material may involve either explicit or nonexplicit depictions of sexual activity.

It is important to note that our typology includes materials that would not be considered obscene or pornographic in a legal sense. The six categories also do not *completely* classify the materials examined by researchers interested in the effects of pornography or violence against women into mutually exclusive categories. It is often difficult to fit specific stimuli into an appropriate category because of the vague descriptions given in research reports. The scheme does, however, allow for ready classification of the vast majority of stimulus materials.

Throughout this book we will be describing studies that have found that individuals exposed to certain types of materials respond with blunted sensitivity to violence against women, calloused attitudes about rape, and sexual arousal to rape depictions and laboratory simulations of aggression against women, among other antisocial effects. For the most part we will not be describing studies that have examined the relationship between exposure to pornography and sexual violence or rape. Not because we wish to ignore these types of inquiries, but because so few of them exist. Most of what we describe in this book are experimental studies in which investigators have compared the responses of individuals deliberately exposed to pornographic or sexually violent materials with the responses of other individuals either watching neutral fare or seeing no materials at all. To a lesser extent we will be describing field studies that have examined rates of sexual violence and rape (e.g., by examining the correlation between the availability of pornography and crime rates across states of societies). But these studies suffer from the fact that they are not experiments. Indeed, it would be highly unethical to design an experiment in which we knew the primary outcome might be higher levels of sexual violence inside or outside the laboratory.

The fact that the primary outcome variables in most of the research described in this book have either been changed attitudes or simulated aggression has made it difficult for those interested in formulating precise legal policies to arrive at definitions of harmful effects that capture what social scientists have demonstrated in their studies. In attempting to use social science evidence as the basis of legal policy, the formulators have butted up against several important criticisms of the procedures used by social scientists to investigate the connection between pornography and aggression.

To provide a more concrete illustration of the problems encountered when attempting to claim that certain forms of media result in significant societal or individual harms, we will describe two legal cases. One involved an attempt to link a sexually violent but nonexplicit media portrayal with the rape of a young girl, the other an attempt to link exposure to pornography with increases both in sexual violence and in certain attitudes that may foster discrimination against women. These cases bear directly on the question of what social science investigations would have to tell us in order for the findings to be used as evidence that a significant social harm emanates from exposure to these materials. Rather than delaying the discussion of these policy issues until later in the book, we have chosen to comment on them right away. It is our hope that the criticisms of the methods used and the findings that emerge when scientific data from social-psychological investigations are used to guide new social policy or to reinforce already established policy (as well as our attempts to answer these criticisms when possible) will serve as a context within which to evaluate the research discussed in the remaining chapters.

Several years ago the courts were confronted with an important and novel case involving violence in the media — *Olivia* v. *National Broadcasting Company, Inc.*[10] In *Olivia*, a minor brought a civil suit against NBC, claiming that a television drama, *Born Innocent,* had stimulated certain juveniles to inflict injury on her by an "artificial rape" with a bottle. The suit alleged that the juveniles had viewed a similar artificial rape scene in the television drama and the scene had caused them to decide to perform a similar act against the minor girl. The plaintiffs sought to convince the court that the producer of the media violence should be held legally responsible for the victim's injury.

The defense attorneys for NBC argued that while it was true that certain forms of speech are not protected by the First Amendment —such as speech directed to inciting or producing imminent lawless action — the television broadcast of a rape scene did not qualify as speech of this type. Eventually, the case was dismissed on the grounds that the violent television depiction was protected speech and thus there could be no grounds for the plaintiffs' suit against the network.

Over the last 75 years, Supreme Court decisions involving advocacy of harmful or criminal acts have attempted to distinguish between speech advocating unpopular ideas and speech actually threatening public safety. The Court has rejected the notion that the majority of citizens have the right to suppress speech that is alleged to have merely a "bad tendency" to cause a general harm to a particular group or institution.

In *Schenck* v. *United States*[11] — one of a series of cases arising from the prosecution of public speeches advocating opposition to United States participation in World War I — Supreme Court Justice Oliver Wendell Holmes proclaimed that "the question in every case is whether the words used are used in such circumstances and are of such a nature as to create a *clear and present danger* that they will bring about the substantive evils that Congress has a right to prevent."[12] The clear and present danger test as originally formulated allowed the government to punish speech that merely had a tendency to produce lawless or otherwise harmful behavior. In the 1927 subversion case of *Whitney* v. *California*,[13] Justice Brandeis articulated a narrower interpretation of the clear and present danger test. This more limited test required a showing "either that immediate serious violence was to be expected or was advocated, or that the past conduct furnished reason to believe that such advocacy was then contemplated."[14] The same basic theme was sounded in the 1969 case, *Brandenburg* v. *Ohio*,[15] where the Court ruled that advocacy of subversive action fell outside First Amendment protection only if the speech was "directed to inciting or producing imminent lawless action and is likely to incite or produce such action."[16] Similar language can be found in nonsubversion cases such as *Bridges* v. *California*.[17] Clearly, this language is aimed at speech posing an immediate and highly likely threat of harm.

Thus, in determining whether media portrayals can be held legally accountable, the reader must consider whether the research presented in the following chapters (particularly the research on exposure to violent materials that are not sexually explicit) must establish a link between viewing sexual violence and harmful behavior sufficient to meet the "incitement standard" laid down in Brandenburg. To satisfy the requirements of the incitement doctrine, the social science literature must at least demonstrate the following: (1) The portrayal of violence must result in an identifiable, particularized, and specific harm. Note that most legal scholars also agree that the perceived harm has to be more than the "shock value" or offensiveness of the material; instead, the material must incite a "tangible" harm. (2) The likelihood of the harm's occurrence, given the inciting depiction, must be relatively high.[18]

In 1984 the City of Indianapolis held hearings in which it concluded that in addition to creating other harms, pornography is a discriminatory practice based on sex that denies women equal opportunities in society; is a systematic practice of exploitation and subordination of women; promotes bigotry and contempt for women; impedes women's opportunities for equality of rights in employment and education; and promotes rape, battery, child abuse, kidnapping, and prostitution.

In challenging the constitutionality of the ordinance, the American Civil Liberties Union (ACLU) maintained that the touchstone of First Amendment doctrine has been an insistence on a close causal connection between speech and the harm it is alleged to create. Only when the causal connection is a virtual certainty and not expressed as mere speculative possibility or a "bad tendency" can free expression be limited under the Constitution. According to the ACLU, the City of Indianapolis had failed to adequately demonstrate this connection.

In response to these assertions, the attorneys for the City of Indianapolis argued that there was a sufficient causal relationship between men's exposure to violence against women in the media and harms to women to justify creating the ordinance. One major tenet of their argument was that all women (not just those coerced into performances or abused) are harmed by the distribution of pornography, and that this harm is evident if one examines evidence from experimental social psychological laboratory studies. In the legal brief submitted to the Federal District Court,[19] the city contended:

There is a plethora of empirical data in the social science field which indicates that exposure to pornography as defined in the ordinance has a negative impact on the behavior of the viewer in terms of his attitudes and perceptions toward women as well as his willingness to aggress against them. By mixing misogyny and violence with sexuality, pornography exerts powerful behavioral conditioning on its male viewers which in turn affects the treatment of women in our society. This becomes quite apparent when some of the major studies in this area are examined.[20]

The brief then went on to describe in some detail several of the studies described in the following chapters.

The ACLU responded to the city's assertion that scientific studies have demonstrated a casual connection between exposure to violence against women and subsequent antisocial attitudes and behavior by securing affidavits from several experts who critiqued the social-psychological evidence. In total, four affidavits were submitted.[21] One was from psychiatrist Martha Kirkpatrick, who teaches in the Department of Psychiatry at UCLA. With regard to the experimental studies she stated:

Even accepting these studies at face value, none of them purports to show that the availability of, or exposure to, pornography usually, or even more probably than not, causes harms such as rape, sexual harassment, or other harms of comparable gravity. To the contrary, the most any of them claims is an extremely weak effect in a very few persons under carefully controlled clinical settings. In my judgment, no scientifically valid predictions or assumptions can be drawn from such studies on the effects of pornography and actual behavior in the real world.

On the other hand, there are studies which find, based on my professional expertise, convincing evidence that the availability of and exposure to pornography in the real world does not increase the likelihood of anti-social acts. For many years, social scientists in Scandinavia have examined the effects of anti-social behavior caused by the legalization of pornographic materials there in the 1960's. Those studies have found no increase in such anti-social acts as child molestation, rape, and the like.[22]

Another affidavit, submitted by Wardell Pomeroy, Academic Dean at the Institute for Advanced Study of Human Sexuality in San Francisco, echoed this opinion but added the following:

Moreover, the studies . . . are so methodologically flawed in conception, execution, and analysis that even the meager conclusions reached by those researchers cannot, in my professional judgment, be accepted. To the contrary, it is my judgment, reviewing the studies attempting and purporting to show a relationship between the availability of or exposure to pornographic materials and the commission of anti-social acts, that no causal relationship, or meaningful association has been demonstrated

One can make just as good an argument that exposure to pornography or sexually violent materials can act as a substitution or release from acting out.[23]

John Money, Professor of Medical Psychology and Associate Professor of Pediatrics at Johns Hopkins University goes even further, claiming the studies have no validity in the "real world" at all:

The result [of certain assumptions that Donnerstein and others make] is that they design an oversimplified experiment of cause and effects, namely an experiment in which subjects, usually college students, look at or listen to selected pornographic stimuli, and then are quizzed in order to find out what effect, if any, was produced —e.g., aggression against women. The criticism which invalidates such an experiment (and its findings) is that it fails to take into account the extremely simplified and artificial nature of the conditions of the experiment as compared with the complex and multiple determinants of events in real life. The results of an experimental quiz or other test do not necessarily have any bearing on what causes people to do what they do in real life. It is not scientifically permissible to generalize from one oversimplified experiment to the complexities of real life. Nonetheless, this is precisely what is done by those who use the Donnerstein type of experiment to buttress their argument, e.g., that pornography creates and maintains discrimination against women. Scientifically, there is not a shred of evidence to support the logic of such argument.[24]

As is evident from this exchange, there is considerable disagreement about the ability of currently available social-psychological data on the effects of exposure to pornography to establish a causal connection between depiction or advocacy and a harmful outcome. Before examining the specific criticisms, it is necessary to make a general point about the laboratory studies cited as evidence of harm by the proponents of the ordinance in Indianapolis. Many of the findings cited in the Indianapolis brief were based on the experiments described in this book. As we have noted, most of them were conducted in the laboratory, although a few were conducted in the field. These experiments are not valid according to critics such as the ACLU because they do not take into account the simplified and artificial nature of the conditions of the experiment as compared with the complex and multiple determinants of events in real life.

The issue of whether or not researchers examining sexual violence are justified in extrapolating from their laboratory experiments to the real world is an important one and raises the question of why researchers employ laboratory experiments in the first place. After we answer this question we will turn our attention to the specifics of laboratory experiments in this area that allegedly render them invalid.

The primary advantage of an experiment conducted in the laboratory under controlled conditions is the unambiguous assignment of causality. When an experiment is conducted, the researcher is justified in making a strong statement concerning the relationship of factor A to factor B. In no other form of systematic research can such a claim be made. (Thus, when Kirkpatrick claims that she finds correlational evidence from Scandinavia—showing an opposite result—more compelling than experiments, as she did in her affidavit, she makes a statement that might be puzzling to many scientists.) Even if we were to observe a nearly one-to-one relationship between viewing violent pornography and committing a sexual assault or rape in the real world, this finding is not as compelling in a causal sense as is an experiment. Even with a perfect one-to-one correlation in the real world we could never be sure if viewing violent pornography leads to harmful behavior, or that those people already predisposed to violence were also drawn to violent pornography. Similarly, even if every violent rapist we could find had a history of exposure to violent pornography, we would never be justified in assuming that these materials "caused" their violent behavior. On the other hand, this observation, in conjunction with the findings from well-controlled laboratory experiments, may allow us to be vastly more confident about our choice of one hypothesis over another.

The experiment is a powerful device for making a causal statement because the experimenter can randomly assign subjects to "conditions." In a typical study such as those reviewed later in this book, men might be randomly assigned to a condition in which they saw a violent pornographic movie, to a condition where they viewed a pornographic movie with no violence, or to a condition where they saw a neutral film. Because the men in these experiments are chosen randomly to view one of the film types, we can be confident that there was no unique background feature (i.e., some men may already be predisposed to aggressive behavior, some men may start out with negative attitudes toward women, and some men might even be predisposed to rape) that is systematically associated with viewing a certain kind of film. In other words, those men predisposed to behave aggressively are just as likely to be selected to view a neutral film as they are to view a violent or nonviolent pornographic film. Once we eliminate this sort of bias we can safely attribute the differences we detect in aggression after men have viewed the films to the type of films they have viewed, not to their backgrounds (or any other factor).

Despite the higher level of causal certainty available to the laboratory experimenter, laboratory assessments of the effects of mass media, particularly violent mass media, on behavior are susceptible to many criticisms.[25] Among these are: (1) Laboratory subjects do not really perceive themselves as inflicting harm when experimenters ask them to perform very artificial forms of aggression in their interactions with a confederate. (2) In the real world, people are subject to punishment for violence; in the laboratory, aggression is condoned, even encouraged, after the subject has viewed violent material. (3) All of the studies examine subjects from a very narrow segment of the general population. (4) Laboratory experiments in general are susceptible to what has been termed an "experimenter demand effect," wherein subjects attempt to guess and then confirm the experimenter's hypothesis. (5) Only studies that obtain positive results are published. (6) No one yet has been able to come up with either an acceptable operational definition of aggressive behavior on the part of the subject who is supposedly reacting to the film or other media event, or an acceptable definition of what actually constitutes violence in the media depiction itself. We will address each of these criticisms next.

1. *Laboratory subjects do not really perceive themselves as inflicting harm.* Many studies of the effects of pornography measure laboratory aggression on an "aggression machine."[26] Typically, subjects are seated before the machine and asked to play the role of an experimenter in a "learning experiment." The subject is asked to administer a shock whenever the other subject in the learning experiment makes an incorrect response. The second subject is, of course, an accomplice of the experimenter. In the typical aggression experiment, a subject may view a violent film and then be asked to participate in a learning experiment involving the aggression machine. As we describe the research using this machine in subsequent chapters, the reader may ask whether subjects using the aggression machine perceived themselves as inflicting any real harm.

In defense of this measure, it is important to point out that studies have found substantial associations between aggression as measured by devices like the aggression machine and other less "artificial" measures of aggression. This research suggests that devices such as shock machines or aversive noise machines may be more valid indices of aggression than would first appear. Here, researchers have demonstrated that certain physiological and attitudinal measures dealing with real-world aggression significantly relate to laboratory aggressive behavior. In one study, for example,[27] male attitudes about rape and physical responses to rape (penile tumescence) were measured in the first phase of a two-part experiment. In the second phase of the procedure the men participated in what they believed was a completely different experiment — subjects were told they were participating in an ESP study — in which aggression was measured by having men transmit aversive noise to a woman confederate of the experimenter if she could not correctly guess a number the subject had in mind. The results of this experiment revealed strong positive relationships between attitudes facilitating hostility and violence against women, physical arousal to rape assessed in the first session, and the delivery of aversive noise. Furthermore, when additional questions were asked of subjects in phase 2, it was revealed that their motivations for delivering aversive noise were clearly to hurt the receiver. The results of this study suggest that men who are hostile toward women and physically aroused by rape will manifest that hostility in the laboratory when asked to participate in an experiment using a device like the aggression machine.

2. *In the laboratory there are no sanctions against engaging in violent behavior.* Violence in the real world is viewed as deviant and is often punished. In the laboratory studies of aggression discussed in the following chapters, subjects may not be inhibited by these real-world sanctions. If the laboratory places the subject in an atmosphere that is conducive to or tolerant of aggressive, antisocial behavior, laboratory experiments may overestimate the effects; this might be particularly true for studies of filmed violence against women.

There is empirical evidence indicating that this criticism may not be extremely well-founded. In fact, the evidence from these studies indicates that, if anything, laboratory environments are perceived as being more restrictive and inhibiting than the real world by subjects who participate in the experiments. Investigations designed to evaluate the degree to which subjects behave differently in the laboratory than in the real world have demonstrated that most subjects are apprehensive about being evaluated negatively and are interested in looking "good" or in appearing healthy and well adjusted to the experimenter. For the subject in the typical aggression experiment, appearing healthy means appearing nonaggressive. The evidence further suggests that many people taking part in psychological experiments are inclined to be restrained in attacking their victims if they suspect that the researcher is interested in their aggressive behavior. This means that whatever high levels of aggression are obtained may come about in spite of the subjects' attempts to present themselves favorably.[28]

An experiment conducted by Turner and Simons[29] provides a good illustration of the effects of evaluation apprehension on subjects' behavior in the typical aggression experiment. In this experiment the researchers created several levels of sophistication in their male subjects by revealing more and more about the experimental hypothesis (in this case, that the presence of a gun on a nearby table in the room would serve as an aggressive cue and would facilitate greater violent behavior). Half the men in the experiment were also led to believe that the experimenter was concerned with evaluating their psychological adjustment, while the remaining half were made

to feel less apprehensive. All the men were then deliberately provoked and given the opportunity to shock another man while in the
presence of a weapon. The results of this experiment revealed that
men who were sophisticated about the hypothesis delivered significantly fewer shocks than the less sophisticated men, and men who
are apprehensive about the experimenter's evaluation were also
significantly less aggressive than the less apprehensive men. The
findings from Turner and Simons[30] led Berkowitz and Donnerstein
to conclude:

Rather than being more compliant to the (experimenter's expectations) . . . subjects tended to hold back on the shocks they delivered. The reason for this restraint
is obvious: Aggression is frowned on in our society and the subjects did not want to
exhibit "bad" behavior. We can also see this in the evaluation apprehension findings: The subjects who were made to be concerned about their psychological
adjustment gave fewer shocks than their less apprehensive counterparts.[31]

Thus, aggression experiments conducted in the laboratory may
well underestimate a subject's aggressive response to a given stimulus because the subject is very concerned with complying with societal norms and values and does not wish to appear overly aggressive
or deviant.

3. *Most of the research on the effects of pornography is done with a
narrow segment of the population.* Virtually all the laboratory experiments described in the following chapters used college students
usually between the ages of 18 and 22 years. We cannot say with
complete confidence that the conditions that produce aggression in
the laboratory among subjects 18 to 22 years old will necessarily
produce the same responses in older or younger groups of people.
Social scientists are always safest in generalizing only to the type or
class of persons similar to those who were actually used in the laboratory experiments.

Fortunately for pornography researchers, however, this criticism
is not the problem it would be for researchers in other domains. The
typical subject in the pornography experiments just described, as in
much other psychological research, is male and between the ages of
18 to 22 years, precisely the population to which it is most important
to apply or generalize the research findings. The National Crime
Survey (NCS) for 1973–1977, conducted by the U.S. Bureau of the
Census, has revealed that the highest incidence of rape occurs
among males 18 to 20 years of age. In fact, all forms of violent crime
or personal crime (rape, robbery, assault, and larceny from the

person) are committed more frequently by males 18 to 20 years old than any other age group.[32]

The claim by critics that most laboratory findings are applicable only to a narrow segment of the population is problematic only if we wish to generalize the research findings on violent pornography to persons outside the age range of the typical subject used in these experiments. Unfortunately, there have been very few studies of differences between college student subjects and other populations in the area of media effects and aggression. Consequently, we should be cautious about generalizing the findings of experiments cited in the subsequent chapters beyond the college-age subject groups used in most of the research.

Recently, social psychologist David O. Sears has raised some serious questions about applying the results of studies that have used college students to other populations.[33] He notes that the field of social psychology, in general, may have too narrow a view of human nature as a result of the biases inherent in results obtained from college students tested in academic laboratories. Sears notes that social psychologists may overestimate the degree to which people readily change their attitudes, overestimate people's tendency to behave inconsistently with their attitudes, and underestimate the extent to which they rest their perceptions of themselves on introspection because they use college students as subjects. College students as a group may be more likely than others to have very mutable attitudes, low attitude-behavior consistency, and reflect little on why they hold the attitudes they do. Studies on pornography and aggression cited in this book are not exempt from this criticism.

But that does not necessarily mean we must limit the generalizability of the findings to college students only. We are probably safe in generalizing the results of the laboratory work cited in this volume to groups who may be similar to college students in some critical ways. In other words, even if our experimental subjects do, in fact, exhibit a tendency to be more changeable in their attitudes or less self-reflective than the population as a whole (and we believe they probably do), we are still safe in generalizing our research findings to other groups in the population who possess the same characteristics. Specifically, because most of the laboratory work on the relationship between exposure to pornographic and violent materials and antisocial attitudes and behavior has been undertaken with a group who may have rather mutable attitudes about sexuality or low levels of correspondence between attitudes about sex and behavior (college students), we are probably safest in generalizing to persons in the general population who have the same characteristics. It is probably most prudent to limit the media effects found in the laboratory to those persons — college students or otherwise — who have relatively ill-formed beliefs about sexuality or have some confusion about the inappropriateness of sexual violence. Depictions of pornography and violence may have the greatest impact on persons already predisposed to favorable attitudes about sexual violence or who have very poorly formed attitudes, such as adolescents or school-age children. The media depictions described in this book will probably only have a minimal effect on those who are completely confident of their attitudes regarding women and sexuality and on those who have had a great deal of experience with normal healthy sexual behaviors.

4. *Experimenters' attitudes sometimes affect their findings.* Critics of research on the effects of media violence have asserted that much of the research may be questionable because of experimenter demand effects. The problem, simply stated, is that the attitudes of the experimenter can have an effect on the outcome of the experiment without either the experimenter or the subjects realizing it. Some critics have theorized that in many experiments the experimenter and associates might convey certain expectations about the outcome of the experiment and that subjects may be eager to cooperate with these expectations — perhaps behaving in such a way as to confirm the experimenter's hypothesis.[34]

There have been studies of demand characteristics in aggression research. The results have indicated that, if anything, subjects are more inhibited about behaving aggressively when they know the experimenter is interested in this type of behavior. We have already cited a study conducted by Turner and Simons designed specifically to examine experimenter demand effects in aggression research in the laboratory. In that experiment, several levels of sophistication about the experimenters' hypothesis were created either by subtly suggesting or explicitly stating that the experimenter was interested in the subjects' aggressive responses in the face of certain stimuli. The results of this study revealed the opposite of what proponents of the experimenter demand hypothesis would expect. Subjects told the most about the experimenters' hypothesis behaved least aggressively. Other studies in other research domains, designed to test the impact of experimenter demand, have also produced results indicating that awareness of the experimenter's expectations does not have a systematic effect on subjects' behavior. Subjects in these studies who were informed about what the experimenter expected tended either to disconfirm this expectation by changing less in the direction advocated than did subjects to whom no comparable expectation was expressed, or showed no differences between themselves and uninformed subjects.

5. *Only studies that obtain positive results are published.* The critics of media violence research have maintained that academic publications in this field are themselves subject to an effect much like the experimenter demand effect. None of the published research supports the "null hypothesis" that there is no difference in behavior between persons exposed to media violence and those not exposed. Instead, only studies that have found positive relationships between viewing and aggression are published. As these critics properly point out, journal and book editors prefer to publish some results rather than no results. However, this process of selection does not necessarily distort our knowledge in a given field of inquiry.

Scientists in the social sciences tend to publish results that achieve a rather stringent level of statistical significance. In all the research on media violence in general, and in the research on violent pornography in particular, the investigators generally only report findings that are statistically significant at the .05 level. This means that they require the difference between an experimental group and the control group to be sufficiently large and reliable that the difference would be found by chance only 5 times if we were to run 100 experiments. This level of statistical significance is set precisely to guard against the possibility of too readily rejecting the null hypothesis and claiming that an effect exists when it does not.

Implicit in the critics' argument concerning academic demands is that there may exist, perhaps tucked away in researchers' files throughout the country, many studies of media violence that found no observed differences between the groups exposed to filmed violence and those not exposed. Rosenthal[35] has devised a simple formula designed to calculate the number of new, filed, or unretrieved studies averaging null results required to produce an unacceptable level of statistical significance (i.e., higher than the .05 criterion) if we were to combine these studies with those already published. Using this formula we selected 4 studies[36] in the area of violent pornography and calculated the number of unpublished studies needed in order to make us believe that the results from these 4 studies were unreliable. We found we needed 28 studies that found no relationship between viewing violent erotica and aggressive behavior against women to render these 4 studies questionable. If one were to consider all the studies done by the growing number of researchers in the field of sexual violence, the number of null findings needed to overturn these results would be astronomically large.

We should also note that we have taken pains in this volume to report on studies whose outcomes show no effects. We have attempted to make it apparent in each chapter when conflicting results have been obtained.

6. *No one has come up with an acceptable definition of media violence or aggressive behaviors.* Most damaging to the research conducted on media violence, according to many critics, has been the failure of investigators to arrive at a suitable operational definition of media violence or a suitable definition of what constitutes aggressive behavior once a person is exposed to media violence. According to some critics:

To be useful as a basis for policy making, studies of the causes of violence must rest upon a definition incorporating normative, social connotations . . . these definitional difficulties go to the very heart of the meaning and utility of the reported empirical research because what the behavior-observers have studied are acts of "violence" only under mutually inconsistent and fiercely debatable definitions of the term.[37]

There is, according to these critics, an objective and determinable definition of violence that includes the following:

The purposeful, illegal infliction of pain for personal gain or gratification that is intended to harm the victim and is accomplished in spite of societal sanctions against it.[38]

Contrary to these critics' assumptions, the majority of social scientists have agreed on a definition of violence strikingly similar to their own. One of the leading researchers in the field of aggression, Robert Baron,[39] has summarized the definition acceptable to most social scientists and implicit in most research on the effects of violent pornography:

Any form of behavior directed toward the goal of harm; or injuring another living being who is motivated to avoid such treatment.[40]

Both of these definitions include the notion that to be objectively defined, aggression must be some sort of goal-directed or purposeful behavior. Further, it is assumed in both definitions that either the individual victim or the members of society at large are, or would be, sufficiently distressed by the aggressive action to be motivated to avoid it on the individual level or to devise sanctions at the group level to prohibit it. The question for researchers and critics alike is: To what extent do the activities portrayed in the media and the behavior of subjects measured after exposure to these media depictions conform to the definition of violence agreed upon by both social scientists and members of the legal community? The researcher who attempts experimental work in the domain of media violence and aggressive behavior cannot ethically devise an experimental manipulation that will cause a subject to actually inflict harm upon another. Thus, social science research is continually subject to the criticism that it is impossible to investigate adequately the effects of media violence as just defined because it requires that the experimenter create exactly the kind of behavior that no researcher in a laboratory may seek to cause and that no real-world observer can hope to witness systematically.

While behavioral scientists cannot inflict actual harm in the laboratory, scientists in this area are not prohibited from leading subjects to believe that they are actually inflicting harm on another person, as long as the subject is thoroughly debriefed after participating in an experiment. This is important for two reasons: First, there is good evidence that subjects in laboratory aggression experiments do in fact perceive themselves as inflicting actual harm although they recognize, of course, that the harm is of a rather unique variety (i.e., administering shocks or blasts of noxious noise). Second, although the violent act committed by the laboratory subject is rather unique, it is far from meaningless or inconsequential to the aggressor. Intending to hit someone with an axe handle but resorting instead to a baseball bat because axe handles are less available does not change the meaning of the aggressive act. It is this meaning — the idea of inflicting harm, the intention behind the aggressive act, whether it be shock, pricking someone with a pin, or shoving someone — that can be generalized from the laboratory to the real world.

The basic point here is that the generalizability of laboratory results of aggression experiments to real-world aggressive acts does not depend solely on the physical similarity between the aggressive activity performed in the laboratory and an aggressive act outside the laboratory.[41] The validity of a laboratory study — the degree to which its results can be generalized to the real world — depends upon the meaning that subjects assign to the situation they are in. The available evidence points strongly to the fact that subjects define the act of giving someone an electric shock as aggressive, as a means of inflicting harm. Second, there is a heightened tendency to inflict harm as a result of exposure to violent media depictions. There is good reason, then, to believe that people exposed to violent media depictions outside the laboratory will exhibit a greater tendency toward harmful behavior.

The validity of an experiment does not hinge on whether or not the setting has surface realism.[42] It is quite appropriate to generalize from the results of a laboratory experiment on aggression to real-world aggression if we can be sure that persons inside and outside the laboratory assign the same meaning to events around them. In the case of research on violent pornography, the male participating in a laboratory experiment in which he is asked to administer shocks or aversive noise knows that his victim is female, understands that the shocks are painful, and believes that his female victim is in fact receiving them.

While most of the damage done by sexually violent media appears not to meet the rigid notion of imminent harm defined by the *Brandenburg* standard, violent pornography influences attitudes and behaviors in more subtle and indirect ways. Viewers come to cognitively associate sexuality with violence, to endorse the idea that women want to be raped, and to trivialize the injuries suffered by a rape victim. As a result of these attitudinal changes, men may be more willing to abuse women physically (indeed, the laboratory aggression measures suggest such an outcome). The social scientist would have a difficult time asserting that the *immediate* outcome of exposure to sexual violence is *actual* violence to women because, as we stated earlier, it is not possible to design an experiment in which subjects are exposed to sexually violent materials, then allow those individuals to engage in any behavior that may threaten public safety.

It is becoming increasingly apparent to social scientists that the best way to describe the effects of exposure to violent media is to say that "for some people, some of the time," exposure to violence will result in aggressive behavior. Very few people actually attack anyone after they watch others fight.[43] There are simply too many environmental and personal factors operating to restrain the individual from actually engaging in aggressive behavior. The main effects of observed violence for the average viewer most of the time probably are aggressive ideas that might come to mind for a brief period, harsh judgments that might be made of others, or hostile words that might be uttered to some offending party soon after exposure. The likelihood of actual violence among most viewers is certainly very low. On the other hand, if conditions are right, exposure to media violence may lead to aggressive behavior. Aggressive behavior following a violent media depiction will most often depend on both exposure to the depiction itself and a combination of individual viewer characteristics and features of the environment.

Whether or not a person will choose to expose himself or herself to media violence in the first place might depend on several factors: prior histories of personal aggressiveness[44] or apprehension about crime and violence that may be alleviated by exposure to crime shows in which "good guys" win.[45] The approval or disapproval of media violence by fellow observers also appears to play a role in whether or not aggressive reactions are displayed or restrained.[46] The simple availability of a victim after seeing violence, as well as more subtle victim characteristics such as similarity between available targets after exposure and victims portrayed in the media event, may influence subsequent aggressiveness.[47]

In addition, there is a consensus among aggression researchers that people who are angry at the time of their exposure to media violence are especially likely to respond aggressively.[48]

Other studies have demonstrated that the degree to which viewers believe the media depictions to be realistic influences subsequent aggression. In general, subjects who view what they believe is realistic violence behave more aggressively.[49] Finally, even simple attentional factors such as whether the viewer attends primarily to the violence depicted in the story or focuses instead on a myriad of other scenes and stimuli present in most media depictions will determine if an individual will behave aggressively after exposure.[50]

Other researchers[51] have pointed to demographic characteristics such as age and sex that may affect aggressive responding after exposure to media violence. Investigators have noted, for example, that older children are more likely to comprehend violent TV shows in terms of the "aggressor"'s intentions or motivations rather than in terms of raw outcomes.[52] In other words; if the character meant well but the result nonetheless was violent, older children will not necessarily become more aggressive following the depiction. Young children who are less able to make these subtle distinctions seem to respond in "all or nothing" fashion to violence, becoming increasingly aggressive no matter what the content of the violence depiction. On the other hand, older viewers, such as college-age subjects, may be especially reactive to certain types of portrayals (e.g., revenge scenarios) and not particularly aggressive after viewing others. Sex differences in reactiveness to aggression — males more likely than females to show increased aggression after exposure to a violent film[53] — are also apparent, although these differences may be diminishing because of changes in the pattern of socialization for girls in our society.

In brief, exposure to media violence promotes aggressive behavior only under certain conditions and for certain persons. Each of these variables plays a role in heightening the probability that actual violence will ensue after exposure to media violence. Most often, however, media effects are relatively weak — they may result in a temporary tendency to verbal hostility or irritability. Personal and environmental restraints make it unlikely that an observer will actually engage in violent behavior.

We have chosen to begin this book by taking a critical approach to the social-psychological research on the effects of exposure to pornography and other mass-media depictions. Our objective has been to provide readers with a basis for formulating their own assessment of the research presented in the following chapters. We feel that the consequences of taking action on the basis of research findings in this area are extremely important. To act too quickly on the basis of a less-than-thorough consideration of the social science research could have a disastrous effect on our First Amendment right to free speech. Only when we are confident about exactly what depictions will affect what people and under what conditions will it be appropriate to consider new laws to curb the harmful effects of certain media depictions. Anything less than a fair examination of the social research — its strengths as well as its shortcomings — is unacceptable.

2

Research of the 1970 Presidential Commission

In this chapter we will examine the work of the 1970 Presidential Commission on Obscenity and Pornography. This commission was established to study the effects of exposure to nonviolent sexually explicit materials on a wide range of attitudes and behaviors.[1] We have decided for two reasons to devote a separate chapter to the social science research conducted for the 1970 commission. First, the commission's report made a significant advance in our knowledge of the effects of nonviolent sexually explicit pornography. Prior to the formation of the commission there was very little systematic research on the effects of pornography.[2] In fact, this was one of the major reasons for the establishment of the commission. Even though virtually all the research conducted for the commission investigated the influence of nonviolent sexual stimuli — a decision later criticized by members of the academic community[3] — the commission's work generated for the first time a body of knowledge to which the scientific community and others could turn for answers.

Second, and perhaps most important, the report, which basically gave pornography a clean bill of health, was considered the definitive statement on pornography's effects for many years. These findings became "cultural truths" or standards to which researchers and even later commissions were held.[4] Whenever researchers had findings that were contradictory to those of the 1970 commission, they needed to be reconciled. Even the most recent Attorney General's report on pornography makes it quite clear that its findings will "inevitably be compared with the work of the President's Commission on Obscenity and Pornography . . . reported in 1970."[5] We want readers to have knowledge of the 1970 report so that they can compare its findings with those of subsequent research.

In Chapter 1 we presented a rough but handy typology of the six types of stimuli used by researchers. We noted that these stimuli could be categorized under three major headings: Nonviolent Sexually Explicit materials; Violent Pornography, and R-Rated Eroticized Violence. This chapter and the next two will be devoted to the effects of exposure to Nonviolent Sexually Explicit materials. It is important to keep in mind while reading these chapters that the stimuli used by researchers in studying this category of materials have ranged from pictures of female nudes, such as those found in *Playboy* magazine, to films of explicit sexual behavior such as intercourse, fellatio, and cunnilingus. We have tried, whenever possible, to point out exactly what materials have been used by researchers whenever we discuss a particular research study.

THE RESEARCH FINDINGS OF THE 1970 PORNOGRAPHY COMMISSION

The Commission on Obscenity and Pornography was interested in nearly every facet of pornography. Investigative panels were commissioned to study the distribution and traffic of sexually explicit materials, legal issues, sex education, and the effects of exposure to pornography. The research on the effects of exposure to pornography as studied by social scientists is described in detail in Volumes 6, 7, and 8 of the nine-volume technical report published in 1970, and summarized in the final report of the commission.

The panel was charged with three responsibilities: review and evaluate the existing research in the field, conduct new research, and evaluate and report on these new findings. The research program funded by the commission had several limitations, however, and the commission itself, to its credit, noted many of them. The commission acknowledged the extremely short time span in which the research was conducted (in fact, it encompassed much less time than the two-year life of the commission itself). This made it very difficult to conduct studies on the effects of continued exposure to pornography. Also, there was no way to examine ethically the effect of pornography on children. Both of these problems still plague researchers today.

Research evidence published prior to the commission was sparse and suggested only that erotic materials influenced sexual arousal under varying conditions. Most of the statements regarding the effects of pornography were found in popular literature. On the one hand, pornography was deemed offensive and assumed to be harmful; on the other hand, there were those who called it harmless and even touted it as beneficial.

To many, pornography was considered to be "a stench in the public nostril"[6] or, as noted by Gagnon and Simon, "quite analogous to keeping a goat in a residential area, or urinating in public."[7] The panel noted that people often assumed offensiveness was directly related to harmful effects:

I am convinced that this traffic in hard-core pornography is indeed an evil of considerable magnitude. This stuff is pollution, as surely as sewage, and it ought to be equally subject to Federal control through the commerce clause. I cannot prove that it is harmful even to young people, but I doubt that the contrary can be proved either — that it is not harmful. There are times when reasonable men have to rely upon their instincts and upon their common sense.[8]

Another theme found in the popular literature was that exposure to pornography is harmful to individuals (both adults and children alike) and to society as a whole: it has negative effects on behavior, attitudes, character, and emotions.

Eroticism frees the imagination not only of children but of the child that is in the hearts of all men, leading them to go much further than they would go on their own. Inflamed fantasy leads to inflamed action.[9]

Pornography deindividualises and dehumanises sexual acts. . . . This de-humanisation eliminates the empathy that restrains us ultimately from sadism.[10]

These pornographic materials are bound to produce in the lives of the teenagers acts of masturbation, acts of self-abuse, acts of unnatural things between fellows and girls . . . and reveals itself in emotional problems in the classroom. [11]

There was also the suggestion that pornography either had no effects or could in some way be beneficial. There were suggestions that exposure to pornography would be helpful in sexual expression or have a cathartic effect by actually reducing sexual crimes:

People who read salacious literature are less likely to become sexual offenders than those who do not, for the reason that such reading often neutralizes what aberrant sexual interests they may have.[12]

It is possible that obscene materials provide a way of releasing strong sexual urges without doing harm to others.[13]

The open distribution of pornography and obscenity would thus encourage heterosexuality, and discourage impotence and frigidity.[14]

Because of this wide diversity of opinion on the effects of pornography, the panel put together a research plan to study (1) public opinion about pornography; (2) changes in sexual arousal and sexual behavior following exposure to pornography; (3) changes in attitudes and perceptions after exposure to pornography; (4) increases in aggressive behavior; and (5) the impact of pornography on delinquency and criminal behavior.

In an attempt to approach the topic as objectively as possible, the effects panel decided that because of the problem of defining exactly what was meant by pornography, the term itself was not to be used when referring to sexually explicit materials. Instead, they substituted the terms "erotic" and "sexual." Also, standard sets of slides or films were used by many of the researchers to achieve consistency across investigations. The visual materials used depicted activities ranging from nudity to actual sexual acts (e.g., coitus, fellatio, cunnilingus, bondage). There are, of course, differences in meaning for some people between the terms erotic and pornographic, as we noted in Chapter 1. However, in describing the research conducted for the commission we will use its terminology.

In the following sections we will review the effects panel's findings. In Appendix 1 we have assembled a brief annotated bibliography of all the studies conducted by this panel.

The American Public's View of Pornography

The panel funded a public opinion survey of 2,486 adults (aged 21 and up) and 769 young persons (aged 15–20) to determine whether Americans thought the availability of erotic materials was a social problem. Only 2% of the responses to the question, "Would you please tell me what you think are the two or three most serious problems facing the country today?", included a concern over the availability of sexually explicit materials (the war in Vietnam was at the top of the list, with 54%). However, a majority of individuals did favor some form of restriction on these materials if they were shown to have harmful effects. When asked about the effects of exposure to erotic materials on themselves, individuals were more likely to list effects the commission termed "socially desirable" than socially undesirable ones. For example, virtually none of those surveyed reported that it led them to commit rape or made them "sex crazy," while 24% said it gave them information about sex, and 10% said that it improved their sexual relations. Even in situations where respondents believed that erotica had negative effects, they assumed that these effects happened to other people, not themselves. Table 2–1 contains a summary of these findings.

TABLE 2–1

Summary Findings from 1970 Survey on Opinions About Sexually Explicit Materials

Percent of respondents (N = 2,486) indicating what are the two or three most serious problems facing the country as of 1970

Problem	%
Vietnam War	54
Economy, inflation, taxes	32
Breakdown of law and order	20
Poverty	12
Moral breakdown in society	9
Overpopulation and birth control	4
Concern about erotic materials	2

Percent of respondents (N = 2,486) indicating that exposure to sexual materials had the following effect on themselves

Effect	%
Provide sex information	24
Provide entertainment	18
Improve sex relations	10
Excite people sexually	15
Become bored with sexual materials	20
Want to do new things with wife	7
Breakdown of morals	1
Commit rape	<1/2
Make people sex crazy	<1/2
Lose respect for women	5

SOURCE: Adapted from Abelson, Cohen, Heaton, & Suder. Technical Reports of the Commission on Obscenity and Pornography, Vol. 6.

It was also found that those individuals who reported recent exposure (during the previous 2 years) to erotica claimed that this exposure resulted in neutral or even positive effects; respondents with less recent exposure reported less positive effects. Reports of more positive effects were also observed for individuals who were more highly educated, younger, and more liberal in their sexual attitudes.

The panel also gathered the opinions of experts in the areas of juvenile delinquency, psychiatry, psychology, and sex education. The large majority of these individuals believed that exposure to sexually explicit materials did not have "harmful" effects. For example, only 12% of professionals who worked with juvenile delinquents believed the reading of obscene books played a significant role in causing delinquency. Further, only 14% of psychiatrists and psychologists believed exposure to pornography would make it more likely that an individual would engage in antisocial sexual acts.

The Impact on Sexual Arousal and Behavior

The studies done for the panel showed that a large proportion of the adult population is sexually aroused by exposure to erotica. This arousal, however, was dependent upon two main factors. The first was the medium of presentation. The results showed that males tended to report more sexual arousal to films and photographs, while females tended to report more arousal to written materials. The second factor influencing arousal was the type of "theme" portrayed in the materials. As might be expected for the general population, heterosexual activity (intercourse, fellatio, nude petting) was considered more rousing than images of homosexual activity or sadomasochism.

Homosexual males showed more arousal to pictures of nude males than did heterosexual males, and for pedophiles (individuals with a sexual orientation to children) the age of the depicted characters rather than their gender was the critical element determining arousal. Certain personality characteristics also tended to influence arousal. Individuals who were low in sex guilt (did not feel anxious about sexual matters), more liberal, and more sexually experienced tended to find sexually explicit materials more arousing.

One question specifically considered by the commission was

whether repeated exposure to sexual stimuli results in increased sexual excitement or boredom. It found that individuals do not become more sexually aroused with more exposure. Rather, there is a tendency for individuals to become less "excited" and more "bored" with continued viewing of sexually explicit materials. A study by Howard, Reifler, and Liptzin[15] illustrates this effect. Men were first shown a sexually explicit film. During the following 3 weeks they were given the opportunity to view sexually explicit materials for 90 minutes a day, 5 days a week. In the 5th week, and again about 8 weeks after that, the men were shown the same sexually explicit film. Results showed that with the passage of time the men were less physiologically responsive to sexual materials (over the period of the study) and showed less interest in the materials (as measured by time spent viewing erotica). In addition, the men became more "liberal" in their attitudes regarding pornography. Following massive exposure to sexual materials, they felt that pornography would not harm adults or stable adolescents, and were less inclined to endorse controls on sales and distribution of pornography.

Most surveys reviewed by and conducted for the panel found that people with more exposure to and experience with sexually explicit materials tended to have had their first sexual experience at an earlier age and tended to be more sexually active. The experimental research done for the panel, however, demonstrated that exposure to erotica did not significantly change previously established sexual patterns.

People who were sexually active before exposure remained so afterward, and those inactive before exposure remained so afterward. Studies by Byrne and Lamberth; Davis and Braucht; Kutchinsky; Mann, Sidman, and Starr; and Mosher all found no antisocial changes in sexual behavior after short- or long-term exposure to erotica.[16] When married couples were exposed to erotica, normal sexual activity increased temporarily (up to 24 hours after exposure), then returned to normal levels. For people not currently involved in a sexual relationship, there was no evidence of increased heterosexual activity. There was evidence of increased masturbation in a minority of study participants (up to 30%) who already had a history of frequent masturbation. Generally, any increase in heterosexual activity following exposure to pornography depended upon the presence of a consenting partner with whom the participant was already engaged in sexual activity.

A few of the studies done for the panel also examined the influence of erotica on "low-frequency" sexual activity such as homosexuality, anal sex, group sex, and sadomasochism. Both a short-term exposure study (one exposure) and a long-term study (4 weeks) found no evidence of increases in sexual activity immediately or within 6 months after exposure to materials that included depictions of these activities.[17]

After reviewing the evidence of these studies, the panel reached the following conclusion about the relationship between exposure to erotica and sexual arousal and sexual behavior:

> The findings of available research cast considerable doubt on the thesis that erotica is a determinant of either the extent or nature of individuals' habitual sexual behavior. Such behavioral effects as were observed were short-lived, and consisted virtually exclusively of transitory increase in masturbation or coitus among persons who habitually engage in these activities.[18]

Impact of Exposure to Sexual Materials on Attitudes and Perceptions

The findings of the panel's national survey showed that individuals who have viewed more erotic materials are more tolerant of homosexuality and premarital intercourse. These individuals also tend to be more highly educated and to support fewer restrictions on the availability of erotica. As with all types of correlational studies, however, there was no way to determine if exposure to these materials caused these attitudes. Studies done for the panel that measured people's attitudes before and after exposure to erotica also showed no antisocial changes in attitudes.[19]

In order to examine the effects of erotica on attitudes, Mosher[20] developed a scale to measure "sex-calloused" attitudes regarding women, in which respondents were asked about their views about women as sex objects and exploitative techniques they may have used to obtain sexual intercourse. Some of the items from the Sex-Calloused Attitudes Scale are: (1) "Pickups should expect to put out"; (2) "A man should find them, fool them, fuck them, and forget them"; (3) "A woman doesn't mean 'no' unless she slaps you"; and (4) "If they are old enough to bleed, they are old enough to butcher." Men who watched two erotic films did not show any increase in these attitudes 1 day or 2 weeks after exposure. However, those men who scored high on the scale before watching the films reported that they were more sexually aroused by the films.

There was no indication of any behavioral changes in these sex-calloused males after film exposure.

If the studies done for the panel discovered anything, they discovered changes in attitudes about the acceptability of pornography itself. Generally, exposure to erotic materials tended to produce more liberal or tolerant attitudes regarding restrictions on pornography. However, these changes in attitudes occurred primarily among persons who were low in sex guilt and who did not have feelings of "disgust" from viewing the films.

One ambitious goal of the panel's research was to attempt to determine which materials are judged pornographic or obscene. On the basis of empirical analysis the commission concluded that these judgments appear to depend upon a combination of factors: the sex acts depicted in the materials, emotional and physiological reactions to the materials, and certain characteristics of those making the judgments. For example, in studies by Mosher[21] and Byrne and Lamberth,[22] images of oral sex, anal sex, and homosexuality were considered more obscene than images of heterosexual intercourse. This difference, however, was more pronounced in people low in sexual experience. The educational background of the viewers also seemed to influence judgments, with less-educated viewers rating the sexual materials as more pornographic. Sexual stimulation or arousal were also found to be related to higher ratings on an "obscenity" scale, but so did the degree of "pleasantness" reported. It seems that materials that are both highly arousing and seen as "disgusting" or "unpleasant" are considered the most pornographic or obscene.[23] This interaction between arousal and emotional reaction is interesting because these two dimensions of erotica tend to play an important role in determining later aggressive behavior in the laboratory. We will discuss this issue in more depth later in the next chapter.

The Impact of Sexual Stimuli on Aggressive Behavior

Surprisingly, only one series of studies (Tannenbaum[24]) examined the effects of exposure to erotica on aggressive behavior (willingness of a person to administer electric shock to another person). Tannenbaum found that if people were exposed to highly arousing erotica, they acted more aggressively toward another person who had angered them earlier. However, the same erotic material in-

creased positive behaviors toward this person if the previous interaction was friendly. We will say more about the theory behind these
findings in the next chapter.

Another study done by Tannenbaum[25] for the panel was not fully
described in the panel's summary report. In this study, men viewed
a silent erotic film accompanied by one of three different audio
descriptions prepared by the experimenter. The first description
was purely sexual: A woman discusses an upcoming visit by her lover
that focuses on the sexual aspects. The second description had an
aggressive focus: The women discusses her negative treatment by
her lover and how she intends to kill him (poison him, shoot him,
stab him) when he arrives. The third version was similar to the
second, with the addition of visual displays of the weapons she would
use for her aggressive act. It was found that when subjects were
angered, the two aggressive films led to the highest levels of
aggression.

It would be almost 10 years before the effects of combining sex
and violence in pornography were examined again (see Chapter 5).
One can only speculate on why this study did not receive attention
from the effects panel. Perhaps it was that only one study examined
the effects of erotica on aggressive behavior, and that portrayals of
violence in erotica were not very prominent in the 1960s. Consequently, the commission's concern with such images was minor.

*The Impact of Exposure to Sexual Materials
on Delinquency and Criminal Behavior*

Prior to the commission, the only evidence regarding the effect of
erotica on delinquency was nonempirical and primarily opinion. In
trying to determine the effect of erotica on sexual criminal behavior, the panel relied mainly upon two types of data: crime statistics
and self-report questionnaires from various populations of known
sex offenders.

These studies found that in the 10-year period from 1960 to
1969, the availability of sexual materials increased almost seven-
fold, yet the actual number of sexual crimes by juveniles *decreased*.
Comparisons of delinquents with nondelinquents showed that the
age of first experience with erotic materials and total experience
with erotic materials seem to be the same for both groups. While the
effects panel noted that much more systematic research was needed

on the effects of exposure to erotica on delinquency, it offered the following tentative conclusion: "Taken together, these data provide no particular support for the thesis that experience with sexual materials is a significant factor in the causation of juvenile delinquency."[26]

The available research upon which this conclusion was based included studies of crime statistics in the United States between 1960 and 1969, such as a study by Kupperstein and Wilson.[27] They found that while sex crimes *did* increase during this period, the increase was smaller than the increase in the availability of erotica during the same period. Furthermore, many other violent crimes increased more than the crime of rape. With respect to these data, the panel was somewhat cautious in its conclusions relative to statements made about other types of effects discussed earlier. It noted:

Thus, the data do not appear to support the thesis of a causal connection between increased availability of erotica and the commission of sex offenses; the data do not, however, conclusively disprove such a connection.[28]

This displays a different tone than might have been expected given the clean bill of health on pornography the panel endorsed. The investigation into the relationship between the availability of erotica and sex crimes like rape would lie dormant for almost 15 years, after which new and more sophisticated research would emerge. Given the ambiguous findings in the United States, the panel relied upon the research done in Denmark, which removed all legal prohibitions on the availability of erotic materials during the period 1967–1969.

Studies on sex crimes in Copenhagen by both Ben-Veniste[29] and Kutchinsky[30] showed a reduction in reported sex crimes throughout the 1960s, with fairly large reductions from 1967 to 1969. There was no evidence that these reductions in reported sex crimes were significantly influenced by a change in attitudes about sexual crimes or in attitudes regarding the reporting of such crimes. Thus, the Copenhagen data were fairly strong evidence for the position that laws removing restrictions on the availability of erotica would not increase the rate of sexual crimes. These data and the continuing monitoring of sexual crimes (particularly rape) in Copenhagen over the years would be a topic of debate for the next decade and beyond.

There was also research comparing individuals who had committed sex crimes with groups of non-sex offenders and individuals drawn from the general population to determine if there were differences in the frequency of exposure to erotica, sexual arousal to erotica, and behavior in response to erotica.

Goldstein et al.[31] compared a group of convicted rapists with a normal control group and found that the rapists had had less exposure to erotica during adolescence and less recent exposure than the nonoffender control group. Walker[32] found that a control group of nonoffenders had had their first exposure to erotica at an earlier age than a group of rapists. The rapists indicated more often than the non-sex offenders that erotica had more to do with their crime and being in prison. Johnson, Kupperstein, and Peters[33] found that sex offenders' first exposure to erotica was at a later age than controls. Both groups reported exposure to similar materials, with the exception that sex offenders reported more experience with materials of a violent nature (whips, belts, spankings). None of the rapists reported that erotica was related to their crime. Cook and Fosen[34] compared sex offenders with non-sex offenders and found that the two groups did not differ with regard to exposure to erotica during the 24 hours immediately prior to their crime. There was also no indication that they considered pornography responsible for their crimes.

Based upon these findings, and upon data collected before the commission was formed, the panel concluded:

Research to date thus provides no substantial basis for the belief that erotic materials constitute a primary or significant cause of the development of character deficits or that they operate as a significant determinative factor in causing crime and delinquency. This conclusion is stated with due and perhaps excessive caution, since it is obviously not possible, and never would be possible, to state that never on any occasion, under any condition, did any erotic material ever contribute in any way to the likelihood of any individual committing a sex crime. Indeed, no such statement could be made about any kind of nonerotic material. On the basis of the available data, however, it is not possible to conclude that erotic material is a significant cause of crime.[35]

The final report of the commission makes it clear from the first sentence that censorship of sexually explicit materials is fundamentally misguided if it is based on the findings of scientific inquiry: "If a case is to be made against 'pornography' in 1970, it will have to be made on grounds other than demonstrated effects of a damaging personal or social nature.[36] According to the commission, the safest conclusion to be drawn from the research would have to be that pornography has not been shown to have a dangerous effect. Given the nature of pornography in the 1960s and the state of scientific inquiry about pornography at that time, there was probably no other conclusion the commission could have drawn. The totality of the evidence suggested no effects.

Those liberals whose preconceptions were that pornography was not harmful embraced the findings, but to say that the pornography commission report was criticized after its release by conservatives is an understatement. It was immediately rejected by President Nixon, who said, "I have evaluated that report and categorically reject its morally bankrupt conclusions and major recommendations."[37] As we noted in Chapter 7, Chief Justice Burger, a Nixon appointee, cited the minority report issued by dissenting members of the commission (which asserted that there was at least an arguable correlation between pornography and harmful behavior) rather than the commission report itself as partial justification for more strict obscenity laws.

Several social scientists were openly critical of the research conducted by the effects panel.[38] The two best-known critiques of the commission report come from Cline in his book *Where Do We Draw the Line?*,[39] which was aimed primarily at the social science community, and from certain chapters in the feminist anthology, *Take Back the Night.*[40] It was Cline's belief that the social science data were not objectively evaluated because of the liberal political views and biases held by certain members of the commission. After reviewing 16 specific problems with the studies conducted by the commission, Cline concludes:

In the Commission's presentation of the scientific evidence, errors and inaccuracies occur in their reporting of research as well as in the basic studies themselves. Frequently, conclusions which are not warranted are drawn from data. Notable are frequent failures to distinguish or discriminate between badly flawed, weak studies and those of exceptional merit. But most serious of all is the Commission's failure to report data from a number of studies showing statistical linkages between high exposure to pornography and promiscuity, deviancy, and affiliation with high criminality groups.[41]

In *Take Back the Night,* Diamond, and Bart and Jozsa also elaborate upon the problems with various studies conducted by the commission. Like other critics, Diamond was concerned with the discrepancy between the findings of the Surgeon General's Report on Television Violence and those of the pornography commission. It seemed implausible to Diamond that people imitate violent behavior viewed on TV, but are unaffected by pornography. Bart and

Jozsa argue that the research on pornography was implicitly guided by a catharsis model, which assumes that exposure to sexually explicit materials acts as a safety valve for males' aggression against women. Bart and Jozsa note that recent research has not demonstrated sufficient support for the catharasis model. Instead, research has demonstrated that the most likely effect of viewing violence is imitation. Bart and Jozsa go on to conclude:

> We need an alternative feminist model—a conflict model, which would assume that men's interest and women's interests are not always the same and, in fact, may be largely *in conflict*. The speedy dissemination and incorporation into textbooks and other publications of the findings of the Commission on Obscenity and Pornography—findings which have been shown to be patently biased and based on shockingly sloppy research (and certainly not relevant to the violent pornography of today, although it is referred to allay our concern about such pornography) —should warn us to examine carefully what is presented as "scientific truth." The history of science demonstrates that science is not value-free. Neither are scientists.[42]

One theme running through all these critiques of the commission's report is the discrepancy between the Surgeon General's Report on Television Violence and the report of the pornography commission. It seemed contradictory that the Surgeon General's report accepted the view that people could learn to be violent from the mass media, while pornography, according to the commission's report, had no effects.

In an article entitled *Sex and Violence: Can Research Have it Both Ways?*, Richard Dienstbier tried to reconcile these two views.[43] He noted that perhaps one should not expect similar findings for exposure to sex as for exposure to violence when one considers the way these two behaviors are viewed in our society. In our society, violence is seen as an acceptable way of dealing with conflict, particularly by children. On the other hand, sex is rarely discussed, and at an early age conjurs up feelings of guilt, anxiety, and shame. Dienstbier notes that exposure to televised violence will in many ways reinforce our attitudes and values regarding the use of violence, while exposure to sexual images may act to reduce feelings of guilt and shame—in a sense acting in a cathartic manner. More important, there is constant, everyday exposure to violent content, thus promoting an easy acceptance of violence. This is not the case for sexual materials, which are seen much less frequently. Furthermore, the inhibitions in society regarding aggression are much lower than those against the expression of sex, particularly in children. The position that Dienstbier takes, however, is premised on the idea of exposure to normal sexuality. He does not indicate how learning may develop when people are exposed to more deviant forms of sexuality, which may include violence. His assumption, supported by available research at the time, was that these more deviant images occur at an extremely low frequency.

The other major criticism raised by both Cline and feminists is that there has been a significant increase in violent images over the years. We will examine this in a later chapter.

It was attacks like these on the commission's findings that eventually led to the establishment of a new investigation into the effects of pornography by the Attorney General of the United States some 15 years later.

The availability of sexually explicit material increased dramatically in the 1970s. By the end of the decade, *Playboy* and *Penthouse,* as well as numerous spinoff publications, were available at nearly every convenience store in nearly every neighborhood. During this time psychologists, most of whom were convinced by the findings of the commission studies, turned their attention elsewhere. When they studied the effects of sexually explicit materials at all, it was usually in the context of one of many sources of arousal that may faciliate increases in aggressive behavior. To that research we turn our attention in the next chapter.

3

Nonviolent Pornography
and Aggressive Behavior

FOLLOWING the report of the Commission on Obscenity and Pornography, there was a substantial decrease in empirical research on the effects of pornography. Many of the studies done for the commission were published in scientific journals, and although many debated their findings, most of the scientific community accepted the commission's conclusions. It would not be until the late 1970s, when researchers turned their attention to violent forms of pornography and political groups became outspoken against pornography, that there would be a resurgence of interest in the relationship between sexual materials and violence. The period following the commission was not completely devoid of research, however. A series of studies conducted primarily to validate theoretical ideas concerning human aggression began to show that, contrary to the prevailing opinion, there *was* a relationship between pornography and aggression. These early studies were concerned primarily with same-sex aggression, mainly aggression by males toward other males. In the late 1970s the emphasis changed to aggression against women, then to violent pornography, which we will discuss in Chapter 5.

Our discussion in this chapter of the research on nonviolent pornography and aggression will be divided into two subtopics. First, how does exposure to nonviolent pornography influence same-sex aggression (men's aggression against other men and women's aggression against other women)? Second, how does nonviolent pornography influence men's aggression against women? The first question was addressed more in terms of theoretical issues about aggression than as a question about the effects of pornography per se. Within the scientific community these studies were more often brought up in the context of "what increases or decreases aggressive behavior" than in discussions of the harmful effects of pornography. Researchers were primarily concerned with the effects of arousal on increases and decreases in aggression. They were only interested in sexually explicit materials in so far as they were a source of physiological arousal. It was not until research turned to the topic of aggression against women by men that the issue of pornography came back to center stage.

CONDUCTING RESEARCH ON AGGRESSION

Many of the studies we will be discussing in this chapter and in Chapter 5 used similar procedures. Therefore, we will relate in some detail how these studies were conducted and define some terminology they all share.

The individuals selected for participation in these studies are primarily undergraduate college students. They volunteer in order to fulfill a course requirement in departments of psychology, communication, or other university departments. For their participation they are normally given either extra course credit or, less frequently, financial payment. When they are initially recruited they generally do not know that the study involves exposure to sexual materials.

After they arrive for the experiment, subjects are usually told that the researcher is interested in the effects of stress or reinforcement on learning memory. The subject is informed that he or she will be required to perform some task that will be evaluated by another subject in the experiment and will be given an opportunity to evaluate the other subject's performance afterwards. The other subject, sometimes called a confederate, actually works for the experimenter.

One of the primary interests of researchers in this area was the effect of pornography on individuals who are predisposed, ready, or "primed" to behave aggressively. In order to anger subjects so that they would be instigated to aggress, the experimenter has them perform a task. The subject is told that his or her performance on this task will be evaluated by another student, who is actually the confederate. The evaluation often takes the form of written comments and sometimes includes the delivery of electric shocks to the subject. For example, if the experimenter wanted to anger the subject, both a negative written evaluation and several shocks might be given.

At this point in these studies, subjects would be exposed to the sexual stimuli. A common procedure is to tell subjects there will be a break in the experiment to allow the confederate time to study for a task. Given the free time, the subject is asked if he or she would be willing to help the experimenter in another, unrelated study. Subjects are then asked to examine and evaluate various types of pictorial stimuli or films. These materials could be anything from nonsexual scenes to nudity and explicit sexual behaviors. The actual exposure time is usually no more than 5 minutes.

Following exposure to the various films or pictures (depending on the study), subjects are given an opportunity to evaluate the confederate's performance. The typical procedure is for the subject to administer a varying number of shocks or administer certain levels of shock to the confederate for errors made on a bogus task. The number of shocks or average level (intensity) of shock delivered by the subject is the measure of aggression in these studies. The reader should keep in mind that no shock is actually administered, but rather the subject believes that he or she is delivering some form of punishment to the other person.

While there is variation in the experimental studies to be discussed, these are the general procedures used by most experimenters. Keeping this description of the methodology employed in mind, let us now take a look at the findings of experiments in this area.

MEN'S AGGRESSION TOWARD OTHER MEN

The studies in this section are concerned with how exposure to nonviolent pornography affects one man's aggression against another man. The findings from these studies generally fall into one of three categories. First, there are studies that found an increase in aggression following exposure to pornography. Second are studies that found that exposure to pornography actually reduced aggressive behavior in men who were angered or predisposed to aggression. Third, there are studies that attempted to reconcile the apparent differences between these two types of effects. We will review each type in turn.

Several early studies found that when male subjects were angered and then exposed to sexually arousing materials, their level of aggression would increase.[1] A study by Dolf Zillmann of Indiana University published in 1971 serves as an example of this finding.[2] Zillmann was not really interested at the time in the effects of sexual stimuli on aggression, but was concerned with a different theoretical interpretation of the effects of aggressive stimuli on later aggression. His model, which is called *excitation transfer,* points to the arousal properties of a film as the causal factor in film-facilitated aggression. When an individual is predisposed to aggress, the level of aggression will be a function of the amount of anger arousal felt toward the object of the aggression. This arousal comes not only from being angered by someone, but from "residual" arousal from other sources the individual will label as anger. If some external arousing stimulus (like pornography) is presented between the time the subject is angered and the opportunity to aggress, the subject's dominant response (aggression) should be facilitated. Studies in which subjects have done arousing physical exercise[3] or have been exposed to arousing noise[4] or to highly arousing humor[5] have lent support to this model. To further test this model, Zillmann wanted to expose subjects not only to an aggressive film that would be arousing, but to a nonaggressive film that would be even more arousing. He predicted that a nonaggressive, but highly arousing film would increase aggression more than an aggressive film.

In his study, male subjects were first angered by a confederate. They were then shown one of three film clips (about 7 minutes long) that varied in their physiological arousal level. The first film, *Marco Polo's Travels,* was considered to be nonarousing. It contained no aggressive or sexual content. The second film, *Body and Soul,* was not only more arousing than the first film but also contained scenes of aggression (a boxing match). The final film was the most arousing. It was called *The Couch,* and contained scenes of a young couple engaged in intimate, tender, precoital behavior. It did have scenes of female nudity, but no aggressive content, implied or otherwise. Figure 3–1 shows the results of this study. The highest level of aggression was exhibited by subjects who were exposed to the sex-

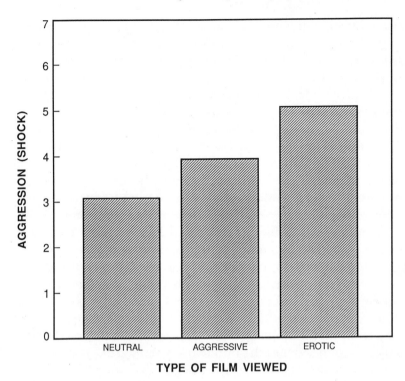

FIGURE 3–1
Men's aggression toward other men after viewing a neutral, aggressive, or erotic film clip. (Adapted from Zillmann, 1971.)

ual film. It is important to remember that although the sexual film increased aggression, the explanation for this increase is not that there is something special about the sexual content (nudity or sexual acts) other than the fact that sexual content is arousing. It is this arousal—whether from sexual, humorous, or aggressive materials —that accounts for the results.

The idea that arousal from sexual stimuli can increase dominant responses (i.e., aggression) in angered individuals has some interesting implications. If subjects were in a positive or prosocial state (rather than being angered) before they see highly arousing sexual materials, would there be an increase in prosocial behavior? According to a study by Charles Mueller and Edward Donnerstein the answer seems to be yes.[6] In this study, subjects were either angered or treated in a very positive manner by a confederate. They were then shown either a highly arousing sexually explicit film or a non-arousing neutral film. When later given an opportunity to reward the confederate (with money), those subjects treated in a positive manner *and* shown the sexually explicit film were the most rewarded. This suggests, again, that sexual stimuli do not directly determine aggressive or prosocial behaviors, but rather affect the level of arousal and *mood* of the subject, which in turn determine the behavior of the individual.

Several studies found that when male subjects were angered and then exposed to sexually arousing materials, they displayed less aggression later.[7] A study conducted in 1974 by Robert Baron gives an example of this effect.[8] In this experiment, male subjects were either angered or treated in a neutral manner by another male. Before being given an opportunity to aggress against the other male, they were exposed either to pictures of a nonsexual nature (scenery, abstract art) or sexually arousing pictures (from *Playboy* magazine). The results of this study are shown in Figure 3–2. When subjects were not angered, exposure to sexually arousing pictures

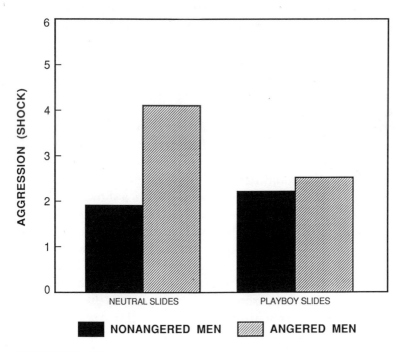

FIGURE 3–2

Men's level of aggression toward other men after being angered or treated in a neutral manner, then exposed to neutral or Playboy *pictures. (Adapted from Baron, 1974.)*

had no effect on their level of aggression. More interesting, however, are the results for the angered subjects. Instead of showing an increase in aggression, which is what Baron really expected would happen, subjects reduced their level of aggression. How might we account for this reduction in aggression? One explanation comes from Baron:

In general, many persons find exposure to mild erotic stimuli (and the sexual titillation they induce) pleasurable. That is, they seem to enjoy exposure to such materials as photos of nude or seminude attractive members of the opposite sex. To the extent this observation is accurate (and the continued popularity of soft-core magazines and films suggests that it is), it seems possible that the positive affect induced by mild erotica may prove incompatible with anger, and so tend to inhibit overt aggressive actions.[9]

This explanation seems reasonable, and is supported in several other studies.[10] But what about the studies that found *increases* in aggression following exposure to sexual stimuli, or the fact that some individuals may not find sexual materials pleasurable? To deal with these inconsistent findings, two models were proposed in the mid-1970s to explain the effects of sexual stimuli on male-to-male aggression.

The two models were called *arousal or attention shift model* and the *arousal and hedonic valence (or affect) model*. The first model was proposed by Donnerstein and his colleagues,[11] and suggested that sexual or erotic materials contain two types of properties that act to influence aggressive behavior. The first property was the arousal level of the sexual materials. It was believed that as erotic stimuli became more arousing, the level of aggression in angered subjects would increase. An examination of those studies that found increases in aggression following exposure to erotica showed that the types of materials to which subjects were exposed were more arousing (more explicit) than the erotica used in studies that did not find increased aggression. For example, studies finding increased aggression used films depicting (frequently) explicit sexual behavior. Those studies finding a decrease used pictures of attractive nudes or seminudes, usually taken from popular magazines like *Playboy*. There is evidence in the scientific literature that filmed sexual material is more arousing than still photographs.[12] It would therefore be predicted that as the sexual material individuals were exposed to became more arousing, the level of aggression displayed by these people, particularly if they were angered, would increase.

While this seemed to account for increased aggression following exposure to highly arousing sexual materials, how would we account for the decrease in aggression for exposure to less-arousing erotica? To explain these findings, Donnerstein proposed a second property of sexual stimuli, which he called *attentional shift.* It was reasoned, based upon work by Bandura,[13] that certain absorbing activities could shift an individual's attention away from being angered and reduce his or her level of anger. The reduced anger would result in a lowered level of aggression. Research by several authors has shown that angered subjects who are exposed to interesting absorbing films will reduce their aggression.[14]

Based upon this reasoning, several predictions could be made regarding the effects of exposure that mildly or highly arousing sexual materials have on men's aggression against other men. First, if these men are angered, being exposed to mildly arousing sexual materials should act to reduce aggression because of the ability of the erotica to shift attention away from anger. One could also argue, based upon Baron's notion discussed earlier, that the mild erotica is incompatible with anger. In either case, though, the prediction is that aggression will be reduced. Being exposed to highly arousing sexual material, however, should lead to a higher level of aggression. Although this material could also act to distract the individual's attention from being angered, its high level of arousal would be predicted to outweigh the distraction.[15]

To examine these possibilities, Donnerstein, Donnerstein, and Evans conducted a study in which men were exposed to one of three types of photographs.[16] One-third were shown pictures of nonsexual materials such as advertisements for book clubs, cigarettes, and soft drinks. Another third were shown pictures of mild erotica from various issues of *Playboy* magazine. The pictures were primarily nude women posed alone. Finally, a third of the subjects were shown pictures of highly explicit sexual scenes from a magazine bought in an adult bookstore. Subjects were shown these pictures after they were angered or treated in a neutral manner by another male. As we can see from Figure 3–3, when subjects were not angered, being shown any type of sexual material did not influence their level of aggression. This finding was consistent with other studies that have shown that being predisposed to aggress (angered) is crucial in order for exposure to sexual materials to have an effect on aggression.

In the case of men who were angered before they were exposed to these pictures, exposure to the mild erotica (*Playboy* pictures) actu-

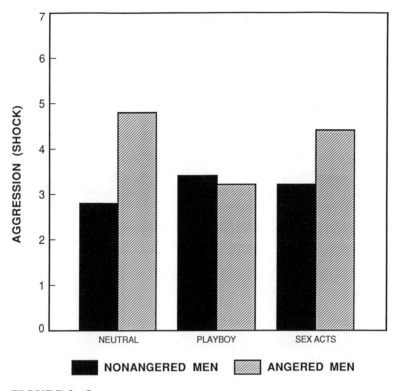

FIGURE 3–3

Men's level of aggression toward other men after being angered or not angered, then exposed to nonsexual(neutral), mildly sexual (Playboy), *or highly sexual* (Sex Acts) *pictures.* (Adapted from Donnerstein, Donnerstein, and Evans, 1975.)

ally reduced aggression. Note that contrary to predictions, even exposure to highly arousing erotica did not increase aggression beyond the level of angered males exposed to neutral stimuli. This would suggest that even this type of material can be incompatible with aggression or can shift an individual's attention away from being angered. It might be expected, however, that as the erotic material becomes more and more arousing (i.e., explicit), this arousal would eventually outweigh the capacity for the material to distract the individual, and the level of aggression will increase.[17]

An alternative explanation for the conflicting results on the relationship between erotica and aggression has been offered by Dolf Zillmann and his colleagues[18] in what is termed the arousal and affect model. These researchers also believe that the level of arousal produced by the erotic materials plays an important role in aggressive behavior. Another important factor, however, is the *affect* produced by exposure to sexual materials, or how pleasing or displeasing the materials are to the individual.

Like Donnerstein, these researchers also noted that those studies that found decreases in aggression usually had subjects view pleasing, mildly erotic materials, while studies showing an increase in aggression used highly arousing, perhaps displeasing or disgusting erotica. The negative affect of this erotica was considered by Zillmann to be compatible with anger, and would consequently increase the level of aggression.

The model offered by Zillmann makes several predictions regarding aggressive behavior in angered individuals as a function of the arousal level and affect level of the sexual materials they observe. Basically, the individuals who would act the most aggressively would be those exposed to highly arousing sexual depictions they find displeasing or disgusting. In order for aggression to be reduced, these individuals would need to be exposed to mildly arousing sexual materials they perceive as pleasurable.

Research reviewed by Sapolsky[19] tends to support the arousal and affect model. An interesting aspect of this model, however, is that any type of highly arousing and negatively affective stimuli should be able to increase aggression in angered individuals; they need not be sexual materials. For example, when subjects were exposed to a highly arousing eye operation in a study by Zillmann et al.,[20] the increase in aggression was the same as in subjects exposed to highly arousing, but displeasing erotica. These authors note:

The findings challenge the view that the effect of erotica is mediated by a specific sex-aggression incompatibility or by the generalization of disinhibition from sex to aggression. The pattern of the effects of excitationally and hedonically matched erotic and nonerotic stimuli on motivated aggression was identical. According to the findings, then, the effect of erotica is not due to their sexual theme per se (or to the *sexual* arousal they may induce), but rather to their impact on autonomic arousal, and their evocation of pleasure or disturbance. Erotica, in other words, affect aggression because they are arousing and pleasant or irritating – not simply because they display *sex*.[21]

This is an important point, for it suggests that even if exposure to nonviolent erotic materials can increase male-to-male aggressive behavior, the immediate causal factor for this increase *is not the sexual content.* Rather, it is the arousal the material produces in the individual, as well as how the individual feels about the particular sexual depiction, that will determine how aggressively he acts. More important, any type of arousing, displeasing image, whether it is sexual or nonsexual, can produce the same amount of aggression.

FEMALE AGGRESSION

Only a limited number of studies have been done on women in the type of procedures discussed earlier.[22] For the most part, the research appears to indicate that men and women are quite similar in their aggressive behavior following exposure to explicit sex. Women exposed to highly arousing sexual materials will show an increase in aggression. Whether the target of aggression is male or female does not change this aggression level. Mild erotica, on the other hand, tends to reduce aggression, as it does in male subjects.

One interesting difference between males and females, however, is that the increase in aggression seems to occur in response to erotica that would not be that highly arousing nor increase aggression for males. This is shown in a study by Robert Baron[23] in which female subjects were either angered or treated in a neutral manner by a female confederate. They were then exposed to one of four types of pictures. The nonerotic pictures were scenery, art, and other nonsexual items. In what was called the "beefcake" condition, the pictures were of handsome men in bathing suits. In the "nudes" picture condition, subjects were shown pictures of nude men taken from *Playgirl* magazine. The remaining subjects were exposed to pictures of couples engaged in sexual acts. After the women were allowed to view the pictures, they were given an opportunity to aggress against another female. When women were not angered, they did not increase their aggression after exposure to any of the types of sexual stimuli. When they were angered, exposure to the beefcake pictures reduced aggression. Women exposed to pictures of nudes showed neither increases nor decreases in aggression. Exposure to the picture depicting sexual acts, however, increased aggression.

In a similar study with men discussed earlier, we saw that exposure to nudes reduced aggression. One explanation offered for this difference between males and females is that women in the study first discussed found this material more displeasing than men. This idea would support the affect model discussed earlier. Generally, however, the small number of studies done on women on the effects of erotica and aggressive behavior in the laboratory have similar findings to studies on men.

AROUSAL, AGGRESSION, AND PROLONGED EXPOSURE

All the studies on laboratory aggression discussed in this chapter had two factors in common — exposure to erotica was of short duration (no more than a few minutes) and aggressive behavior was measured immediately after exposure. An important question, then, is what is the effect of more prolonged exposure to pornography on same-sex aggression? As we noted in our discussion of the findings of the 1970 commission, there was evidence that prolonged exposure to nonviolent pornography resulted in decreased levels of sexual arousal. If physiological arousal (sexual or otherwise) is an important contributor to aggressive behavior, we might expect that continued exposure to erotica will reduce aggressive behavior.

Only one study has directly examined the impact of prolonged exposure on same-sex aggressive behavior.[24] Male and female college students participated. For the first 6 weeks of the study, subjects were exposed to one of three conditions. Subjects in a *massive exposure* condition saw six 8-minute sexually explicit films 1 day a week for 6 weeks. Over the 6-week period they were exposed to 36 sexual films. Subjects in the *intermediate exposure* condition saw three sexual films and three neutral films each week. Subjects in the *no-exposure* condition were shown only neutral films. Two weeks following the first exposure, all the men and women were angered by a confederate of the same sex, then exposed to a sexually explicit film. Subjects were then given an opportunity to aggress against the confederate.

Table 3–1 presents the major findings of this part of the Zillmann and Bryant study. The first significant result is that subjects who were exposed to massive doses of erotica during the first 6 weeks were *less* aggressive than subjects who had been given no exposure to erotica. This was true for both males and females. Subjects given intermediate exposure also showed a slight decrease in aggression. Men and women in the massive exposure condition showed less physiological arousal, less repulsion, and more enjoyment in reacting to the sexual film viewed during this session than subjects in the no-exposure condition.

TABLE 3–1

Reactions of Male and Female Subjects to a Sexually Explicit Film Two Weeks After They Were Exposed to Varying Amounts of Sexually Explicit Materials Over a 6-Week Period

	Exposure During First Six Weeks		
	None	Intermediate	Massive
Aggression[a]	63.8	53.2	48.8
Heart rate[b]	81.1	78.7	77.4
Repulsion[c]	75.4	65.0	54.8
Enjoyment[c]	22.8	40.2	45.0

SOURCE: Adapted from Zillmann and Bryant, 1984.

[a] Measured in "excessive pressure time," the amount of pressure that subject administered to another subject with a blood pressure cuff multiplied by the length of time the pressure was applied.

[b] Measured in mean beats per minute.

[c] Measured on a scale that ranged from 0 to 100.

To account for these results, Zillmann points to his *arousal and affect* model that we discussed earlier. It was noted that increased aggression following exposure to erotica is a function of how arousing the sexual material is to an individual, as well as of how he or she feels (positively or negatively) about the material. Repeated exposure to erotica tends to reduce physiological arousal and also reduces negative feelings about the sexual stimuli (less repulsion and more enjoyment).

PORNOGRAPHY AND AGGRESSION AGAINST WOMEN

So far, we have discussed the effects of exposure to pornography on same-sex aggression. Now we will turn our attention to the effects of pornography on men's aggression toward women. Even though until recently no one had undertaken a systematic investigation of changes in men's aggression toward women following exposure to nonviolent pornography, many people have expressed opinions on the matter. For many years, feminist and conservative writers, as well as scientists, have often commented on the effects assumed to occur as a result of exposure. According to feminist writer Robin Morgan, for example: "Pornography is the theory, rape is the practice."[25] Susan Brownmiller has called pornography:

The undiluted essence of anti-female propaganda . . . does one need scientific methodology in order to conclude that the anti-female propaganda that permeates our nation's cultural output promotes a climate in which acts of sexual hostility directed against women are not only tolerated but ideologically encouraged?[26]

British psychologists Hans Eysenck and D.K.B. Nias have theorized:

Even when they do not overtly depict scenes of violence and degradation of women in the hands of men, such as rape, beatings and subordination, the tone is consistently anti-feminist, with women only serving to act as sexual slaves to men. . . . The intention would seem to be simply to degrade women, and it is noteworthy that in many cases of rape the men involved . . . acted in the same manner.[27]

We will begin this section with a discussion of the research on men's aggression against women in a laboratory context following exposure to nonviolent pornography. This will be followed by a brief survey of research on the relationship between pornography and naturalistic forms of aggression against women (i.e., sexual assault).

Even at the time of the 1970 pornography commission, researchers undertook investigations of the effects of pornography with the assumption that exposure to pornography could trigger aggression against women. The research conducted for the commission and in later years accepted this premise. In some sense, it was as if the supposition that pornography increases mens' aggression against women were determined first and the research was designed to prove it. As we will see, this assumption turned out to be harder to prove than many experimenters anticipated.

Among the research studies conducted for the 1970 pornography commission, only one study investigated the effects of exposure to erotica on aggression toward women. In this study (Mosher[28]), male subjects were found to increase their level of verbal abuse against a female after viewing erotica (e.g., "I've never seen a woman as ugly as you. When I look at you I want to puke."). But this effect only occurred when the men were told that if they increased their verbal abuse they would be allowed to see another erotic film. Some scientists who have examined the commission's report interpreted these findings as evidence for the contention that pornography leads to violence against women.[29] Other scientists, however, take a different stand. British social psychologist Dennis Howitt has commented that while some scientists may be correct in asserting that this study shows increased aggression following exposure to pornography:

It conceals the fact that "aggression against women" is a shorthand for saying the subject was required as a part of the experimental procedures to verbally aggress against a female experimenter. Seeing pornography as such definitely did not increase aggression. Telling subjects that they could take part in a further piece of research if their aggression levels against the female experimenter were high enough did. The subjects were perhaps merely keen to take part further in the research. General conclusions about the effects of pornography on aggression against women are meaningless when the truth is revealed.[30]

Two studies done after the commission's report (1973–74) also examined the effects of nonviolent erotica on males' and females' aggression against women. In the first study, UCLA researchers Jaffe et al.[31] had male and female subjects read erotic passages, then provided them with an opportunity to aggress against either a male or female confederate of the experimenter. The results of this study showed that aggression increased as a function of reading the passages, but males and females did not differ in their level of aggression, no matter who was the target. In other words, there was no evidence that men increased their aggression differentially toward women after reading erotica. A study by Robert Baron and Paul Bell[32] examined the same issue, but with male subjects only. They gave male subjects an opportunity to aggress against either a male or female confederate after viewing *Playboy* nudes. The results of this study showed that exposure to erotica actually *reduced* aggression against both men and women. In fact, overall, there was less aggression directed at the female than at the male confederate. The conclusion, at least from this early research, is that exposure to erotica does not increase aggression against women.

There were several features of the procedures of these studies that might have made it difficult to establish a fair test of the relationship between pornography and aggression toward women. First, in the studies just discussed, subjects were not angered by a woman before viewing erotic materials. The research on male-to-male aggression reviewed in the last chapter showed that subjects needed to be angered and thus predisposed to aggression in order for sexual stimuli to increase later aggression. Also, given the usual inhibitions that men have about aggressing against women in laboratory experiments,[33] it would appear to be extremely important that males be angered as part of the experimental procedures. Of course, aggression against anyone is viewed as wrong by most persons, but there may be particularly strong sanctions against displays of aggression by men against women. Any apprehensions males might have about aggression would be accentuated in the labora- tory environment, where there they are being watched by an exper- imenter. Without the instigating effects of anger, it is doubtful that males would behave aggressively. Angering the subject not only may increase the predisposition to aggress but also may provide legitimation for male aggression against women that could be in- strumental in reducing the usual inhibitions.

Second, the research on male-to-male aggression discussed ear- lier in this chapter also showed that relatively high levels of sexual arousal were needed to increase aggression. Except for the Mosher study, the materials used in the early studies were for the most part only mildly sexually arousing (i.e., erotic passages or nudes). It would seem, therefore, that to examine accurately the impact of pornography on aggression against women, one or both conditions (anger, arousing materials) would need to be manipulated in a study. Donnerstein and his colleagues began a series of studies in 1978 to examine pornography and aggression against women that took these two factors into account.

In their first study, Donnerstein and Barrett[34] attempted to show that angered males exposed to highly arousing pornography would become disinhibited and thus more aggressive toward women. These experimenters had a male or female confederate anger male subjects or treat them in a neutral fashion. Following this, subjects were shown one of two 4-minute films: a highly explicit "stag" film depicting various forms of sexual behavior (oral and anal inter- course and female homosexuality). The other film — in the neutral condition — was a wildlife documentary. After exposure to one of these films, all subjects were given an opportunity to aggress (de- liver shocks) against a male or female confederate. Throughout the entire procedure, subjects' physiological reactions (e.g., blood pres- sure) were measured. The results of this study showed that angered subjects who viewed the sexually explicit film were more aggressive than the subjects shown the neutral film. However, there was no more aggression against females than males. These results suggest that exposure to nonviolent pornography does not differentially influence men's aggression against women.

However, when Donnerstein and Barrett looked more closely at their male subjects, they found that men who were angered by a female and exposed to the pornographic film showed high levels of physiological arousal throughout the study. Yet they were not more aggressive against women. The experimenters expected to find the most aggression among these highly aroused males, but this did not happen. Why? One possibility is that, despite the fact that the men were aroused and angered and thus predisposed to aggress, they were inhibited from doing so. Perhaps they were afraid of displaying aggression against women because of social disapproval from the experimenter, and this fear overrode the predisposition to aggress.[35] This suggested that additional disinhibitors might be needed in the laboratory in order for nonviolent pornography to increase aggression against women. It is possible for researchers to create conditions, beyond making subjects angry, that may act to disinhibit them. Once subjects were "truly" disinhibited, perhaps the relationship between exposure to pornography and aggression against women would be revealed. The next two studies, done by Donnerstein and his colleagues, were designed to create conditions that could be combined with anger for the purpose of further disinhibiting their male subjects.

Donnerstein and Hallam[36] argued that if male subjects were exposed to an aggressive model before being exposed to pornography, viewing this model in combination with being angry might reduce aggressive inhibitions. If this were the case, then exposure to pornography under these conditions would increase aggression against a female. Other research has shown that aggressive models can act as a facilitator of aggression in people.[37] A study by Baron in 1977, for example, suggested that when individuals observe others behaving aggressively, their inhibitions about aggression are lowered.[38]

To examine the possibility that aggressive models may affect violence against women following exposure to pornography, Donnerstein and Hallam had one group of men observe the behavior of an aggressive model. Control subjects were not exposed to the male model. The model was shown delivering high levels of electric shock to either a male or female confederate, against whom the men would also have the opportunity to aggress against later in the study. Following this observation period, all subjects were angered by the male or female confederate. The men were then exposed to one of two 5-minute film clips that were either sexual in content or neutral. The clips were the same as those used in the Donnerstein and Barrett study discussed earlier. Subjects were then given an opportunity to aggress (deliver electric shock) against the confederate. As in the Donnerstein and Barrett study, subjects who were angered by a female and exposed to the pornographic film showed the highest level of physiological arousal. Given this increased arousal, we might have expected that the highest level of aggression would be directed to a female, particularly after exposure to an aggressive model. But, as in the earlier study, this was not the case. When male subjects observed the aggressive model and viewed the pornographic film, they acted more aggressively toward the male confederate but not toward the female. This study, like the Donnerstein and Barrett study, again showed that exposure to nonviolent pornography does not increase aggression against women.

One interesting finding from this study, however, was that just viewing the aggressive male model increased aggression toward a female. This would suggest that depictions of violence against women, even without any sexual content, might be an important contributor to violence against women. In the next chapter we will explore this issue further.

In a second study, Donnerstein and Hallam[39] were interested in the possibility that certain males in our society may be more prone to aggress against women than other males after exposure to pornography. This idea that there might be individual differences in how people react to pornography is not new, but until recently has not received much research attention. For example, in their review of the media violence and pornography research in 1978, Eysenck and Nias noted:

Curiously enough, individual differences, particularly those related to personality, have not attracted much research interest; this is all the more puzzling as not only are they so obvious as to defy anyone to notice them, but in addition they make it impossible to come to any clear-cut decision which would have universal relevance about the portrayal of pornographic and violent scenes in the media.[40]

Donnerstein and Hallam speculated that men's attitudes toward women's roles in society might be a relevant variable to examine. Men who hold traditional values (e.g., women have a subservient role in society) might be expected to consider aggression against women defensible. Men who have more traditional sex roles have been shown, for example, to be more accepting of violence against women and myths about rape.[41] The *Attitudes Toward Women Scale* developed by Spence and Helmreich[42] provides a means of distinguishing men who hold traditional values regarding women from those who are more egalitarian in their beliefs. This scale is composed of a series of statements in which men can indicate their attitudes about the rights, roles, and privileges that women in our society should be permitted (e.g., women should worry less about their rights and more about becoming good wives and mothers; on the average, women should be regarded as less capable of contributing to economic production than are men). Donnerstein and Hallam predicted that traditional males would be less inhibited about aggressing against a woman, and that exposure to pornography would increase their level of aggression, particularly in combination with being angered by a woman.

In this study, male subjects classified as traditional or liberal by their scores on this scale were first angered by a male or female confederate of the experimenter. Subjects were then exposed to either the pornographic or neutral film used in the previous study. The results of this study showed that there were no effects on aggressive behavior as a function of subjects' attitudes toward women. Second, there was no evidence that exposure to pornography increased aggression. In this study, as in previous studies, men were not more aggressive toward females after exposure to pornography. There was also no effect for both variables in combination with one another.

In the experiments discussed so far, subjects were exposed to pornography for only a short period of time. It is quite possible that prolonged exposure could act to disinhibit aggression in males because pornography may convey the message that women are open to all forms of sexual activities, including rape and other forms of aggression. In 1986, Neil Malamuth and Joseph Ceniti[43] conducted a study that investigated the relationship between long-term exposure to nonviolent pornography and males' aggressive behavior against women. In this study, men viewed about 3 hours of sexually explicit films a week for 3 weeks. During the fourth week of the study they were given various sexually explicit materials to take home and view. A week later they were given an opportunity to aggress against a female confederate who had angered them. This study also found that subjects exposed to the sexual materials were no more aggressive than subjects given no stimuli to view.

Up to this point there was no evidence that even when males were angered, exposed to aggressive models, specially selected because of their traditional attitudes toward women, or exposed to pornography for long periods of time, even highly arousing pornography increased violence against women. Perhaps if males were given more than one opportunity to aggress against women in the experiment they would show higher levels of violence after exposure to pornography. Donnerstein and Hallam[44] tested this idea by using a procedure suggested by Green, Stonner, and Shope[45] in which subjects are given multiple opportunities to aggress. These researchers noted that providing male subjects with several opportunities to be aggressive not only increased their aggressive behavior, but also reduced feelings of restraints about aggressing.

As in all studies in this series, male subjects were first angered by a male or female confederate. The men were then shown one of two films or were assigned to a no-exposure control condition in which they viewed no films. Men who observed a film saw either a 5-minute clip of explicit sexual activity used in previous studies or a 5-minute clip of aggressive behavior. The aggressive clip was from the movie *The Wild Bunch,* and depicted only male-to-male aggression. Subjects were then given two opportunities to aggress against the male or female confederate who had angered them. The first opportunity occurred immediately after the subjects had viewed one of the films. Following this first chance to aggress, subjects were told there would be a 10-minute delay and that they would then be given a second opportunity to aggress against the same confederate.

The results indicated that *immediately* after viewing the pornographic film, aggression increased equally against both the male and female confederate. This result is similar to those found in other studies that indicated that women are not differentially the victims of aggression after male subjects are exposed to pornography. The most significant results of this study, however, occurred during the second aggression session, 10 minutes later, and are shown in Figure 3–4. Exposure to pornography led to an increase in aggression against the female, while levels of aggression remained about the same for men in the other two conditions. This larger increase in aggression against women only, after exposure to pornography, was the first published finding of its kind in the social science literature.

Apparently, providing males with more than one opportunity to behave aggressively can reduce aggressive inhibitions in a laboratory setting, and is one condition in which we are able to find increased aggression against women after exposure to highly arousing pornography. But we must be cautious before we jump to the conclusion that giving men multiple opportunities to aggress in the laboratory is representative of how men might behave outside the laboratory. As Quanty has commented:

Laboratory studies that deliberately lower restraints against aggression (e.g., Geen et al., 1975) may be seen as representing a reversal of the normal socialization process. After a subject has been angered, he is allowed (actually told) to attack his adversary. The victim emits no pain cues . . . and the subject not only feels better

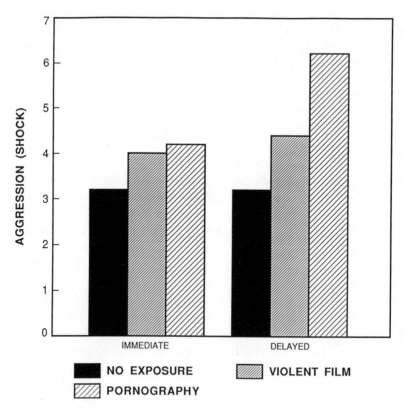

FIGURE 3–4

Men's aggression toward women immediately after exposure to a neutral, aggressive, or pornographic film, then after a 10-minute delay. (Adapted from Donnerstein and Hallam, 1978.)

but learns that, in this laboratory situation, aggression is permissible and socially approved (i.e., condoned by the experimenter). When given a second opportunity to aggress, this subject is more aggressive.[46]

Another study by Leonard and Taylor[47] also found that exposure to nonviolent pornography could increase aggression against women under certain conditions. In this study, male subjects were first exposed to sexually explicit or neutral slides. They were informed that a female subject in an adjacent room was also being exposed to these slides simultaneously. During exposure to the sexual slides, the subject could overhear the female make comments about the slides. In one condition, called *permissive cues,* the female made remarks like, "That looks like fun" and "I'd like to try that." The reason for this manipulation was to reduce inhibitions about other inappropriate behaviors, like aggression. As Leonard and Taylor note:

Clearly, an individual, by his actions, can convey an attitude of permissiveness or nonpermissiveness. Such attitudes could serve to inform others whether the individual will be rewarding or punishing about prohibited behavior. As a result, an individual who conveys a permissive attitude toward one prohibited behavior may provide discriminative cues that facilitate other prohibited behaviors.[48]

In another condition, men heard the female make *nonpermissive cues* about the slides (e.g, "Oh, that's awful" or "This is disgusting"), while a third group heard no comments. Subjects were then placed in a reaction-time game with the female. The game involved each subject's setting a shock level for the other player that would be delivered if the player had a slower reaction time. The game is actually manipulated by the experimenter so that the subject will loose on half the game trials. The female confederate consistently delivers higher and higher shock levels to the subject over the course of the game. This type of procedure is used to anger the subject.[49] There were two important results from this study. On the first trial of the game (before the subject knew the female would deliver high shocks), subjects in the permissive cues condition administered the highest shock level. Also, subjects in this condition and the *no-cues* condition increased their levels of aggression over the course of the game. In other words, subjects exposed to pornography were more aggressive than subjects exposed to neutral materials when the female expressed "permissiveness" about pornography or made no comments.

While the results of this study might appear to suggest that exposure to pornography can increase aggression against a female, several problems must be considered. First, we do not know if the increases in aggression observed against a female would have also occurred if male subjects had been provided with a male target. It is difficult to determine whether pornography *differentially* affects aggression toward women. It is possible that the increased aggression observed in males in this experiment was due to the fact that the men were highly aroused in the permissive condition. Some support for this comes from subjects' ratings of the pornographic slides. Subjects in the permissive cues condition rated the slides more erotic, exciting, and arousing than other subjects. As we noted earlier in this chapter, levels of arousal and aggression are closely related to each other. The more highly aroused the male subject, independent of the source, the more he may behave aggressively.

Finally, we do not know if the subjects exposed to films other than pornography (like violent films) and given permissive cues would also act more aggressively. Given these problems, one must be cautious about generalizing from this study.

PORNOGRAPHY AND VIOLENCE AGAINST WOMEN OUTSIDE THE LABORATORY

What we have described so far are laboratory studies on the relationship between nonviolent pornography and aggression toward women. There are other ways to examine this relationship. Predominantly, researchers have attempted to measure the correlation between the availability of pornography and the incidence of aggression and crime. A correlation is an index of the association between two variables. When two variables are shown to regularly occur together, they are said to be correlated. It is important to keep in mind as we examine this research that the fact that two variables occur together does not imply that one necessarily caused the other. It is always possible that another variable is the cause of the relationship. For example, we will discuss research on the relationship between rape rates in the United States and the consumption of popular pornographic magazines that finds a relatively high correlation between the two. However, as we will see, this relationship can be accounted for by a third variable that has nothing to do with pornography per se. Only in laboratory experiments, like those discussed earlier, are we ever confident about cause and effect because only in an experiment can we randomly assign one group to a pornography condition, the other to a control condition, and compare the two.

Two approaches have been used to investigate the relationship between exposure to pornography and antisocial behavior. The first is to examine the crime data in countries that have made changes in their pornography laws; the second is to interview individuals convicted of sexual crimes. The first approach assumes that if pornography has any influence on sexual crimes, we would expect to see changes in the sexual crime rates (e.g., rape) within a particular locale as pornography laws were changed. As restrictions on pornography are relaxed, sex crimes should increase. The opposite should occur if the availability of pornography is restricted. The second approach assumes that if pornography influences sexual crimes, individuals convicted of these crimes should differ from nonoffenders in their history of exposure and reactions to pornography.

We will begin our review with a discussion of research that has focused primarily on changes in pornography laws and all forms of sex crimes in Denmark. This research has been conducted by Berl Kutchinsky (whose early studies were mentioned in Chapter 2). Next, we will review the work of John Court, who has examined changes in pornography laws and rape rates (rather than all types of sex crimes) for Denmark and several other countries. Finally, we will look at more recent research on the consumption of popular pornographic magazines (*Playboy* and *Hustler*) and rape rates within the United States.

DO CHANGES IN PORNOGRAPHY LAWS INCREASE OR DECREASE THE CRIME RATE?

Between 1967 and 1969, the laws banning pornographic books, pictures, and films were repealed in Denmark. This change provided a unique opportunity to examine the effects of the new legislation on sex related crimes. As we noted in Chapter 2, every indication from the research for the 1970 commission on pornography was that sex-related crimes began to decline during the late 1960s as pornography became more available.[50] At the time, critics argued that any increase in sex crimes following the liberalization of pornography laws could only occur years after the legal changes.[51] Thus, it would have been unlikely that immediate effects would be observed, and the decrease must be due to something else.

Kutchinsky, who has now followed the pornography and crime data for the last 20 years maintains, however, that sex offenses (particularly against children) in Denmark have continued the downward pattern reported to the 1970 commission.[52] Figure 3–5 shows the Denmark data. This time, critics have argued that the decrease stems from the decriminalization of many sexual offenses once considered more serious.[53] They argue that if we look at one offense that has not been decriminalized — rape — there has actually been an increase since lifting the bans on pornography. Danish crime experts, on the other hand, argue that this change is actually the result of a greater willingness to report rape because of increased public awareness.[54] In addition, Kutchinsky[55] points out,

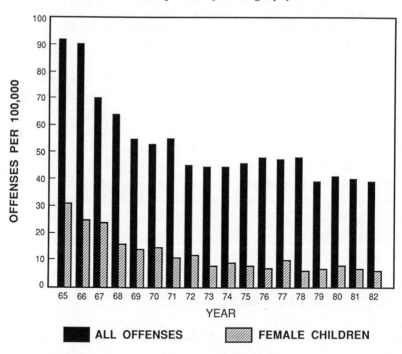

ALL OFFENSES   FEMALE CHILDREN

FIGURE 3-5

Reported total sex offenses and sex offenses against female children in Denmark between 1965 and 1982. (Adapted from Kutchinsky, 1985.)

ironically, that this increase in rape rates has occurred while the production and consumption of pornography in Denmark has actually *decreased*—just the opposite of what would be expected if more pornography led to more crime. He notes that in West Germany, for example, the incidence of reported rape has remained about the same since the repeal of pornography laws in 1973, while there has been a steady rise in other violent crimes (see Figure 3-6).

In a series of widely publicized papers, John Court of Flinders University of South Australia has argued that with the legalization of pornography there have been corresponding increases in sex-related crimes, specifically rape.[56] According to Court, the content of pornographic materials has also influenced rape rates. He argues that because pornography has become more violent (a contention we will address in the next chapter), more recent sex crime statistics should reflect this increase in violence, revealing a pattern different from that reported by Kutchinsky and the U.S. pornography commission. As Court points out:

It is important . . . to note that studies of sex crimes up to 1970 were conducted in settings where porno-violence was relatively unusual. Hence it was too soon for evidence from sex crime rates to be attributable to porno-violence.[57]

In his most recent article on the subject, Court[58] formulates several propositions to support his position that the repeal of pornography laws is related to increases in rape. We will examine the most important of them.

PROPOSITION: *Rape reports have increased where pornography laws have been liberalized.*

Several countries that changed their laws regarding pornography have seen a corresponding increase in reported rape. Table 3–2 shows these changes from 1964 to 1974 for several countries. Court argues that in these countries, both the availability of all forms of pornography and the increase in violent pornography in particular has been accompanied by an increase in rape reports.

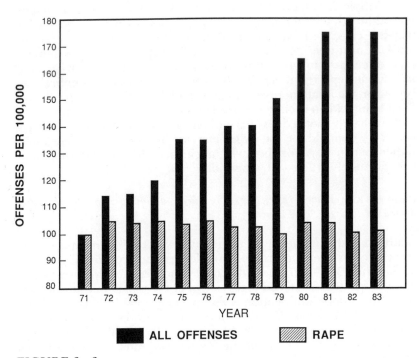

FIGURE 3–6

Reported total crime and rape in West Germany between 1971 and 1983. (Adapted from Kutchinsky, 1985.)

TABLE 3–2

Rape Rates in Selected Countries and Cities Between 1964 and 1974 per 100,000 Persons

	1964	1974	% Change
United States	11.00	26.30	139
England & Wales	1.10	2.13	94
Copenhagen	8.88	16.32	84
Stockholm	10.64	15.05	41
Australia	2.35	6.10	160
New Zealand	4.40	9.12	107
Singapore	2.01	3.40	69
Japan	11.50	6.28	−45

SOURCE: Adapted from Court, 1984.

PROPOSITION: *Areas where porno-violence is not liberalized do not show a steep rise in rape reports.*

For example, Singapore, which maintained strict controls on pornography, although it experienced increases in rape, experienced a smaller increase compared with other countries during this 10-year period (69%). Court does note, however, that Singapore has tough laws for rape offenders, and that this could account for the relatively small increase in reported rapes. But he feels that this does not entirely account for the small increase. A closer look at Table 3–1 reveals that Stockholm had an even lower percent increase (41%) than Singapore. Unfortunately, Court does not consider this fact. If Court's reasoning is correct, we should see the larger increase in rape rates in Stockholm rather than in Singapore because this city had liberalized pornography laws during the 1964–1974 period.

PROPOSITION: *Where restrictions have been adopted, rape reports have decreased.*

Court notes that in Japan, pornography laws have become more strict and there has been a corresponding decrease in reported rape (45%) during the 1965–1974 period. Court concedes, however, that there was also a downward trend in all violent crime in Japan. Interestingly, what Court does not mention is that pornography in Japan depicts a great deal of violence. If there is a direct connection between violent pornography and rape, we would expect to have a high level of rape overall. Yet Japan has one of the lowest rape rates in the world. Of course, as scientists who have commented on the prevalence of violent pornography in Japan have noted: While theoretically there could be a relationship between exposure and rape behavior, the high degree of public shame associated with even the accusation of rape in Japan may result in strong internal restraints against such behavior.[59] Yet, if Court's theory is true, we would expect it to hold across cultures. That it does not in the case of Japan suggests that cultural norms about rape and the treatment of rapists in a society are far more important than the prevalence of pornography.

| PROPOSITION: *Intermittent policy changes are reflected in rape report data.*

To support this proposition, Court examined the rape data from Hawaii. Rape reports were on the increase until 1974, when restraints were placed on pornography. During the 2-year period of restraints, reported rape decreased, only to begin to rise again after restrictions were removed in 1976. While this is indeed compelling, it should be remembered that Court argued that when decreases in rape rates were found after the liberalization of pornography laws in Denmark, these findings should be dismissed because they followed to closely on the heels of the change in legislation. Why does this argument hold for Denmark but not for Hawaii?

| PROPOSITION: *The increase in rape reports does not parallel the increase in serious nonsexual offenses.*

Court makes the following argument:

If changes in rape reports coincide closely with changes in other types of offenses, then nothing specific can be advanced to explain such changes. Fluctuations in crime levels are undoubtedly multifactorial; thus, to advance the influence of a particular factor such as porno-violence, the trends for rape must be in some way discriminable.[60]

This is an interesting proposition, yet Court provides no empirical data to support his contention. In fact, the argument raised by Kutchinsky[61] with the crime data in West Germany (see Figure 3–3) would go entirely against Court's proposition.

There have been many critiques of Court's analysis in addition to those we have mentioned. These critiques have most often focused upon the problem of inferring cause and effect relationships from correlational data, but have also raised several other issues. For instance, there is no indication that Court randomly selected countries for his analysis.[62] This makes any type of generalization to other countries impossible. Second, because Court has not devised any measure of the actual consumption of pornography in these countries,[63] the implicit argument that decreased regulation leads to increased consumption (presumably a critical step in the process) has not been verified. In order to tell if Court's arguments are valid, we need an index of pornography consumption to test whether higher consumption of pornography in any country (particularly violent materials) results in higher rape rates. Third, there is the problem of imprecise crime statistics which, as noted by Nelson,[64] are difficult to collect.

Other critics have been more harsh, suggesting that Court misuses statistics and draws conclusions that are either overstated or incorrect.[65] After reviewing the Court data, the Committee on Obscenity and Film Censorship in England[66] noted the following:

It is not possible, in our view, to reach well-based conclusions about what in this country has been the influence of pornography on sexual crime. But we unhesitatingly reject the suggestion that the available statistical information for England and Wales lends any support at all to the argument that pornography acts as a stimulus to the commission of sexual violence.[67]

RAPE AND PORNOGRAPHY CONSUMPTION IN THE UNITED STATES

It is interesting to note that during all the years of debate on the relationship between pornography and sexual crimes, there have only been two inquiries using data from the United States. The first, which we discussed in the pornography commission review, showed that between 1965 and 1969 there was an increase in sexual crimes, but a smaller increase than would have been predicted given the vast increase in the availability of pornography.[68] More recent studies, however, have suggested something different. Several studies by Larry Baron and Murray Straus[69] show that pornography and rape rates are positively related. In this research, Baron and Straus tried to account for the differences in reported rapes across the 50 states. They developed several indices to measure the state-by-state differences in rape rates. The one of most interest to us is a measure of the number of copies of sex-oriented magazines sold in each state. This index was calculated by looking at the sales (subscription and newsstand) of the following eight magazines: *Chic, Club, Gallery, Genesis, Hustler, Oui, Penthouse,* and *Playboy*. An examination of rape rates in 1979 found a correlation of .63 between sex magazine circulation and rape rates.[70] The correlation between rape rates and magazine circulation in 1980 was .55.[71] A more recent analysis of rape rates between 1980 and 1982 showed a correlation of .64 with sex magazines circulation .[72] Table 3 – 3 presents the state-by-state rape rates plus the sex magazine circulation index.

Do the findings of this research mean that pornography is the *cause* of rape? Baron and Straus note the following:

This is a plausible interpretation. However, it must be remembered that, despite the controls of confounding variables, the evidence presented shows only that there is a strong association between sex magazine readership and rape, not that one causes the other. Even more caution is required because there are a number of other plausible interpretations of what underlies the tendency for rape to be highest in states with the highest circulation of sex magazines.[73]

It is possible that a third variable may explain the correlation between pornography and rape. The authors suggest that a variable that might underlie state-to-state differences in both pornography readership and rape, even though there is no causal relationship, is an aspect of culture that has been labeled as a "hypermasculine" sexual and sex-role orientation.[74]

The presence of a third variable that accounts for the relationship is found in an analysis the researchers undertook with a measure they labeled the Violence Approval Index. This index consists of 14 questions taken from the *General Social Survey* published by National Opinion Research Center, in which respondents are asked about the degree to which they approve of certain violent situations (e.g., Are there any situations that you can imagine in which you would approve of a man punching an adult male stranger).[75] When this index is introduced into the analysis, the relationship between magazine circulation and rape becomes statistically nonsignificant – it disappears. This suggests that attitudes favorable toward violence may account for both sex magazine circulation *and* rape rates across the states. Baron and Straus[76] believe that the Violence Approval Index measures part of what they call hypermasculinity — or macho personality characteristics. Men predisposed to hypermasculinity may engage in acts of sexual aggression to validate their masculinity.[77] The discovery of a third variable that may account for both rape rates and sex magazine circulation must be viewed with caution, however. The study in which the violence approval index was used is based on a 40 state rather than 50 state analysis (because the index, while nationally representative, is not representative within each state). Until these and other problems are sorted out, the conclusions will have to remain speculative.

In another study, Joseph Scott at Ohio State University also examined state-by-state rape rates and pornography.[78] Scott at-

TABLE 3-3

Rape Rates per 100,000 Persons and Sales of Leading Sex Magazines per 100 Males in All 50 States

	Rape Rates	Magazine Sales
Nevada	67.2	44.8
Alaska	62.5	53.2
California	58.2	24.8
Florida	56.9	20.8
Washington	52.7	24.6
Colorado	52.5	26.6
Texas	47.3	22.2
Michigan	46.6	20.8
Arizona	45.2	28.7
Louisiana	44.5	18.0
Georgia	44.3	21.6
New Mexico	43.3	23.4
Oregon	41.5	28.8
Maryland	40.1	20.9
S. Carolina	37.5	14.5
Tennessee	37.4	14.8
Oklahoma	36.3	21.7
Hawaii	34.7	29.8
Ohio	34.3	18.5
Indiana	33.1	18.5
Missouri	32.6	13.6
Kansas	31.5	25.4
New York	30.9	16.4
New Jersey	30.7	19.0
Alabama	30.0	15.3
Vermont	29.1	22.0
Wyoming	28.6	34.3
Utah	27.7	16.7
Virginia	27.4	20.0
Mass.	27.3	17.7
Illinois	26.9	21.5
Arkansas	26.7	12.6
Miss.	24.6	12.3
Delaware	24.2	21.1
Nebraska	23.2	20.9
Minnesota	23.2	21.2

TABLE 3–3 *(continued)*
Rape Rates per 100,000 Persons and Sales of Leading Sex Magazines per 100 Males in All 50 States

	Rape Rates	Magazine Sales
Pennsylvania	23.0	16.1
N. Carolina	22.7	15.3
Idaho	22.4	25.1
Connecticut	21.6	16.8
Montana	21.0	23.2
Kentucky	19.2	14.8
New Hamp.	17.3	23.4
Rhode Island	17.1	14.8
W. Virginia	15.8	13.7
Wisconsin	14.9	18.0
Iowa	14.3	19.9
Maine	12.9	17.2
South Dakota	12.5	19.8
North Dakota	9.5	18.1

SOURCE: Adapted from Baron and Straus, 1986.

tempted to correlate the 1982 rape rates in all 50 states with the number of adult theaters and adult book stores in these states. Neither of these showed any relationship to rape. One index that *did* relate to rape reports, however, was outdoor magazine circulation rates (e.g., *Field and Stream* and *American Rifleman*). We might speculate that consumption of these materials is related to Baron and Straus' hypermasculinity, and that it is this factor that would ultimately account for both outdoor magazine readership and rape rates. Before we can be sure of this, more research is obviously needed.

SEX OFFENDERS AND PORNOGRAPHY

Another way of looking at the relationship between pornography and crime is to consider its effect upon known sexual offenders. The pornography commission had reached the conclusion that known sexual offenders had less exposure to and experience with erotic materials than persons from comparable control groups. Research since the commission report seems to support this conclusion. For example, Kant and Goldstein[79] found that sex offenders had less exposure as teenagers, and continued to have less frequent exposure as adults. Further, these researchers found that a family background in which discussions of sex are repressed and conservative sexual attitudes prevail seems to be a better predictor of sex crimes and other deviant sex practices than self-reports of the influence of pornography consumption on their own activities. Cook, Fosen, and Pacht[80] found sex offenders to have less experience with pornography than nonoffenders. More recently, Abel, Mittelman, and Becker[81] found that frequency of sex crimes, number of victims, ability to control deviant urges, age of offender, and degree of violence was unrelated to the use of pornography among child molesters.

While the data seem to support the conclusion that sex offenders have less exposure to pornography, some researchers have suggested that this does not mean that pornography has no effect on their behavior. For example, Check and Malamuth[82] have suggested that because rapists have less sex education than normals, they may be more influenced by pornography because they are unable to distinguish appropriate from inappropriate behaviors that might be learned from pornography. More important, it is possible that sex offenders may be unduly influenced by certain forms of pornography.[83] For example, pornography that depicts acts of aggression (e.g., rape) may be more influential with this group than simple depictions of sexuality. Nicholas Groth, a psychologist who has had extensive experience with rapists, notes that a certain type of sex offender, the sadistic rapist, may be particularly drawn to pornography, especially violent pornography:

This type of rapist exhibits the strongest preoccupation with pornography but specifically of a sadomasochistic nature. Material that is simply erotic he finds uninteresting, and he is more drawn to the covers of detective/crime magazines, for example, than to the centerfolds of adult magazines.[84]

This suggests that to the degree that sadistic rapists are drawn to pornography, they are attracted not by the sexual explicitness of the material but by the violent nature of some pornographic depictions. As Nelson[85] notes, aggression is a necessary component for sexual arousal in this type of rapist. Rather than looking to pornography to explain rapists' behavior, we might find greater effects were we to examine rapists' consumption of materials that are explicitly sadistic toward women. Detective magazines, for example, contain stories that graphically detail violence against women, with titles such as "Anna took the blade 90 times" or "Ordeal of the Kidnapped Girl in the Pit." Park Dietz (a member of the Meese Commission on Pornography) postulates that detective magazines serve as pornography for sexual sadists:

Detective magazines may contribute to the development of sexual sadism, facilitate sadistic fantasies, and serve as training manuals and equipment catalogs for criminals. We recommend that detective magazines be considered during policy debates about media violence and pornography.[86]

The idea that rapists may be more influenced (at least in terms of sexual arousal) by aggressive pornography has been a topic of investigation by many researchers over the years.[87] This research, which we will discuss more fully in Chapter 5 on aggressive pornography, does suggest that images of aggression are as arousing or sometimes more arousing that nonviolent sexual images.

It seems to be a generally held opinion that pornography, whether violent or nonviolent, is not the causal link for sexual crimes. As noted by Cox:

Such complex phenomena as sex offenses are always over-determined, and personality characteristics, organic factors, modified inhibition due to drugs or fatigue, the detailed circumstances of the offense (including the specificity of the victim), together with the patient's previous life-experience, may all contribute to the . . . particular moment when he assaulted his victim. [88]

This does not imply that pornography may not have some form of indirect influence, but with the present state of knowledge on known sex offenders the data are still lacking on what this influence might be. In his well-known book, *Men Who Rape*, Groth presents, we believe, the most appropriate summary for this section:

Rape is sometimes attributed to the increasing availability of pornography and sexual explicitness in the public media. Although a rapist, like anyone else, might find pornography stimulating, it is not sexual arousal but the arousal of anger that leads to rape. Pornography does not cause rape; banning it will not stop rape. . . . This is not to suggest that pornography should be encouraged, however, or allowed at all, because from a cultural rather than a clinical perspective, it is not only an insult to women (and to men), but it appears to validate sexist attitudes and support the position that women are legitimate targets of sexual abuse and humiliation. . . . From a cultural perspective, pornography is one of the dimensions that must be addressed in efforts to resolve the complex problems of rape, but from a clinical point of view, it is no excuse for an offender's accountability for his behavior. [89]

One point we have tried to emphasize in this chapter is that although nonviolent pornography may sometimes increase same-sex aggression, it probably does so simply because it is arousing, not because it is sexually explicit. In this sense, there is nothing special about the content of nonviolent pornography (i.e., the fact that sexual acts are portrayed) other than it is arousing. Any arousing stimuli (e.g., a very humorous or otherwise exciting depiction) will have the same effect of increasing aggression.

The totality of the experimental evidence to date suggests that the question of whether nonaggressive pornography has an influence on aggression toward women is not easy to answer. The results from the few studies that have examined this issue are inconsistent. Even under conditions where we might have expected aggression by men against women to occur, it did not. For example, when men were angered and exposed to highly arousing pornography, their aggression did not increase. When they were angered, shown arousing pornography, and exposed to an aggressive male model, their aggression did not increase. Even subjects specially selected for their traditional sex-role attitudes who were angered and exposed to highly arousing pornography did not increase their aggression toward women. Even 4 weeks of exposure to pornography failed to elicit aggression against women in angered males. Only in a situation where males were given multiple opportunities to aggress did we observe an increase in aggression toward a female after exposure to pornography. But, as we mentioned, one must be cautious about generalizing from this study because the nature of the multiple-aggression procedure puts the subject in a permission-giving situation he would normally not be in outside the laboratory. Likewise, we must be cautious about the only other study finding increased aggression toward women after exposure to pornography. As we noted, the study by Leonard and Taylor[48] did not include a proper control group for comparing aggression toward both men and women following exposure. Thus, we would have to conclude that among the various techniques to elicit aggressive acts tried in the laboratory, only one, or possibly two, have produced results.

At this point there is not enough evidence from laboratory experiments to conclude that exposure to nonviolent pornography leads to increases in aggression against women under most circumstances. Of course, experimenters have not exhausted all possibilities, but have examined only the more immediately obvious factors that might reduce inhibitions about aggression. As we noted earlier, there are many ways in the real world for such inhibitions to be reduced. Further research in this area will need to find analogues to these real-world conditions so that we may articulate more clearly in which situations aggression against women may occur following exposure to pornography.

The research outside the laboratory is even less conclusive. Data that have been collected by Court on the relationship between liberal pornography laws and increased rape rates is basically uninterpretable for numerous reasons. The research by Kutchinsky on Danish society reaches the opposite conclusion to Court. While this research is, methodologically speaking, on sounder footing, its findings are necessarily limited to Danish society. The only way to be certain that the same findings would hold for the United States would be to conduct a study here with methods identical to those used by Kutchinsky in Denmark. The research on sex magazine circulation and rape rates in the United States suggests at first glance that pornography and crime are related. But, we should also be cautious in interpreting these data. The investigators have presented evidence that a third variable involving the level of hypermasculinity among residents of a state might account for both pornography consumption *and* rape rates. This finding must be taken into consideration by those wishing to claim a relationship between pornography consumption and violent behavior. But what about antisocial attitudes and beliefs about women? While there appear to be serious doubts about a direct relationship between nonviolent pornography and violent behavior, this does not preclude the possibility that exposure to this form of pornography has a detrimental effect on how men think about women. Perhaps exposure to pornography results in greater "callousness" about violence against women. Perhaps exposure predisposes men to believe that women in general are open to a wide range of sexual activities including deviant forms of sexual activity such as rape. If these changes in attitudes and beliefs did occur after viewing pornography, it could be argued that nonviolent pornography does not contribute directly to increases in aggression, but does lead to changes in the attitudes men have about violence against women, and that men who come to have antisocial attitudes would be more likely to behave violently in the long run. We explore these possibilities in the next chapter.

4

Changes in Viewers' Attitudes and Beliefs

WHILE there has been a good deal of research on the effects of nonviolent pornography and aggressive *behavior* over the last decade, only in the last few years have studies been undertaken to examine changes in attitudes and beliefs about women following exposure to pornography. Zillmann and Bryant[1] have suggested that this new interest in the effects of pornography on attitudes may be due in part to the belief that any attitudinal changes that occur as a function of exposure could mediate aggressive behaviors. Among the research studies undertaken for the Commission on Obscenity and Pornography in 1970, three experiments examined attitudinal effects — specifically, attitudes about sex crimes and certain attitudes toward women. There was no indication that shorter-term exposure to pornography had any effect on either attitudes about sexual assault[2] or sex-calloused attitudes toward women.[3] One study on the effects of long-term exposure to pornography indicated that prolonged exposure resulted in more liberal attitudes regarding the legalization of pornography.[4]

More recently, a few studies have suggested there are some negative effects on people's attitudes and perceptions following exposure to nonviolent sexual materials. Generally speaking, two types of studies have been conducted. The first set of studies conducted by Zillmann and Bryant[5] have exposed men and women to what the investigators have termed "massive" doses of pornography in order to assess the effects of this exposure on perceptions and attitudes.

74

The second type of study has examined the effects of shorter-term exposure on satisfaction with the attractiveness of one's own sexual partner and the quality of one's sexual relationship.

Zillmann and Bryant wondered what would be the effect of exposing men and women to depictions of heterosexual activities such as fellatio, cunnilingus, coition, and anal intercourse over several weeks. Would longer exposure to materials that were not overtly violent (but perhaps demeaning or debasing in some way to women) produce effects different from those found in previous experiments? While previous research projects conducted for the 1970 commission had exposed subjects to pornographic materials for comparable periods and found few negative effects, there were several problems with these studies. As Zillmann and Bryant have pointed out, one of these studies had used couples who were married for at least 10 years (couples with such histories might not detect any new activities that were not already part of their sex lives).[6] In the other study, Zillmann and Bryant noted, male subjects were free to choose the amount of material they wished to view; thus all subjects did not receive an equal dose of pornography. To remedy these problems, Zillmann and Bryant exposed all the unmarried male and female subjects to uniform doses of pornography.

They showed men and women 8mm stag films that, while not physically aggressive, did depict women as sexual objects for exploitation by men. According to the researchers, these films depicted women as "socially nondiscriminating, as hysterically euphoric in response to just about any sexual or pseudosexual stimulation, and eager to accommodate seemingly any and every sexual request."[7] Subjects in this study participated in a *massive exposure* condition where they viewed this material over a 6-week period (six 10-minute films a week), a *moderate exposure* condition (three films a week for 6 weeks), or a *no-exposure* control condition.

As shown in Table 4–1, both male and female subjects in the massive exposure condition: (1) became more tolerant of bizarre and violent forms of pornography; (2) became less supportive of statements about sexual equality; and (3) became more lenient in assigning punishment to a rapist whose crime was described in a newspaper account. Furthermore, extensive exposure to this material, according to the authors, significantly increased males' sexual callousness toward women, as reflected in increased acceptance of statements such as, "A man should find them, feel them, fuck them, and forget them"; "A woman doesn't mean 'no' until she slaps

TABLE 4–1

*Perceptions and Attitudes of Male and Female Subjects After Exposure to
Varying Amounts of Pornography Over a 6-Week Period*

	Exposure During First Six Weeks		
	None	Intermediate	Massive
Recommended prison sentence for a man who raped[a]	9.9	7.4	5.2
Support for the Women's Liberation Movement[b]	76.5	54.0	38.6
Men's sexual callousness toward women[c]	10.5	15.6	23.8

*Estimates of the percentage of adults
engaged in the following types of sexual
behaviors:*

	None	Intermediate	Massive
Fellatio-cunnilingus	34.0	49.6	67.2
Anal intercourse	12.1	19.6	67.2
Group sex	10.9	18.2	28.5
Sadomasochism	7.4	8.4	14.8
Bestiality	6.6	7.9	12.0

SOURCE: Adapted from Zillmann and Bryant, 1984.

[a] Years.

[b] Measured on scale from 0 to 100.

[c] Results of 72-item inventory. A response of "agree" = 1, "do not agree" = 0. All terms are summed for each subject.

you"; and "If they are old enough to bleed, they are old enough to butcher."

It is important to note that long-term exposure to this type of pornography did not increase aggressive behavior. In fact, as we saw in Chapter 3 where we also discussed this study, subsequent aggression *declined* with continued exposure.

Why did long-term exposure produce negative changes in attitudes when shorter exposure periods used by other experimenters did not? Zillmann and others[8] have offered a possible explanation for these effects. While the films do not feature infliction of pain or suffering, women are portrayed as extremely permissive and promiscuous, quite willing to accommodate any male sexual urge. Brief periods of exposure to this view of women may not be enough to bring viewers' attitudes into line with these messages. However, attitudinal changes might be expected under conditions of long-term exposure. Continued exposure to the idea that women will do practically anything sexual may encourage similar thoughts that would be more available in memory and easier to recollect than they were before exposure to pornography. We know from other psychological investigations that the ease with which people can dredge up instances of a particular event will inflate their estimates of the frequency of that event.[9] This increase in the "availability"[10] of thoughts about female promiscuity, or the ease with which viewers can imagine instances in which a female has been sexually insatiable, may lead viewers to inflate their estimates of how willingly and frequently women engage in such behavior. The availability of thoughts about female insatiability may also inflate judgments about the frequency or normality of sexual behaviors such as rape, bestiality, or sadomasochism. Further, these ideas, once instated, may be enduring. Zillmann and Bryant,[11] for example, found that male subjects still had a propensity to trivialize rape 3 weeks after exposure to nonviolent pornography.

Unfortunately, we can only speculate about the role that images of female promiscuity and insatiability, specifically, play in fostering callous perceptions of women. This is because Zillmann and Bryant did not systematically manipulate film content in their experiment in order to observe the differential effects of these images versus those that are not sexually explicit or pornographic at all but that are sexually demeaning to women. It is possible that long-term exposure to the latter type of images would produce the same negative attitude changes in viewers. In other words, it may not be the fact that the material is sexually explicit but that the material is demeaning to women that accounts for the effects.

A recent experiment by James Check of York University, Toronto, Canada,[12] was intended as a step toward disentangling the effects of prolonged exposure to sexually explicit images from the effects of exposure to images that are dehumanizing or degrading. In Check's study, a sample of male college students and other adult males from the greater Toronto metropolitan area was solicited through newspaper advertisements. Subjects were assigned to one of three conditions. Two of these conditions consisted of 90 minutes of sexually explicit film clips — what authors labeled "nonviolent dehumanizing pornography" and "nonviolent erotica." The third condition was a no-exposure control group. Check describes a scene from the sexually dehumanizing condition in which a male who is waiting to be treated by a female physician sexually harasses her in the following way:

In spite of the male's abuse (e.g., aspersions regarding her promiscuous nature, obscene language, and the exposing of his genitals), the doctor merely threatens action. The doctor, for the most part, ignores the abuse. When the male exposes his penis, the doctor becomes mesmerized or entranced. She becomes, as described by Zillmann and Bryant,[13] hysterically euphoric and, in fact, cannot delay the sexual gratification offered by the male. Later, the doctor even wonders why she initially put up such a fight. [14]

The results showed that exposure to pornographic film clips of this kind affected subjects' later self-reports about certain antisocial behaviors. Compared with control subjects and subjects exposed to the erotic film clips, subjects exposed to the dehumanizing material were more likely to report that they might commit a rape if assured that no one would know and they would not be punished. A similar result was found for a scale constructed to measure the degree to which subjects would use force to coerce a female into other forms of unwanted sexual activity. This study suggests that relatively long-term exposure to sexually explicit depictions of mutually consenting sexual activity (erotica) probably does not facilitate negative changes in antisocial attitudes among males. However, long-term exposure to dehumanizing or demeaning depictions may have such effects.

Unfortunately, several aspects of the procedures used in Check's study undermine the confidence that might otherwise be placed in its results. First, the subjects in this study were recruited through newspaper advertisements rather than being sampled from some specified population. We must wonder what type of men would volunteer to participate in a study on pornography. As Check himself notes, the likely volunteer for a study of this sort is someone who is already a pornography consumer. Second, subjects in this experiment were told that the evaluations of pornography they would be giving in the study would be used by the Parliament of Canada to help decide policy on the issue of pornography. Subjects were told: "This is one of the rare opportunities which you will have to say something *directly* to the government of Canada" (emphasis in the original). With instructions such as these given to subjects, it is quite possible that the effects observed in the experiment arose, not from the types of material that subjects viewed, but their perception of how socially desirable their ratings might appear. If subjects believed that their responses were going directly to the government, they might rate violent (deviant) forms of pornography as less arousing, more degrading, and more obscene. Third, the time periods during which subjects viewed the stimulus material, and the interval between the last pornographic film presentation and completion of the dependent measures, varied across subjects. Because there is no assurance that the time intervals were randomly distributed across film viewing groups, and because these varying time periods are not considered as a factor in the analyses of the results, it is difficult to assess their potential impact on subsequent self-reports. Finally, Check used a series of sexually explicit excerpts taken from feature-length X-rated films. The end result (as in Zillmann & Bryant[15]) is a long series of sexually explicit images with no context that could provide viewers with information about the characters' motivations, goals, and so forth.

Recent work by Linz,[16] in which male college student subjects were exposed to nearly 8 hours of unedited, feature length X-rated films (five complete films, e.g., *Debbie Does Dallas*) over a 2-week period, does not yield the same results. These films contain portrayals similar to those used by Check in his dehumanizing, nonviolent conditions. The difference is that these portrayals were embedded in the context of larger, feature-length films, rather than as a series of sexually explicit scenes strung together by the experimenter. After exposure to these films, subjects exhibited no significant increases in the tendency to (1) hold calloused attitudes about rape, (2) view women as sexual objects, (3) judge the victim of a reenacted rape trial as more responsible for her own assault, or (4) view the defendant as less responsible for the victim's assault.

Likewise, Malamuth and Ceniti,[17] in an independently conducted study, found no changes in self-reported likelihood of raping if the subjects were assured of not being caught, after 4 weeks of exposure to full-length commercially released nonviolent pornographic videotapes with male subjects.

Interestingly, a study conducted by Krafka[18] with female subjects, using the same experimental procedures as Linz, yielded results very similar to Linz's. Krafka expected that the view of human sexuality portrayed in most pornographic films would not only reflect patterns of socialization that encourage sexual inequality, but might reinforce these inequalities among female viewers. Krafka had also presumed that pornography might cause women to become dissatisfied with their own body image. Viewing pornography might, for example, foster the idea in women that any female phy-

sique that deviates from those depicted in materials is not sexually
desirable to men. Traditional female socialization might also be
considered training for the adoption of the role of victim. Thus,
many women may already subscribe to the view that women victims
"get what they deserve." Pornographic films, insofar as they depict
women as willing participants in nearly any sexual activity no matter
how demeaning, might reinforce the view that even victims of sexual assault deserve whatever happens to them. Surprisingly, Krafka
found that women exposed to approximately 8 hours of sexually
explicit degrading materials over a 4-day period did not engage in
more sex-role stereotyping; experience lower self-esteem, less satisfaction with body image, or more negative beliefs about rape; or
show greater acceptance of violence against women than control
subjects who did not view films.

The films used in the Krafka and Linz experiments contained
many scenes that portray women in a degrading or dehumanizing
fashion, like the clips excerpted from the full-length movies in
Check's study.[19] Failure to find the effects for the nonviolent but
degrading depictions of women embedded in these feature-length
films suggests that it may not be frequency of exposure to images of
female promiscuity that produce the effects, but rather the ratio of
these images to other (not necessarily sexually related) images that
might account for negative changes in attitudes about women. In
other words, the commercially released X-rated films used in the
studies by Linz,[16] Malamuth and Ceniti,[17] and Krafka,[18] while just as
sexually explicit and at times as dehumanizing as the stag films used
by Zillmann and Bryant[11] and the excerpts used by Check,[12] contain
a plethora of other scenes and ideas about women (sexual and nonsexual) that are unrelated to depictions of promiscuity and
insatiability.

This is not to say that the plots contained in any of the films used
in these studies are anything but predictable and sophomoric. But
the films are shot in scenic locations, and women are depicted as
traveling in cars, eating in restaurants, going to movies, holding
jobs, and so forth. While the films contain scenes that are insulting
and demeaning to women, other ideas compete or interfere with
notions about female promiscuity and insatiability that may be acti-
vated by the films. This suggests that either a more concentrated
dosage of scenes depicting women as sexually insatiable, like the
ones to which viewers were subjected in the Zillmann and Bryant,[11]
and Check[12] studies, or a longer term of exposure (more than the

five films used by Linz), is necessary for the trivialization of rape to occur.

The lack of effects detected in the Malamuth and Ceniti[17] study, the study by Linz,[16] and the Krafka[18] study must be reconciled with the results obtained by Zillmann and Bryant,[11] and Check.[12] We have suggested some explanations here, but because so little research has been conducted on the effects of exposure to nonviolent pornography and negative attitudes, it is difficult to reach any firm conclusions. The most prudent course would be to wait until additional evidence has been collected before either indicting or vindicating pornography as a cause of negative attitudes about women.

Zillmann and Bryant[20] have also argued that in pornography portrayals, "sexual performances are highly enthusiastic and athletic" and participants react "euphorically" and often appear to be in sexual "ecstacy." They wondered if persons exposed to pornography would report less satisfaction with their own intimate partners, their partners' physical appearance, and sexual performance. They conducted a study[20] in which male and female subjects were exposed to 1 hour of nonviolent pornography each week over a 6-week period. After exposure, this group was compared with another group of subjects who had seen 6 hours of prime-time sexually innocuous comedy shows.

The results appeared to confirm these expectations. Subjects exposed to pornography were less satisfied with their mates' physical appearance and judged their mates' performance to be less gratifying than control subjects. In addition, the researchers found weaker but statistically significant tendencies for those exposed to pornography to consider recreational sexual engagements without emotional involvement or attachment more important than controls. In discussing these results, the authors note:

Adoption of such values can be viewed as the direct result of absorbing the principal message of pornography: great sexual joy and ecstasy are accessible to parties who just met, who are in no way committed to one another, and who will part shortly, never to meet again.[21]

The authors assume that the effects they find are due to exposure to pornography. In this experiment, they appear to be. But pornography is certainly not the only medium for messages about sex without commitment, or the only source for messages about dissatisfaction with one's sexual performance or partner. The depictions that Zillmann and Bryant include in their pornography condition are common to many types of media: soap operas, romance novels, and many commercially available R- and PG-rated films. It is possible that the same effects would have been observed if subjects had been exposed to nonsexually explicit images that have similar messages about others who appear to have more exciting or satisfying sex lives than themselves. In fact, the research on short-term exposure to nonviolent pornography that we review next suggests that it is not sexual explicitness per se but other information in the portrayal that changes subjects' viewpoints.

A recent series of studies by Kenrick, Gutierres, and Goldberg[22] had male subjects view attractive nude pictures from *Playboy* and *Penthouse* magazines or pictures of nude women that were pretested and found to be rated "average" in attractiveness, or photographs of art works. Subjects were later given an opportunity to rate the sexual attractiveness of another photograph of a nude woman who had previously been rated as average in attractiveness. The researchers were interested in how previous exposure to either highly attractive or average attractive nudes would influence their ratings of the second nude woman they were shown. The results indicated that subjects exposed to *Playboy* and *Penthouse* nudes rated the average nude presented to them in the second phase of the experiment as less sexually attractive than subjects exposed first to either the average nude or the art works. It is interesting to note that subjects preexposed to the average nude gave the highest ratings of sexual attractiveness to the second portrayal. This suggests that it is not prior exposure to a sexually explicit stimuli that affects ratings of sexual attractiveness, but exposure to an *attractive* model or person, nude or otherwise, that accounts for the findings.

In a second study, subjects were first exposed to the *Playboy* and *Penthouse* pictures or the art photographs, and later asked to rate the attractiveness of their mate and report their level of love for their mate on the Rubin Love Scale. Results from this study showed that subjects exposed to the *Playboy* and *Penthouse* pictures found their mate less attractive, and had lower scores on a Love Scale (a measure of caring, needing, trust, and tolerance for another's faults developed by Rubin[23]) than the art photograph control subjects. Because the experimenters did not include an average nude preexposure condition in this study, it is difficult to determine if these additional effects, which closely resemble the effects obtained in the Zillmann and Bryant work[20] referred to earlier, are a function of exposure to sexual stimuli or simply of exposure to attractive women.

We suggest that these effects might be expected any time we are asked to compare are own average looks or those of our mates with exceptionally attractive people. Such a comparison creates a "contrast effect." If we are constantly exposed to beautiful people in the mass media, the contrast between them and more ordinary people, such as those we are in personal relationships with, may increase our dissatisfaction with these relationships.

Several other studies suggest that this contrast effect may account for the results found by both Kenrick et al.[24] and the results obtained by Zillmann and Bryant.[25] For example, Kenrick and Gutierres[26] had male subjects watch an episode of *Charlie's Angels* or a slide of an attractive female from a magazine ad (Farrah Fawcett). When subjects were asked to rate the attractiveness of a picture of an average female as a possible date, those who had seen either the *Charlie's Angels* episode or the Farrah Fawcett picture gave lower ratings to the potential date compared with a control group who had not seen the episode or the magazine ad. Also, Cash, Cash, and Butters[27] found that female college students rated their own physical attractiveness lower after exposure to pictures of attractive women taken from magazine ads. It appears that the attractiveness of women in the media, whether in sexual or nonsexual contexts, not sexual explicitness, is the critical factor.

But are these contrast effects always found? No. Some studies have indicated that exposure to nonviolent pornography can favorably enhance ratings of our sexual partners, just the opposite of the effect described earlier. For example, Dermer and Pyszcynski[28] had male subjects read sexually explicit passages from adult magazines. These researchers found that subjects scores on the Attachment, Caring, and Intimacy components of the Love Scale were increased for their mates after reading the erotic passages. Moreover, there is a substantial literature[29] on the effects of nonviolent pornography in the treatment of sexual dysfunctions as well as the improvement of sexual relationships. As Wilson[30] has noted, about 20% of American couples are dissatisfied with their sex life. Discussing the use of pornography by men and women with unsatisfactory sex lives, Wilson indicates that it

provided them with sex information, reduced their sexual inhibitions, increased their willingness to discuss sex with others, caused them to try "new things," and generally improved their sexual relationships.[31]

These beneficial effects from exposure to nonviolent pornography are rarely discussed in reviews of the impact of pornography. Although the effects occur within controlled clinical settings, they nevertheless indicate that under some conditions (e.g., sexual counseling) there can be positive attitudinal effects from the viewing of certain sexually explicit materials.

Even if future research were to fail to substantiate a link between exposure to nonviolent pornography and negative attitudes, or even if future research were to substantiate the idea that pornography can have significant positive effects, would this close the book on the question of the harmfulness of this form of pornography? One could assert that even if there is no immediate harm in consuming nonviolent pornography, that it quickly becomes boring, and that the viewer becomes more likely to seek out other materials for excitement, it could be a potential problem. As we indicate in the next chapter, the research on violent pornography has produced a much more consistent set of findings about increases in antisocial attitudes and behaviors following exposure to these materials. If consumption of nonviolent pornography inevitably leads to the consumption of violent pornography, we would have to conclude that this type of material does have negative consequences.

Does exposure to nonviolent pornography create an appetite for stronger, more arousing forms of pornography, such as those that are violent? There is one study (extensively relied upon by the 1986 Attorney General's Commission on Pornography and conservative antipornography groups) whose findings suggest that it does. But, as with much of the research in this area, the study is not without flaws. Recently, Zillmann and Bryant[32] found that after 6 weeks of exposure to nonviolent pornography, subjects given an opportunity later to choose among other forms of mass media including pornography, both nonviolent and violent, chose to view the more violent forms including bondage, sadomasochism, and bestiality. Unfortunately, as the social scientist for the Attorney General's Commission on Pornography[33] has noted, the results might be attributed to nothing more than "stimulus novelty" or curiosity among the subjects. The results might also be attributed to some form of permission giving, with subjects assuming that because the experimenter had already let them watch nonviolent material, that violent material was also socially acceptable. Furthermore, there is no evidence from this study that individuals actually enjoyed viewing these more violent forms of pornography or had a desire to seek out this material again following the experimental manipulations. Given only this one study, it would certainly be incorrect to conclude that prolonged exposure to nonviolent pornography creates an appetite for more violent types of materials.

What can we conclude about the effects of exposure to nonviolent pornography? Reflecting on the results of experiments examining attitude effects or dissatisfaction with sexual partners discussed in this chapter, and the results of studies that have examined aggressive behavior following exposure to pornography discussed in Chapters 2 and 3, we would have to conclude that the data, overall, do not support the contention that exposure to nonviolent pornography has significant adverse effects. In reaching this conclusion we do not deny that there have been studies finding negative effects or the possibility of finding such effects in the future. We only mean to assert that the evidence, on balance, is mixed. Some studies find negative effects; others do not. Nor does this discount the possibility that the effects of these materials are rather subtle and cannot be detected with the instruments that have been devised by social scientists so far. Perhaps, as we noted in our conclusions to Chapter 3, the key ingredient missing in these depictions is overt violence against women. It may be that only when sex is fused with aggression that serious antisocial effects arise. We turn our attention to this possibility in the next chapter.

5

The Impact of Violent Pornography

BY the latter part of the 1970s, many people were becoming concerned about what was perceived as an increase of violence in pornographic materials. While in retrospect this assumption appears to be questionable, as we will discuss later, violent pornography appeared to be a growing social problem. In addition, there were ample reasons for assuming that violent pornography would have a negative impact on a viewer's behaviors and attitudes. The 1972 Commission on TV Violence had already established to the satisfaction of most of the scientific community that nonsexual violent materials could have a harmful impact on viewers. Feminists, meanwhile, warned that images of male-female relationships seemed to be becoming explicitly perverse in the wide-spread pornography trade.[1]

Social scientists, who also believed that the content of pornography was changing, began systematic investigations into the impact of what was being termed "aggressive" or "violent" pornography.[2] These investigations, which indicated that exposure to violent pornography could produce negative changes in behavior and attitudes, increased the debates among feminists, religious groups, and civil libertarians about the harmful effects of pornography. Many expressed concern that the message in violent pornography—that women enjoy or desire victimization—might foster, at the very least, a calloused attitude toward rape and other forms of violence against women and, at worst, increase levels of sexual violence and rape. Partly as a reaction to these concerns, in 1985 President Ronald Reagan established a new commission within the Attorney General's office to examine the "problem" of pornography. In its final report, the Attorney General's Commission on Pornography noted the following when discussing sexually violent pornography:

It is with respect to material of this variety that the scientific findings and ultimate conclusions of the 1970 Commission are least reliable for today, precisely because material of this variety was largely absent from that Commission's inquiries. It is not, however, absent from the contemporary world, and it is hardly surprising that conclusions about his material differ from conclusions about material not including violent themes. There is a causal relationship between exposure to sexually violent materials and an increase in aggressive behavior directed towards women. . . . we have reached the conclusion, unanimously and confidently, that the available evidence strongly supports the hypothesis that substantial exposure to sexually violent materials as described here bears a causal relationship to antisocial acts of sexual violence.[3]

In fact, many critics of the 1970 obscenity and pornography commission believed that if violent forms of pornography had been the subject of that investigation, many of the conclusions reached by the commission would have been different. Exposure to violent pornography might have resulted in negative changes in attitudes toward women as well as increases in aggressive behavior. As we saw in our review of the 1970 commission's work, one study that did use pornography with aggressive themes found that aggressive behavior was increased in the laboratory. This was the only study, however, that investigated aggressive forms of pornography because, as the commission noted, such materials were not as readily available before 1970. Since that time, social science researchers have undertaken more systematic investigations of violent pornography.

This research has concentrated primarily on four questions. First, what are the effects of exposure to violent pornography on aggressive behavior? Second, how does violent pornography influence the viewers attitudes and perceptions about sexual violence, particularly rape? Third, do men who are exposed to violent pornography find it sexually arousing? Fourth, if there are effects from viewing violent pornography is it due to the fact that the material is sexually explicit or that it is violent?

What do we mean by violent pornography? Consider the following account of a rape that has been used by researchers who have investigated the effects of violent pornography:

It's in the afternoon, and you're in a room. You're in a room with Nancy and you have a knife. You're going to screw her. You tell her you're going to screw her and she might as well give in. She's saying she doesn't want to, that she wants to leave. And you are just taking out the knife. You tell her to take her clothes off. You see her blond hair. She's big. You are telling her to take her clothes off, go on ahead and take her clothes off. She's slipping off her panties. You're going to rape her right there on the bed. She's slipping off her panties and now she is slipping off her bra. You can see her tits there. You tell her to lie back and she's reluctant to, and you just slap her a little, slap her a little as she's lying down now. You feel yourself . . . you've got a nice stiff erection. You're getting right on top of Nancy. She's big. She's got big thighs and you stick your dick into her there. All the way, deep into her. And she's fighting you. You slap her a little. You tell her to quiet down, to remain still. She's starting to scream now and cry. You're holding her down, forcing yourself on her and you can tell that she likes it. She is telling you to stop, to please stop. You can tell that she is really getting excited now. She is really aroused.[4]

The important features of this depiction are: (1) A women is the victim of sexual coercion in a sexually explicit context. A man uses force against the women to obtain sexual gratification. (2) The depiction portrays a positive victim outcome. Rape is depicted as pleasurable, sexually arousing, and beneficial to the female victim. As we will see, it is this unique feature of violent pornography — the presentation of the idea that women find sexual violence arousing — that plays an important role in producing violent pornography's harmful effects.

IS THERE REALLY MORE VIOLENCE IN PORNOGRAPHY TODAY?

As we mentioned earlier, it is popularly assumed that images of violence have become more prevalent in pornography, particularly in recent years. The 1986 Attorney General's Commission on Pornography takes note of this supposed change in pornography since the time of the first commission report 15 years earlier. According to the commission:

The category of material on which most of the evidence has focused is the category of material featuring actual or unmistakably simulated or unmistakably threatened violence presented in sexually explicit fashion with a predominate focus on the sexually explicit violence. *Increasingly, the most prevalent forms of pornography, as well as an increasingly prevalent body of less explicit material, fit this description.*[5]

Even social scientists, ourselves included, often discussed this rise in violence as if it were fact.[6] But to determine accurately if there has been an increase in violence over the years, it is necessary to do a systematic content analysis of the books, films, and magazines published and distributed over at least a 15–20 year period. Interestingly, no all-inclusive analysis have been undertaken. But there are a handful of studies that have concentrated on subvarieties of mass media. Unfortunately, these studies do not provide a definitive answer to the question of whether violence is more prevalent now than in the past.

One of the first systematic content analyses was undertaken in 1976 by Donald Smith.[7] Smith analyzed "adults only" paperback novels between 1968 and 1974. He found that sexual explicitness became more prevalent after 1969, and the level remained constant through 1974. Depictions of acts of rape doubled during this time, and about one-third of the sex depicts in the novels involved the use of force to obtain sex, usually with no negative consequences to the aggressor. A widely cited study by Neil Malamuth and Barry Spinner[8] found that violent images in *Playboy* and *Penthouse* pictorials increased from 1% to 5% between 1973 and 1977. Although a total percentage of 5% is small, the authors suggest that these images could contribute to a "cultural climate" that sanctions violence against women.

A more recent study by Joseph Scott[9] of Ohio State University puts a new perspective on the Malamuth and Spinner study, at least with regard to the level of violence in *Playboy* magazine. Scott extended his analysis to examine violence in cartoons and pictures in *Playboy* from 1954 to 1983, and found that current levels of violence are below the 1977 level. Thus, Malamuth and Spinner may have hit upon those very years when the level of violence in *Playboy* had first ascended, then peaked. Scott's analysis showed what appears to be a curvilinear relationship. That is, for a time there was an increase in violent images, but since 1977 there has been a decrease in the amount of violent depictions. Furthermore, Scott notes that sexual violence occurs in about 1 page out of every 3,000 and in less than 4 out of every 1,000 pictures. The explanation for this curvilinear relationship might reside in an interesting example of how research findings actually influence pornography's content: A personal communication from Dr. Malamuth revealed that shortly after Malamuth and Spinner's study was published, *Playboy* publisher Hugh Hefner (apparently aware of the study's results) contacted Malamuth about his concern with the ascending level of violence in the magazine. Hefner then instructed his editors to be especially vigilant about violent imagery in *Playboy*.

Park Dietz (a member of the 1986 pornography commission) and Barbara Evans[10] examined the covers of 1,760 adult magazines in the Times Square area of New York. They found that in 1981 only 10.7% of covers depicted a women posed alone — the predominant cover format of magazines sold during the time of the 1970 commission. Pictures of bondage and domination constituted 17.2% of the covers. Unfortunately, the authors cannot relate this figure to a comparable figure for 1970 because this information was not collected at that time. It is possible to argue that the aggressive images that are now "above the counter" were in 1970 "under the counter," and thus not as readily available. But, this is only speculation. It is interesting to note that in a recent study by Dietz[11] on the content of detective magazines, which are not the domain of adult bookstores, 76% of the covers depicted domination and 38% bondage.

In an examination of the stag film genre (the 8mm films now shown more often in peep shows), Slade[12] notes that between 1915 and 1972, rape constituted on average 5% of this material. During this period, violence never went beyond 10% of the material, and there was no indication of any increase in violent images over time. Slade does note that the violence since 1970 has become more graphic and more brutal.

While the stag film was a major form of pornography before the mid-1970s, the videotape has all but replaced the stag film for the home viewing of pornography. Recently, T.S. Palys[13] of Simon Fraser University analyzed the content of 150 randomly selected home videos produced between 1979 and 1983 that were available in British Columbia. The videos were rated either "Triple X," in which the sexual activity is explicit and graphic (classified as X-rated in the United States) or "Adult," in which no explicit sex is shown, but nudity and implied sexual behavior is allowed (R-rated in the United States). Palys found some surprising results when he compared these two types of videos. First, Triple X films depicted more "egalitarian" and "mutual" sexual depictions than Adult films. For example, within the Adult video it was usually the male who played the more dominant role in sexual scenes. In the Triple X video, on the other hand, males and females were depicted in the dominant role about equally as often. Even when Palys considered who was being dominated, females were more often found in this role in the Adult videos than in the Triple X videos. Second, the Adult films had more scenes of aggression, higher percentages of aggressive scenes, and more severe and graphic forms of aggression than the Triple X videos. More important, there was no indication of an increase in aggressive images between 1979 and 1983 for either type of video. Third, with regard to sexual violence, the Adult videos included more depictions in which at least one participant did not engage in sex freely or the scene involved overt aggression than did the Triple X videos. In fact, as Palys notes, the difference between these two types of videos may be widening over time primarily because of *decreases* in sexual violence in the Triple X category. In contrast, the amount of sexual violence in the Adult films has remained fairly constant. And this is the case regardless if one examines the total number of scenes of sexual aggression in the films, or the percentage of sexual aggression within each scene. These findings were clearly contrary to initial expectations, and should lead us to a reevaluation of whether pornography is the proper place to be searching for increases in sexual violence. As the author notes:

Because concern has focused on the issues of violence and sexual violence, the place we have looked for "pornographic" material is in the realm of sexually explicit material, perhaps because that is where we have 'always' looked for it in the past. (This) . . . has left concerned individuals with the potentially misleading impression that those who produce 'pornography' hold the monopoly on violent and sexually violent materials. In contrast, the present study reveals that we may have been myopic in our perspective. The analysis of violent and sexually violent content revealed, contrary to expectation, not only that this material had apparently decreased in frequency within the Triple-X sample, but also, if indeed our concern is with violence and sexual violence, that our attention perhaps would be better directed to what is on the shelves rather than what is under the counter.[14]

At least for now, we cannot legitimately conclude that pornography has become more violent since the time of the 1970 obscenity and pornography commission. The results of the few studies that have been done are inconclusive and mutually inconsistent. It is probably the case that the sheer quantity of violent and nonviolent pornographic materials that are for sale or rent in the United States has increased over the last 15 years — we don't need social science research to inform us of this fact. Undoubtedly, the ready availability of all forms of sexually explicit materials makes it much easier today to come into contact with those materials that are sexually violent. In other words, we may be more aware of the sexually violent forms of pornography because all forms of pornography are more prevalent than they once were. Furthermore, regardless of the increase or absolute level of violence in pornography, the violence that does exist is no trivial matter. There are good reasons to assume that the combination of sex and violence present in some forms of pornography are especially harmful.

Neil Malamuth of UCLA notes that violent pornography is likely to influence viewers for a number of very good reasons.[15] First, the antisocial effects — for example, the imitation of aggressive behavior and desensitization to violence — that researchers have found for individuals who observe mass media violence on television[16] are expected to occur when this violence is presented within a sexual context. But aggressive pornography may be more potent than televised violence because it pairs both sex and violence. Coupling of sex and aggression in violent pornography may result in a conditioning process. Aggressive acts become associated with sexual acts in the viewers' minds. The result of this conditioning process would be that viewers become sexually aroused by violence. Several researchers already believe that this conditioning process is responsible for rapist behavior.[17]

A second concern raised by Malamuth is that because many depictions portray women as secretly desiring and benefiting from aggression, the male viewer might get the idea that even if a women resists his advances, if he is forceful and aggressive he will win her over in the end. Further, the male viewer may apply this to real life although he realizes the depiction he has seen is fiction. Research on memory has shown that subjects who imagine an event they know to be totally fiction may nevertheless believe the event more likely to happen than subjects who do not imagine the event.[18] Research on "priming effects" in cognitive psychology suggests that frequent exposure to mass media depictions of the myth that women enjoy rape might increase the likelihood of applying this scenario in a particular situation, and the myth may become belief.

Check and Malamuth note other possibilities.[19] Men who view violent pornography in which others are enjoying rape might come to expect that they too would enjoy rape. Further, most of the aggressors in violent pornography seem to go unpunished for their actions. Observing a man in a pornographic rape depiction going completely unpunished for his actions might disinhibit an already angry or assault-prone observer's own rape behavior.

For these reasons it seemed likely that violent pornography would have an effect upon the viewer, and that that effect would probably be different from that found for nonviolent sexual materials. As was the case with investigations of sexually explicit materials in the past, three types of effects were examined — aggressive behavior, attitudes and beliefs about women, and sexual arousal.

DOES VIOLENT PORNOGRAPHY INCREASE AGGRESSION AGAINST WOMEN?

From a methodological standpoint, nearly all the studies that purport to show a relationship between violent pornography and aggressive behavior are similar to those discussed in Chapter 3. Nearly all use college-age males as participants, expose them to pictures or films, then give them an opportunity to aggress against a male or female accomplice of the experimenter by supposedly delivering an electric shock or an aversive blast of noise. As we cautioned in the first chapter, there are, of course, many questions about the validity of these procedures when it comes to making a statement about sexual violence outside the laboratory. We will not reiterate them here, but they should be kept in mind as we discuss the research on violent pornography.

The first study to examine aggressive pornography and aggressive behavior since the 1970 obscenity and pornography commission was conducted by Neil Malamuth at UCLA in 1978.[20] College-age men read stories accompanied by pictorials that were either sexually aggressive, nonaggressive but sexual, or neutral in content. The aggressive and sexual stories and pictures were taken from *Penthouse* magazine. The sexually aggressive story depicted the rape of a woman in which it was suggested that she responded in a positive manner (in the end she enjoyed the rape). After reading the stories, all of the men were angered by a woman who was actually hired by the experimenter. The men were then given an opportunity to aggress against this woman under one of two conditions. Half of the men were told by the experimenter that it was "ok" to aggress against the woman, while the remaining men were given information to make them more inhibited about aggressing. The results of the experiment showed that when the men were given the inhibitory message, their level of aggression remained the same no matter what type of pictorial they had seen. In the disinhibitory condition, however, males exposed to the aggressive pornography stories displayed the highest level of aggression. These findings suggested to Malamuth that at least under some conditions (when aggression is condoned), aggressive pornography could increase aggression against women.

A series of studies by Donnerstein at the University of Wisconsin were also done to study the effects of pornography on aggression toward women. In the first study,[21] male subjects were angered or treated in a neutral manner by a male or female confederate. After this treatment, all subjects saw one of three films that were about 5 minutes long. The first film depicted a young couple engaged in various forms of sexual activity. It was sexually explicit (X-rated) but contained no aggressive content. The second film showed the rape of a woman by a man who breaks into her house and forces her into sexual activity at gun point. The film was X-rated, and the reactions of the women were ambiguous (the viewer could not tell if she enjoyed or did not enjoy the rape—a scene not atypical for aggressive pornography). The third film was a control film that contained neither sexual nor aggressive scenes. After viewing one of these films, all subjects were given an opportunity to aggress against the male or female confederate. The results of this study are displayed in Figure 5–1.

When subjects were given an opportunity to shock another male, both pornographic films increased aggression. These findings are similar to those discussed in Chapter 3 in which we noted that when individuals are angered, highly arousing sexual stimuli can increase male-to-male aggression. The aggressive porn film was no different from the nonaggressive film. When subjects were paired with a female, however, there were differences between the two sexual films. As has been the case with most research in this area, the nonaggressive sexual film did not increase aggression against a woman. The aggressive pornographic film did. In fact, the highest level of aggression toward a female in the study was displayed by men who were both angered and shown the sexually violent film. Even more interesting, there was an increase in aggression after exposure to aggressive pornography even for those men who were not angered by the female.

A second study by Donnerstein also examined the influence of aggressive pornography on aggression toward women. The focus of this study was on the reactions of the female rape victim in the film. As we noted earlier, one of the common themes in aggressive pornography is that women are shown to derive pleasure from sexual aggression. According to Donnerstein and Berkowitz,[22] it would seem reasonable to assume that viewing an act of aggression in

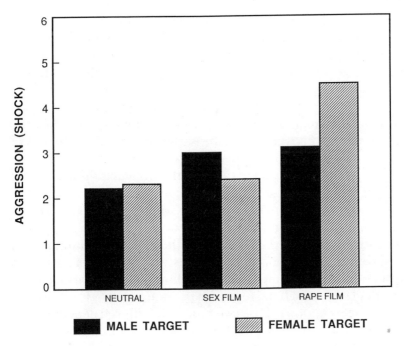

FIGURE 5–1

Men's aggression toward another male or a woman after viewing either a neutral, sexually explicit, or sexually explicit rape film. (Adapted from Donnerstein, 1980.)

which the victim responds in a positive manner would reduce aggressive inhibitions for a male viewer. What about a film that shows a negative reaction by the victim? It is possible that seeing a victim suffer might be rewarding to an angry male? Angry people want to inflict injury.[23] Suppose that the male viewer of aggressive pornography happens to be angry with women as he watches the movie. Seeing the female victim being hurt by the assault on her might be very stimulating for him; her "pain cues" could make his aggressive feelings even stronger.

Donnerstein and Berkowitz[22] predicted that violent pornography would increase aggression against women in men who are already angered, and thus predisposed to aggress. The film showing a positive reaction from the victim will be effective because it can reduce aggressive inhibitions and justify aggression. The film showing a negative reaction will be effective because of its ability to reward or reinforce aggression.

In the first of two studies done by Donnerstein and Berkowitz,[22] male subjects were first angered by a male or female confederate. They were then shown one of four film clips of about 5 minutes duration. The first film was neutral and did not depict sex or violence. The second film was sexually explicit (X-rated) but did not contain any scenes of violence. The third and fourth film were aggressive pornography. They depicted a young woman who comes to study with two men. Both men have been drinking, and when the young women sits between them she is shoved around and forced to drink. She is then tied up, stripped, slapped, and raped by both men. In the *positive ending* version of the film, the woman is shown smiling at the end and in no way resisting. A narrative added to the film indicated that she eventually became a willing participant. In the *negative ending* film, the reactions of the woman are ambiguous, but the narrative indicated that she found the experience humiliating and disgusting. After viewing these films, all subjects were asked to rate them on several dimensions including their "aggressiveness" and the degree to which the female in the film appeared "to suffer."

Subjects' perceptions of the two rape films differed depending on the victims reactions at the end of the film. It is important to remember that both films depicted exactly the same acts of aggression, only the endings differed. Yet, subjects who were exposed to the positive ending film saw the film as less aggressive than those shown the negative ending. Furthermore, the woman in the positive ending film was seen as suffering less, enjoying herself more, and considered more responsible for what happened. (These perceptions of a rape victim who shows a favorable reaction to rape are interesting in themselves, and we will discuss them further later in this chapter).

What were the effects on aggression? The data from this study are shown in Figure 5 – 2. When subjects were angered by a male, there were no effects for exposure to any of the films. However, males exposed to either the negative or positive outcome violent pornography films increased their aggression toward the female who angered them. There were no increases in aggression for men exposed to the sexually explicit but nonviolent film.

These results, like those found earlier by Donnerstein,[24] suggest that violent pornography can increase aggression against women in a laboratory situation. While both types of violent pornography equally increased aggression, it was suggested that they did so for different reasons. The positive ending film, it was reasoned, suggested that aggression was acceptable. This is similar to the Mala-

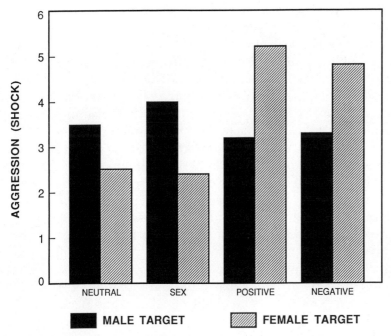

FIGURE 5-2

Men's aggression toward another male or a female after exposure to a neutral, sexually explicit, or rape film. The rape film had either a positive or negative ending. (Adapted from Donnerstein and Berkowitz, 1981.)

muth[25] study that found that when subjects were given information that aggression was OK, exposure to violent pornography increased aggression toward a woman. It appears that a similar process was at work in this study. The negative ending film may have had its influence because the pain and suffering in the film acted as a reinforcement for later aggression by males who were already predisposed to aggress.

Donnerstein and Berkowitz[22] argued that if this reasoning were valid, one might expect a different pattern of results for males who are not angered or primed to aggress. For example, research in the area of human aggression[26] has shown that pain cues act to reduce aggression in subjects who are not angry with the individual they are asked to aggress against. If violent pornography that shows the pain and suffering of a victim increases aggression because it reinforces the anger subjects feel during the experiment, one should see this effect only with men who are angered, not for those who are not angered. But even men who are not angry may be motivated to aggress after exposure to violent pornography that shows a positive victim outcome. Because the positive outcome justifies and reduces inhibitions about aggression, this would suggest that aggression would still be increased after exposure to this type of film.

A second study by Donnerstein and Berkowitz[22] examined these possibilities. In this study, male subjects were angered or treated in a neutral manner by a female confederate. Following this treatment, subjects were shown one of four films that were used in the earlier study. They evaluated the films on several scales and were then given an opportunity to aggress against the female.

The ratings of the rape victim in the positive ending film were similar to those found in the first study. This film was seen as less aggressive, and the victim as suffering less, enjoying more, and having more responsibility. The effects on aggressive behavior, shown in Figure 5–3, are similar to those found in the first study and tend to support the reasoning of Donnerstein and Berkowitz.[22] When subjects were angered, both types of violent pornographic films increased aggression. For nonangered subjects, however, only the positive ending rape film increased aggression.

Results from both studies show that violent pornography can influence aggression toward women, at least in a laboratory situation. While depictions that stress, pain, and suffering seem to affect males who are predisposed to aggression, the common story line of violent pornography — the willing victim — influenced both angered and nonangered males. It is important to note, however, that materials that were merely sexual in nature had no effect on aggressive behavior.

The thoughtful reader might ask how long these effects last. In other words, if individuals have a long enough rest period after exposure to violent pornography, would the observed increases in aggressive behavior still be evident? In all the studies discussed to this point, aggressive behavior is measured almost immediately after exposure to the violent pornographic films. Another question that may be raised is whether the effects of exposure to violent pornography are cumulative. Would viewers exposed repeatedly to such materials become even more aggressive than those exposed only briefly?

Although not designed specifically to answer these two questions, one study has looked at long-term exposure to violent pornography

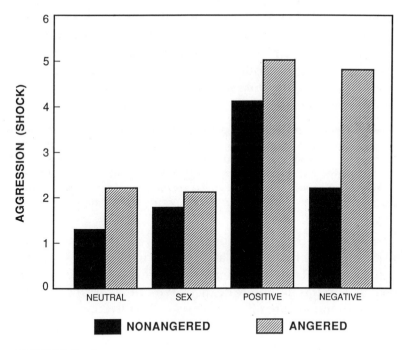

FIGURE 5–3

Aggression toward a female by angered or nonangered men after viewing a neutral, sexually explicit, or rape film. The rape film had a positive or negative ending. (Adapted from Donnerstein and Berkowitz, 1981.)

and later aggression against women with a delay between film viewing and the measurement of aggressive behavior. In this study by Malamuth and Ceniti,[27] male subjects were exposed to violent and nonviolent sexual materials over a 4-week period. This consisted of two feature-length films a week for the first 3 weeks, followed by reading materials in the fourth week. About 1 week after this exposure phase, subjects returned for a session in which they were angered by a female confederate, then given an opportunity to aggress. Surprisingly, the authors found that neither subjects exposed to violent nor to nonviolent pornography displayed more aggression than control (no exposure) subjects. We have to ask why there was no effect for exposure to violent pornography in this study. It is possible that the effects for violent pornography are only short-lived and that they may only activate temporary tendencies toward aggression.[28] Or it is possible that the long-term impact of the exposure is only evident when retrieval cues present in the environment at a later time (such as when a male finds himself in a situation resembling the scene depicted in violent pornography) reactivate the aggressive messages contained in the film. As Malamuth and Ceniti note, if this is true, then the impact of violent pornography may involve two processes:

First, exposure to messages in violent pornography suggesting that aggression against women has positive consequences, is justified or is erotic, may implant and/or strengthen these ideas in the audience as well as stimulate certain arousal processes that might "energize" aggressive responses. Second, behavioral tendencies to aggress may be increased only if effects are measured immediately following exposure or if retrieval cues reactivate violent pornography's messages when a later opportunity to aggress exists.[29]

For the moment, then, we do not know if repeated exposure to violent pornography has a cumulative effects in producing aggression, or if such effects are only temporary. This is one area where additional research is definitely needed. We can say with certainty that there is an immediate effect, however short-lived.

DOES VIOLENT PORNOGRAPHY MAKE MEN THINK DIFFERENTLY ABOUT WOMEN?

Aggressive pornography may foster the belief that women desire and derive pleasure from sexual assault. Images of women eventually succumbing to and finally enjoying sexual violence may suggest to male viewers that even if a woman seems to be first repelled by a pursuer, she will eventually respond favorably to overpowering, aggressive advances.[30] Male consumers of aggressive pornography might come to think, at least for a while, that actually engaging in sexual aggression might be personally profitable, thus reducing their inhibitions about this form of aggression.[31] Beliefs such as these may be important in producing or sustaining violent behavior. Men who subscribe to these beliefs might be more likely to attack a woman after they see the supposedly "pleasurable" rapes depicted in violent pornography.

There is now evidence, mainly from the work of Malamuth and his colleagues[32] that exposure to aggressive pornography alters observers' perceptions of the act of rape and of rape victims themselves. For example, in a study by Malamuth, Haber, and Feshbach,[33] men and women participated in a two-part study. In Part 1 they read either a story about a woman being raped or a nonviolent but sexually explicit story. The rape story portrayed the women as becoming sexually aroused. In Part 2, all subjects read yet another story. This time, all subjects read about a woman who was raped, with no indication in the story that the woman showed pleasure. Malamuth then asked subjects to rate the second story on several dimensions and assign a prison sentence to the rapist. Results showed that males who read the rape story in which the victim showed arousal in Part 1 said the victim in the second story experienced less pain. These men also reported more sexual arousal to this story. Contrary to expectations, these same men were more punitive to the rapist by giving him a harsher prison sentence for his act of rape.

One finding in this study has often been misinterpreted. When subjects were asked how likely they would be to behave as the rapist did in the second story if they knew they would not be caught, 51% indicated some likelihood of behaving that way. This occurred for all males in the study, regardless of whether they first read the violent story or the nonviolent story. It has often been reported that this "increase" happened because of exposure to the violent pornography the subjects read. For example, a document titled *Pornography: Its Effect on the Family, Community, and Culture* (often cited by pornography foes and published by the Free Congress Research and Education Foundation) mentions that even after brief exposure to pornography, particularly violent pornography, one-third of the subjects reported an increased willingness to actually commit rape, and two-thirds an increase in their willingness to say they would force a woman into sexual acts (presumably from a study by Briere and Malamuth).[34] However, there was no direct effect on the "likelihood-to-rape" measure from exposure to either of the first two stories read by the subjects. In fact, in none of the Malamuth studies, including a study with repeated exposure to aggressive pornography over 4 weeks,[35] has there been a change in this rape measure as a function of exposure to pornography. This measure was, however, correlated with self-reported sexual arousal to the first rape story and a general calloused attitude about rape. In other words, males indicating some likelihood to rape were more sexually aroused by the first rape story in Part 1 of the study. As noted by Malamuth,[36] men who indicate some likelihood that they might commit rape (if not caught) are generally more affected by exposure to aggressive pornography, but there are no data to indicate from his studies that exposure to aggressive pornography is the cause of this predisposition.

In another two-part study, Malamuth and Check[37] had men listen first to one of three versions of a sexually explicit story. In the first version, a woman rape victim becomes sexually aroused while being attacked. In the second version she does not become aroused. The third version served as a control and did not depict rape or any other form of aggression. In Part 2, all subjects listened to a rape story in which there was no indication that the woman showed pleasure. Results showed that men first exposed to the rape story in which the woman becomes aroused saw less trauma to the rape victim in the second story, and believed that a higher percentage of men would say they would commit rape. There was no effects on the likelihood-to-rape measure, although there was a significant correlation between sexual arousal to the negative ending rape story and this measure.

It is important to note that the findings in this area have not always been consistent. For example, a study by Malamuth, Reisin, and Spinner[38] in which males were exposed to sexually violent materials from *Playboy* and *Penthouse* did not find any effects of this exposure on perceptions of a rape victim presented to them in a video interview. Malamuth[39] has suggested that the differences between these studies may be due to the endings of the sexually violent stories. The earlier studies found changes in perceptions of a rape victim when the sexually violent story they had earlier been exposed to depicted the female victim as showing a positive reaction to the rape. In the Malamuth, Reisin, and Spinner study, argues Malamuth,[40] the materials were not chosen to reflect this type of positive ending. This supports the idea that the message in violent pornography that women find force or aggression pleasurable seems to be an important factor in influencing perceptions and attitudes about rape.

This particular message seems to have a stronger effect on certain types of men. As we have already noted from Malamuth's work, males indicating some likelihood they might rape if not caught may be more influenced than other males by this message. This is further illustrated in a more recent study by Malamuth and Check.[41] In this study, males were first classified as high likelihood to rape (HLR) or low likelihood to rape (LLR), based on their answer to a question asking their likelihood to rape if they knew they would not be caught. In Part 1 of the story, men read one of several versions of a sexually explicit story, including the typical rape story in which the victim becomes aroused. In Part 2, subjects were exposed to a realistic rape story used in previous studies by Malamuth. The authors found that all males exposed to the positive rape story, regardless of whether they were HLR or LLR, attributed more pleasure to the female victim in the second rape story. While the HLR and LLR subjects exposed to the positive outcome rape did not differ in this measure, they did differ on two additional questions asked by the experimenters: What percentage of women would enjoy being raped; and what percentage of women would enjoy being forced into sex? Malamuth and Check found it was only the HLR men who were affected by exposure to the rape/arousal story in Part 1. In fact, for HLR men, the percentages who said women *would enjoy rape* was 37% and for *enjoy being forced* 38%, after viewing the rape arousal story. LLR men were not as affected by exposure to the positive outcome rape pornography. Their estimates on these same questions following exposure to this material were much lower.

These results are important because they suggest that the effects from exposure to aggressive pornography may be dependent upon an individual's initial attitudes about rape and other forms of violence against women. This may indicate that exposure to aggressive pornography is not necessarily "causing" calloused attitudes about rape, but rather reinforcing and strengthening already existing beliefs and values.

IS VIOLENT PORNOGRAPHY SEXUALLY AROUSING TO MEN?

While it was once believed that only rapists would become sexually aroused by depictions of rape and other forms of aggression against women,[42] research by Malamuth and his colleagues[43] indicates that even nonrapists will show sexual arousal to certain kinds of media-presented images of rape. This increased arousal occurs primarily in response to depictions of rape in which the female victim shows signs of pleasure and arousal. In the research with rapists[44] it was generally found that rapists showed increases in sexual arousal when viewing depictions of rape and consenting sexual behaviors.

Nonrapists, on the other hand, while showing arousal to consenting sex, do not show arousal to rape depictions. Researchers have suggested that sexual arousal to rape depictions may be an objective and reliable index of a proclivity to engage in rape.[45] In other words, an individual whose sexual arousal to rape themes was similar to or greater than his arousal to nonaggressive depictions (consenting sex) would be more likely than other men to engage in aggressive acts against women under certain conditions. But this does not mean that viewing the rape depiction caused or encouraged them to rape, only that the individuals who rape tend also to be aroused by rape scenes.

Why did researchers like Abel find that nonrapists were not aroused by scenes of rape, while studies done by Malamuth showed that many normal males did find depictions of rape sexually arousing? As noted earlier, Malamuth finds that college males are just as aroused by rape scenes as they are by consenting sex scenes, perhaps even more aroused when the rape shows the female victim herself becoming sexually aroused. In his research, Abel always presented depictions of a rape victim to subjects who showed a negative reaction to her assault. As we have already noted in this chapter, a great deal of aggressive pornography (and other media portraying rape) presents rape as something the female victim desires and finds pleasurable, a scenario that nonrapists (as well as rapists) find arousing.

Malamuth has also shown that there is a group within the normal male population that responds to violent pornography in much the same way as rapists respond.[46] This group of men is identified by Malamuth by their answers to the question of whether they would be willing to rape if they were assured of not being caught or punished. These men have been labeled as HLR, and Malamuth finds that they show more sexual arousal to rape depictions no matter what the ending, positive or negative.

The implications for normal males becoming sexually aroused to aggressive pornography is best stated by Malamuth:

To the extent that people perceive that they are sexually aroused by violence, they may infer that they are capable of and would be sexually aroused by rape. For many individuals, this inference may be based on their experience with violent pornography rather than any actual behavior they have personally engaged in. Their reactions to pornography may lead them to believe (probably erroneously) that they would be sexually aroused by actually engaging in rape.[47]

SEXUAL AROUSAL TO RAPE,
ATTITUDES ABOUT RAPE, AND
BEHAVIOR OUTSIDE THE LABORATORY

The research to this point suggests that exposure to violent pornography can influence men's perceptions and attitudes about rape as well as leading to increased sexual arousal. The reader might ask, however, whether these changes in attitudes or arousal patterns have any relation to real-world behaviors. It would be impossible for researchers to expose men to violent pornography and then place them in a situation where they could actually rape a woman. But social scientists can assess the relationship between sexual arousal, attitudes about rape, and later aggressive behavior in a laboratory context. They can also ask men to report on whether or not they have committed acts of sexual aggression against women, then measure the relationship between these self-reports and sexual arousal.

Two studies by Malamuth[48] try to do just that, and strongly suggest that measures of sexual arousal and attitudes about rape do a fairly good job of predicting aggressive behavior toward women. Malamuth[49] designed a study to determine whether measures developed to assess sexual arousal and attitudes about violence toward women would predict normal males' aggressive behavior against women in the laboratory. In Part 1 of the study, Malamuth measured sexual arousal to rape by having subjects listen to a rape story and a consenting sex story, then measuring the difference between their sexual arousal to both stories. As we noted earlier, this difference is considered to be a measure of a general proclivity to rape. Malamuth also measured subjects' acceptance of rape myths and acceptance of interpersonal violence against women.[50] In Part 2 of the study, conducted days later, subjects were given an opportunity to aggress against women in a laboratory setting and were asked about their desire to hurt women. Results of this study indicated that the measures obtained from subjects in Part 1 of the study could successfully predict aggressive behavior and desire to hurt women several days later.

In another study Malamuth,[51] examined the relationship between sexual arousal to rape, rape-related attitudes, and other psychological processes on self-reported naturalistic sexual aggression. Male subjects in this study first completed a questionnaire that measured the following:

1. *Dominance as a sexual motive.* This scale measures the degree to which an individual sees control over a sexual partner as a motivation for sex. Typical items from this scale are, "I enjoy the feeling of having someone in my grasp," or "I enjoy the conquest".

2. *Hostility toward women.* This scale, recently developed by Check and Malamuth,[52] was included because it was believed that it would show which men in the sample would not be inhibited about sexual aggression and a woman's suffering. A typical item from the scale is, "Women irritate me a great deal more than they are aware of."

3. *Attitudes facilitating violence.* The Acceptance of Interpersonal Violence Scale was used to tap this general attitude. An example of an item from this scale is, "Sometimes the only way to get a cold woman turned on is to use force."

4. *Antisocial characteristics.* Malamuth used subjects' scores on psychoticism from the Eysenck Personality Questionnaire to measure this characteristic. Previous research has shown that sex offenders score high on this personality trait, and it appears to be a useful measure to predict some sexually aggressive responses.

Next, Malamuth measured sexual arousal to rape and consenting sexual stories, and constructed the usual rape index by looking at how sexually aroused the men were by the rape story relative to a consenting story.

Malamuth was interested in the degree to which these measures were related to self-reports of actual sexual aggression. To measure this, he used a scale developed by Koss and Oros[53] that measures sexual aggression ranging from the use of psychological pressure to obtain sex to physical force. An example of an item from this scale is, "I have had sexual intercourse with a woman when she didn't want to because I used some degree of physical force (twisting her arm, holding her down, etc.)."

The results of this study showed that all the measures, except antisocial characteristics, were correlated with self-reports of sexual aggression. Further analysis by Malamuth showed that the best predictor of sexual aggression against women was the combination of all of these measures — sexual arousal as well as the others. This implies that both sexual arousal to rape and attitudes about harming women are equally important in predicting aggression. According to Malamuth, however, the fact that a man finds depictions of women being raped sexually arousing does not imply that he will behave aggressively against women in the real world. While sexual arousal to rape is an important determinant of aggression against women, other factors must be present. More important, the study indicates that being sexually aroused by viewing violent pornography need not occur in order to predict aggressive acts against women. The attitudes men have about women, and particularly violence against women, can be important predictors of their aggressive behavior. While these attitudes may develop as a result of exposure to violent pornography, as we will see in the next chapter, they are just as likely to come about from exposure to many types of mass media — from soap operas to popular commercially released films.

Up to now we have seen that exposure to violent pornography may have negative effects on attitudes about women, and appears to increase aggressive behavior against women — at least in the laboratory. We have also seen that normal college age males become sexually aroused to violent pornography, especially if it contains the message that women enjoy being raped. But there remains an important question. Because violent pornography contains both a message about violence against women and is emotionally arousing because of its sexual explicitness, we need to know which of these aspects of violent pornography accounts for these effects. What is the relative contribution of the sexual and aggressive components of violent pornography to changes in attitudes and aggressive behavior? Is it the sexual nature of the material or the messages about violence that are crucial in facilitating laboratory aggression by males against females and influencing attitudes about rape? This is an important question because many policy-oriented discussions of this research omit the fact that the material under study is violent as well as sexually explicit. It is sometimes assumed that the experimental effects occur primarily because the material is sexually explicit and sexually arousing, and secondarily because the material is violent. In the next chapter we will examine studies that suggest this is not true.

6

Is It the Sex or
Is It the Violence?

ONE certainly does not have to delve into the pornographic market to find examples of violence against
women. Let's take a look at the following excerpt:

On the table is a woman about forty-two who owns a local bookstore. Her hands
and feet are tied with soft padded straps, her eyes are blindfolded and a soft white
cloth covers her mouth . . . She suddenly begins to struggle as she becomes
aware of being tied down. I speak to her slowly and softly, telling her she will not be
harmed . . . she is nervous, crying, fearful. She will not calm down and so I cover
her mouth again . . . I unbutton her vest and blouse, pull them both apart and
kiss her chest and neck. . . . I lift her bra up and reveal her little tits. Her nipples
are quite large for the size of her tits and are brown. . . . I continue to lick her and
tease her, occasionally playing with her nipples which now grow hard with my
touch. I slowly work my fingers in and out of her cunt and ask her to tell me what I
want to know about her masturbation. At this point in the fantasy she changes
completely into total cooperation. . . . As she finishes I am licking her cunt fur-
iously, lapping her juice and she is shuddering and responding to my tongue.
Suddenly her hips rise and she comes. I feel her beginning to come again. I stop and
quickly insert my cock to the hilt. I begin to fuck harder and harder and she moves
with me instead of against me. In seconds we are both lost in a fantastic orgasm.[1]

Is this another passage, like the one we presented at the beginning
of the last chapter, from a study investigating the effects of violent
pornography? No. Is it a passage from a paperback book or magazine sold in an adult bookstore? No. It is one of many sexually
aggressive depictions from a popular best-selling book by Nancy
Friday called *Men in Love,* which consists of stories written by men
about their sexual fantasies. The point here is that these ideas about

108

rape are so pervasive in our culture that it is myopic to call them the exclusive domain of violent pornography.

In fact, nonexplicit depictions of rape and sexual violence in which the victim later expresses affection for her assailant have appeared in daytime television soap operas and in movies shown on network television. For example, in the daytime drama *General Hospital,* produced by the American Broadcasting Company, several episodes were devoted to the rape of one of the popular female characters by an equally popular male character. At first, the victim was humiliated; later the two characters married. A similar theme was expressed in the popular film *The Getaway,* used in research by Malamuth, starring Steve McQueen and Ali McGraw. In this film, the protagonist

kidnaps a woman . . . and her husband. He rapes the woman but the assault is portrayed in a manner such that the woman is depicted as a willing participant. She becomes the protagonist's girlfriend and they both taunt her husband until he commits suicide. The woman then willingly continues with the assailant and at one point frantically searches for him.[2]

Malamuth and Check[3] tried to determine whether the nonexplicit depiction of sexual violence contained in *The Getaway* and in a mass-released film with similar content *(Swept Away)* influenced the viewers' attitudes toward rape and their perceptions of women. In their investigation, 271 male and female students participated in what they thought was a study of movie ratings. One group of subjects watched, on two different evenings, *The Getaway* and *Swept Away.* A control group of men and women watched neutral feature-length movies. The movies were viewed in campus theaters as part of the Campus Film Program. Several days later the researchers measured the viewers' acceptance of interpersonal violence against women and rape myths, measures that we saw earlier are related to actual aggression against women. These questions were embedded in a larger questionnaire containing many items as part of a sexual attitudes survey that was distributed several days after the film viewing so that subjects would not become suspicious about the true nature of the study and deliberately distort their answers. When questioned after the study, subjects reported seeing no connection between the survey and the movies they had seen earlier. The results showed that viewing the sexually aggressive films significantly increased male but not female acceptance of interpersonal violence, and tended to increase acceptance of rape myths. The important point here is that these effects happened not with X-rated materials but with images more suitable for prime time television.

In a more recent pair of studies, Donnerstein, Berkowitz, and Linz[4] examined systematically the relative contributions of the aggressive and sexual components of violent pornography. In the first study, male college students were angered by either a male or a female confederate and were then shown one of four different films. The first was similar to the aggressive pornography used in studies discussed earlier. The second was X-rated, but contained no aggression or sexual coercion. Subjects rated it just as sexually and physiologically arousing as the first film. The third contained scenes of aggression against women, but without any sexual content. Subjects rated it as less sexually and physiologically arousing than the previous two films. The last film was of neutral content.

After viewing the films, the men were given the opportunity to aggress against a male or a female confederate of the experimenter. The results showed that the men who viewed the aggressive pornographic film displayed the highest level of aggression against the woman, as was the case in the other studies discussed in this chapter. Most importantly, the aggression-only film, which was devoid of explicit sex, produced more aggression against the woman than the sexually explicit film that contained no violence or coercion. In fact, there were no differences in aggression against the female target for subjects in the sex-only film condition and the neutral film condition. In the second study, the aggressive "cue value" of the female target was strengthened by establishing a name connection between the female victim in the film and the female confederate in the study whom the men would later be asked to aggress against.

Earlier research on nonsexual violence had established that providing the target of aggression with the same name as a victim in a film portrayal of violence increased aggression against that target.[5] The investigators reasoned that the same procedure might increase violence against women following exposure to sexually aggressive films. Subjects were first angered or treated in a neutral manner by a female confederate, then exposed to three versions of the same film. The first version contained a scene of sexual aggression in which a woman was tied up, threatened with a gun, and raped. The second version contained only the violent parts of the scene, with the sexually explicit content removed. The third version contained the sexually explicit parts of the scene, with most of the violence deleted. After viewing the films, it was made apparent to half of the subjects that the female in the film had the same name as the confederate against whom they now had the opportunity to aggress. The other half of the subjects were not encouraged to make this association. Following the viewing of one of these films, subjects completed a questionnaire that measured their attitudes toward rape (Rape Myth Acceptance Scale), their willingness to use force against a woman, and their willingness to rape if not caught. The results showed that while subjects who viewed the combination of sex and violence showed higher levels of aggressive behavior than subjects in the sex-only group, subjects exposed to the violence-only depiction under certain conditions also exhibited higher levels of aggression than the sex-only group. Subjects in the violence-only condition, who were either given the name association cue or who were angered by the experimenter, showed higher levels of aggression against the female target than the sex-only subjects. Interestingly, the most callous rape attitudes and the largest percentage of subjects indicating some likelihood of raping or using force were found in the aggression-only film condition. Subjects in the X-rated sex-only film condition scored lowest on these measures. In fact, 50% of subjects in the violence-only condition indicated some likelihood to rape compared with 11% for sex-only and 25% for the sexual violence film.

It may not be surprising to the reader that certain attitudes and behaviors can be influenced by sexually nonexplicit violence against women. After all, this is consistent with the findings on television and behavior.[6] But what about sexual arousal, a measure that we saw earlier is also a reliable predictor of self-reported aggression against women? Is sexual explicitness needed in depictions of violence against women in order for certain males to become sexually aroused? The answer seems to be no. Research with rapists has shown that nonsexually explicit images of rape can be sexually arousing,[7] and more recent research by Malamuth has shown that for many normal individuals with already existing calloused attitudes about violence against women, just the depiction of a woman as a victim of aggression *devoid of sexual content* can stimulate sexual arousal. Malamuth, Check, and Briere[8] found that males who indicated they would be sexually aroused by "forcing a woman into doing something she did not want" (about 30% of the subjects) were more sexually aroused by aggressive than nonaggressive stories. The aggressive stories were both sexual or nonsexual, with the nonsexual story depicting a man who cuts a woman with a knife and beats her into unconsciousness.

Considered together, these studies strongly suggest that violence against women need not occur in a pornographic or sexually explicit context to have a negative effect on viewer attitudes and behavior.

If this is true, then to focus research efforts primarily on pornographic images of violence against women is somewhat misguided. By doing so, we ignore the substantial quantity of violence against women contained in R-rated movies. What is particularly troubling about these depictions is their tremendous availability. It is safe to assume that many more people have been exposed to violence against women in this form than have been exposed to violent pornography. Because sexually nonexplicit forms of violence are more available to greater numbers of viewers, we need to ask: What are the effects of continued exposure to this material on our perceptions of violence and views about victims? Will viewers become calloused toward violence, not only in the R-rated depictions themselves but also in more realistic circumstances?

DESENSITIZATION TO VIOLENCE

Imagine for a moment a malevolent psychologist who wanted to design a program of therapy, the purpose of which was to enable people to calmly view the torture and dismemberment of women. What steps would be taken? First, the psychologist might have his or her patients read about the torture and mutilation of women. Most of the patients would find this troubling at first, but if they persisted they would probably become less disturbed by it. After the patients became accustomed to these readings, the therapist might employ a stronger set of stimuli. The patients could be asked to view still photographs of mutilated female bodies. Toward the end of this "desensitization" procedure, the patients might be asked to watch actors engaged in the simulated mutilation of human bodies. After viewing scene after scene of mutilation, the patients' tolerance for the material might become quite high. After such "therapy," we might expect that viewing films of actual mutilation and even viewing a mutilated body itself (as a doctor in an emergency room would) would become more tolerable.

To make the procedure more pleasant for the patient, and also to make the desensitization process more efficient, the psychologist might provide the patient with a favorite food, or have the patient imagine something pleasant in the scene. Better yet, the therapist might intersperse the bloody, gory scenes with pleasing scenes, such as mildly erotic depictions of a woman disrobing or a young couple making love.

A whole genre of movies (sometimes called "slasher films" or "splatter films") has emerged over the last 10 years or so. These films play to millions in drive-ins and movie theaters, are readily available on videocassettes, and are not just confined to adult cinema or "dirty" book stores. While the sex is not explicit, but merely suggestive, the violence is graphically displayed and is overwhelmingly directed at women. In these films, women are, among other things, stabbed, beaten, tortured, raped, decapitated, burned, drilled with electric drills, cut with saws, scalped, and shot in the head with nail guns. Each year the films are more graphic than their predecessors in depicting mutilation (particularly of women), and may be doing to viewers exactly what the fictional therapist described above would have done to make his or her patients more tolerant of blood and gore. The possible desensitizing effects of this genre of films have not escaped the attention of some leading film critics. For example, Janet Maslin,[9] film critic for the *New York Times*, has hypothesized:

Violence in the real world becomes much more acceptable after you've seen infinitely greater violence on the screen. And this kind of horror film, in addition to inuring its audience to genuine violence, has a debasing effect as well. In this respect it harkens back to hard-core sexual pornography, the tactics of which it carries to the most extreme. Years ago, when sexual explicitness on the screen seemed to have advanced so far as it possibly could go, it was often remarked that only by actually penetrating the body could the camera go any further. That in a sense, is what the camera does now.

People unaccustomed to viewing slasher films may wonder exactly what they contain and why critics such as Maslin are concerned that real-life violence may become more acceptable after viewing them. The wording of the advertisement on the cover of one particular videocassette in this genre might help the uninitiated appreciate the content of some of these films. This film is quite literally the quintessential slasher film. It distills all of the "best" or most gruesome scenes from several movies into one. The viewer of *Filmgore* is promised

A cosmic cavalcade of bloodthirsty thrills from the most violent movies ever made! An entertainment extravaganza of extreme exterminations, devastating decimations, and delirious decapitations!!

Filmgore is an endless orgy of unimaginable atrocity at an incredible velocity — the most sanguinary sensations ever splashed and splattered across the savage screen![10]

There are many slasher films that, aside from simply presenting unrelenting violence, present violence scenes in a peculiar way. The presentation is quite similar to the procedures used by our malevolent psychologist, in which a pleasant scene is paired with an anxiety-provoking scene to speed up the desensitization process. Critic Maslin has also noted this juxtaposition of pleasant and anxiety-provoking scenes, and speculates that this device is intentionally used by the film maker to make the film's violence more effective:

> The carnage is usually preceded by some sort of erotic prelude: footage of pretty young bodies in the shower, or teens changing into nighties for the slumber party, or anything that otherwise lulls the audience into a mildly sensual mood. When the killing begins, this eroticism is abruptly abandoned, for it has served its purpose, that of lowering the viewer's defenses and heightening the films physical effectiveness. The speed and ease with one's feelings can be transformed from sensuality into viciousness may surprise even those quite conversant with the links between sexual and violent urges.[11]

Social scientists and public health officials, such as Surgeon General Everett Koop, have expressed concern that continued exposure to filmed violence will cause some viewers to become desensitized and thus unconcerned about victims of violence in the real world.[12] These problems become particularly important in the face of the tremendously increased availability of this material due to advances in cable, satellite, and video technology.

The remainder of this chapter examines the scientific research on the impact of prolonged exposure to violence in the media — particularly sexual violence. The research on these films described in this chapter addresses several questions: Do male viewers become desensitized to graphic depictions of violence against women as a result of continued exposure to such depictions? Does this desensitization, if it occurs, spill over into other contexts — that is, will individuals who become desensitized to filmed violence against women have a tendency to perceive the victim as less injured and/or express less sympathy for a female victim of actual violence? Will female viewers experience the same desensitization effects as males? What are the implications of desensitization for violent behavior — will the desensitized person be more or less likely to behave violently? We will first offer a brief overview of the techniques used in desensitization therapy, a procedure developed by psychologists to help people overcome phobias or anxieties. It has been argued that just as a person will become less anxious about snakes or public speaking (two of the many phobias treated by psychologists) with sufficient exposure to these "objects of anxiety" in therapy, viewers exposed to violence that was once anxiety provoking will become less anxious about it.

McCutcheon and Adams[13] designed a clinical experiment to examine the effectiveness of "implosive therapy," a type of therapy in which the therapist "floods" a patient with a series of images or cues in order to achieve high levels of anxiety so that the fear associated with these images or cues rapidly "extinguishes." Male and female students enrolled in an introductory psychology course at the University of Georgia were asked to complete the Fear Survey Schedule III,[14] a questionnaire that asks about a wide range of fearful situations. Women who indicated that they were "very much afraid" of watching a surgical operation (which by the way, according to pilot data collected by the authors is the most common fear among female college students at the University of Georgia) were asked to participate further in the experiment. These students reported to an experimental laboratory where they watched a 16-mm film entitled *Multiple Wounds: Report of a Battle Casualty*. This film could be stopped by a switch made available to the experimenter. Only women who terminated the film before 3 minutes were retained in the study. These subjects then sat in a dimly lit room in a reclining chair wired with galvanic skin resistance (GSR) electrodes. These electrodes were used to continuously record how aroused the study participants became to a 60-minute audiotape recording of fear-provoking imagery (a description of a surgical operation). After the 60-minute flooding session, the women were asked to watch the *Battle Casualty* film again. The results indicated that whereas before exposure to the fear-provoking images the women could watch, on average, only about 50 seconds of the film, after the flooding session the women could tolerate over three times that much. They were now, on average, able to view more than 2½ minutes of the surgical film. In addition, their level of physiological arousal decreased steadily throughout the fear-image flooding procedure.

Desensitization is defined as decreased responsiveness to a stimulus after extensive exposure to it.[15] Continued exposure usually results in a blunting of feelings of fear and anxiety about a stimulus, and reduced physiological arousal in the face of the stimulus. Desensitization also often involves changes in a behavioral or action component—the women watching the surgical film were able to tolerate more of the film before they took action to terminate it. In another situation involving exposure to a feared object like a snake, the desensitized patient may be able to touch and handle a snake he or she could not even look at in the past without an extreme fear reaction.

Desensitization therapy has proven to be the most effective technique for training individuals to engage in behaviors that were previously inhibited by severe anxiety responses.[16] Exactly why exposing people either gradually, or all at once, to the objects they fear will eventually result in less fear in the presence of these same stimuli is not really known. It was first thought that desensitization techniques would only work if the patient could be induced to respond with the opposite of an anxiety response — that is, a relaxation response when in the presence of a feared object.

Research on systematic desensitization therapy has seen shown that desensitization does not depend upon presenting a strong competing response, such as muscular relaxation, in the face of an anxiety-provoking stimuli; it does not depend upon a hierarchical or graded presentation of anxiety-provoking stimuli; and it does not require continual pairing of relaxation with hierarchy items.[17] As a result, most psychologists no longer think of desensitization as a reciprocal inhibition process. A major alternative hypothesis to account for desensitization is the "counterconditioning hypothesis." This hypothesis suggests that fear is reduced by pairing anxiety-provoking stimuli with *any* nonanxiety response — not necessarily an antagonistic one. Supporters of the counterconditioning hypothesis maintain that a graded stimulus presentation paired with elicitation of a competing response is probably the most efficient way of reducing fear with minimum stress, even though these conditions are not theoretically necessary for desensitization to occur. Relaxation, according to this hypothesis, is also not necessary for fear reduction, but it does play a facilitative role.

Counterconditioning is probably the most widely accepted explanation for desensitization at present.[18] However, many psychologists also interpret the effects of desensitization therapy simply as a form of extinction. The idea is that there is reduction in anxiety because of the repeated presentation of emotional stimuli that the patient has been conditioned to fear, followed by no adverse consequences.[19] Repeated exposure to the anxiety-provoking stimulus (a snake — to use our well-worn example) with no aversive consequences (the patient is not attacked or bitten) results in the anxiety response being extinguished in the patient.

Other explanations for desensitization effects are more controversial. Some researchers[20] maintain that desensitization is really a form of *habituation* rather than extinction. Habituation is a term usually applied to temporary decreases in sympathetic arousal responses (unconditioned responses rather than more complex classically conditioned responses) to a stimulus that is repeatedly presented. For example, the decrement in startle responses (to noise or bright light) with repeated exposure to a stimulus is thought to be a form of habituation. Because there are currently no predictions from a habituation perspective that differ from predictions made from an extinction perspective, there is no experiment that can be done to distinguish between the two theories. Other than differences in terminology, the two approaches lead to the same conclusion about exposure to an object or situation that provokes anxiety —continued exposure leads to reductions in anxiety. The extinction explanation may be better because it is not limited to simply physiological phenomena.

Other researchers have tried to characterize desensitization as a form of operant learning. In other words, during the process of imagining oneself in a feared situation, the patient becomes aware of the rewards associated with engaging in "nonavoidant" behaviors. These rewards might be in the form of encouragement and praise from the therapist, vicarious reinforcements from watching a model successfully deal with a feared object or situation, or self-praise as the patient notes his or her progress through the fear stimulus hierarchy. Other psychologists have applied more current terminology to explanations of desensitization by attempting to explain the process in terms of changes in "fear schemas" or mental images of the frightening stimulus. According to Lang,[21] these images are stored in memory as verbal propositions—semantic units comprising memories, behavioral, and physiological reactions. Accordingly, desensitization therapy is successful because a fear schema is evoked from memory and modified in some way— new information incompatible with the old is added to the schema ("I can now sit for 2 minutes in the presence of a snake, where before I could not"). Unfortunately, it is not clear exactly *how* information is added to the fear schema and whether or not the patient actually has any voluntary control over the process. Further, it is not apparent that anything is gained, at least from a scientific perspective, from describing the desensitization process in these new and more complex terms, when simpler processes like extinction or counterconditioning can be posited.

The reader should keep some of these explanations in mind when thinking about desensitization to violence, particularly sexual violence. For example, the process of counterconditioning described here could easily account for reductions in anxiety or desensitization in the face of violent media depictions. In this view, it will be recalled, virtually any nonanxiety response that is paired with the previously anxiety-provoking stimulus will serve to reduce anxiety. Also according to this approach, desensitization is most efficiently produced when stimuli graded by intensity are paired with relaxation responses. Thus, if a film maker were to continually pair violent scenes with relaxing music, or continually pair violence with pleasing stimuli such as mildly erotic scenes, building from the least fearful scenes to a climax of great fearfulness, desensitization may occur very efficiently. The viewer would come to associate, through conditioning, the previously anxiety-provoking stimulus (violence) with the neutral or positive response elicited by neutral scene or a mildly erotic scene.

The process of extinction proposed to operate in desensitization therapy might also account for the effects observed after the prolonged exposure to filmed violence described in the next sections of the chapter. Depictions of physical violence and mutilation that are naturally anxiety provoking for most viewers[22] might become less so with continued exposure because of the extinction process. Even extremely fear-provoking stimuli such as scenes of humans being stabbed, cut up, and mutilated with knives or other objects may lose their ability to provoke an anxiety response if the scenes are continually shown with no aversive consequences to the viewer (i.e., the viewer is not injured or physically hurt).

More than 15 years have passed since the National Commission on the Causes and Prevention of Violence[23] declared a link between violent behavior and viewing violence on television. During that time, the debate over media violence and possible effects on social behavior continued unabated. In 1972 the Surgeon General's Study of Television and Social Behavior[24] reached a "tentative conclusion of the causal relationship." Then in 1976 the American Medical Association[25] claimed that televised violence was a "threat to the social health of the country." Now the National Institute of Mental Health (NIMH) forcefully asserts (after reviewing "hundreds of empirical studies") that there is "overwhelming evidence of a causal relationship between violence on television and later aggressive behavior." The report concludes:

The consensus among most of the research community is that violence on television does lead to aggressive behavior by children and teenagers who watch the programs. This conclusion is based on laboratory experiments and on field studies. Not all children become aggressive, of course, but the correlations between violence and aggression are positive. In magnitude, television violence is as strongly correlated with aggressive behavior as any other behavioral variable that has been measured. The research question has moved from whether or not there is an effect to seeking explanations for the effect.[26]

The conclusions reached by NIMH were based on the accumulation of results from investigations of violent television programs on subsequent aggression in the laboratory,[27] field experiments, and correlational studies.[28]

In light of the volume of research examined by the NIMH report, and in light of recently completed large-scale longitudinal projects,[29] it might seem that the question of media violence and its impact on the viewer is resolved. But the reader should be cautioned that while most behavioral scientists see the accumulated findings as unassailable evidence for a link, a dissenting view — that media violence does not contribute to real-world violence — is espoused by the television industry.[30] Sociologist Joseph Klapper, the director of research for CBS, testifying at congressional hearings, maintained that there was no relationship between exposure to TV violence and antisocial behavior,[31] that there is "still no convincing evidence" that television violence contributes to crime.[32] Moreover, among research psychologists there are those who question the external validity of current laboratory research findings.[33] Many of the criticisms outlined in Chapter 1 concerning the strengths and weaknesses of laboratory investigations into the effects of exposure to pornography apply with equal force to investigations into nonsexual media violence.

In most of the experimental research described in the NIMH report,[26] subjects have only been exposed to violent stimuli for a short time (in most cases only a few minutes). Evidence has been mounting (albeit at a slower rate) regarding the effects of prolonged exposure to *many* violent scenes. We will discuss this evidence next.

Early research by Lazarus et al.[34] suggested that when people were repeatedly exposed to filmed scenes of physical mutilation, they became desensitized to this type of film stimulus. Theses investigators exposed their subjects to films of a primitive tribal ritual, involving painful and bloody genital mutilations. They found that viewers became less emotionally responsive with repeated observations of the scene. On the basis of these findings and the findings of investigations undertaken up to that time on the effectiveness of desensitization therapy, Cline, Croft, and Courrier[35] suggested that when people have been exposed to a great deal of prior violence — either directly, or vicariously as in movies, television programs, or other types of media — there may occur a "kind of psychological blunting" of the normal emotional responses to violent events. Cline and his associates designed a study to determine if children who were relatively heavy consumers of TV violence showed different physiological effects to a clip of filmed violence than would light consumers of TV violence.

Eighty male children between the ages of 5 and 12 years were surveyed on their television viewing. On the basis of their answers, the experimenters divided the boys into two groups: high consumers of television (an average of 42.0 hours per week for the past 2 years); or low consumers (3.8 hours per week for the past 2 years). The experimenters then exposed the boys to one of three clips strung together in a 14-minute film: a 2-minute nonviolent ski film; a 4-minute chase sequence from a W.C. Fields film; and an 8-minute sequence from the Kirk Douglas film *The Champion,* depicting a boxing match. While they were watching these clips, each boy's blood pulse and GSR was measured. The results indicated that the low television exposure boys were significantly more physiologically aroused during selected violent segments of the boxing film than the high exposure boys.

While these results indicated a desensitization effect for exposure to TV violence, it was only an indirect indication clouded by a few troubling issues. First, as the authors' own analysis revealed, the heavy consumption group consisted of more children from families of lower socioeconomic status (SES) than the light consumption group. This confounds the experiment because we do not know if it was exposure to TV or the fact that children of lower SES families have other experiences that would lead them to be less aroused by scenes of violence. Second, although the study purported to investigate the effects of prolonged consumption to TV *violence*, the investigators only asked their subjects about TV viewing habits in general, not how much violence they watched. This also confounds the experiment — we cannot be sure that children who have more experience with watching TV in general, regardless of whether or not they watch violence, would have lower physiological reactions when asked by the experimenters to view films in the laboratory. In fact, there was some evidence in the study that the low consumption children were more aroused by both the nonviolent and the violent depictions than the high consumption children—an indication that exposure to any sort of film is more arousing for light TV viewers. Also, the experimenters did not measure the boys' responsiveness to real violence or even films of real violence, but to films depicting fictional violence. Finally, the experiment was conducted with children only. Would the same effects be observed if adults were studied?

Two experiments conducted by Thomas et al. were designed to remedy these problems. Thomas and her colleagues first randomly assigned both children and adult subjects to view violent or nonviolent TV shows, and collected violence-viewing histories, rather than forming the groups on the basis of their self-reported history of general TV exposure. After exposure to the violent or nonviolent TV shows, the subjects faced filmed scenes if real aggression rather than fictional depictions.

In the first experiment,[36] boys and girls between the ages of 8 and 10 years who were recruited through newspaper ads and elementary school newsletters sat in the laboratory wired with an electrode that measured GSR. While connected to the electrode, the children viewed either an aggressive TV drama (an edited excerpt from the TV police series *SWAT* that contained several shootings, physical aggression, and other forms of violence) or a nonaggressive film (an excerpt of similar length from an exciting championship volleyball game). Immediately after the film, and while still connected to the electrode, the children were asked to do "a favor" for the experimenter. The experimenter told the child that he was helping a friend who was working with younger children, and that this friend had a TV camera in a playroom in another part of the building. The camera, according to the experimenter, "sees" everything that goes on in the room. The experimenter explained that he was supposed to watch the children, but that he had to make a call, so he wondered if the study participants would watch for him. Each child then watched a videotaped sequence that portrayed, according to the authors, preschoolers who upon being left in the playroom "engage in a series of aggressive actions, beginning with an exchange of derogatory comments and escalating to physical aggression and property damage."[37]

The results indicated that the children who had first viewed the violent police drama were less emotionally responsive to the preschoolers' fight (had lower GSRs) than control subjects. Further, the effect was the same for boys and girls. Because the experimenters had also collected self-reports from the children specifically about their TV violence viewing at home, they were able to correlate these reports with the children's GSRs measured when watching the preschoolers. The results showed relatively large negative correlations between self-reports of TV violence viewing and physiological responsiveness to the "real" aggression — meaning that the more violence the child watched outside the laboratory, the less emotionally aroused he or she was to the violence presented in the laboratory.

In the second experiment,[38] the subjects were adults. This time, however, after watching either the violent police drama or the control film, the adult subjects were shown an excerpt from a NBC Huntley-Brinkley television news coverage of the August 28, 1968 riots outside the headquarters of the Democratic National Convention. The film, according to the experimenters, "contained many violent acts of physical aggression such as police officers clubbing and dragging individuals injured during the riots, crowds pushing and shoving, and people screaming."[39] The results were basically the same as those found in the first experiment with children, with one exception: Of those who had been first exposed to the violent police drama, only men were less physiologically aroused by the subsequent news footage of the Chicago riots compared with the controls. The women in the experiment did not show the same desensitization effects.

These studies suggested that one consequence of dampened emotional reactions to filmed violence may be the failure to respond emotionally to, and ultimately a failure to act to prevent, a victim being injured. Throughout our lives we are confronted with many opportunities to intervene in an aggressive exchange. For example, in the typical grade-school classroom there may be one or two aggressive individuals, and the remaining class members are either the victims of aggression or (more likely) bystanders to aggressive acts. As adults we may not be likely to engage in aggressive acts ourselves, but we may witness actual aggression (e.g., an entire apartment building may hear the husband in a neighboring apartment physically abusing his wife). Even more often we find ourselves in the position of evaluating victims of aggression. We often read about victims of violence and rape in newspapers and magazines. Has our perception of these victims been altered by our prior exposure to violence in the media? More important, we are sometimes asked to make critical decisions about circumstances and persons involved in acts of violence. For example, we might be asked to serve as a juror in a case involving a violent sexual assault. Will exposure to sexual violence inhibit our ability to react empathically to the victim, perhaps causing us to blame her for her own plight or to excuse the defendant for the assault?

THE IMPACT OF EXPOSURE TO
MEDIA VIOLENCE AGAINST WOMEN

Data that bear on these questions come from research on exposure to R-rated, full-length commercially released films that contain scenes of explicit violence, primarily directed toward women, often occurring during or juxtaposed to strongly erotic scenes. It would appear reasonable to hypothesize that continued exposure to so-called slasher films might facilitate the processes theorized to operate in desensitization therapy, such as counterconditioning, or extinction, resulting at least in reduced anxiety in response to the film violence. Upon viewing the first movie, viewers will experience a relatively high level of anxiety, which will decline with repeated exposure. A similar process might occur with respect to other indices of being upset by the material, such as feelings of depression. Viewers might then use these feelings as a guide for evaluating the material. With decreases in anxiety and depression, viewers will begin to evaluate the violent depictions differently. They may see the films as containing fewer scenes of violence, as being less offensive, less degrading to the victims of violence.

Becoming desensitized to the violence portrayed in movies, while something most of us would find undesirable, is a limited social harm. The more important effect of exposure to sexual violence would be if these blunted feelings and calloused evaluations spill over into evaluations of a female victim in other, more realistic contexts. Specifically, people repeatedly exposed to filmed violence may come to have less sympathy for, and evaluate as less severely injured, a victim of sexual assault. These hypotheses are tested in two studies with male college students conducted by Linz, Donnerstein, and Penrod[40] and Linz.[41]

The Linz, Donnerstein, and Penrod study was primarily concerned with establishing a desensitization effect of the slasher films themselves (i.e., reduced anxiety and depression with continued exposure to the depictions of sexual violence). Then the experimenters were interested in testing whether or not these reductions would be related to the subjects' evaluations of the material — how violent, degrading, offensive, and enjoyable the material seemed to the men over the course of continued exposure. Finally, the experimenters examined the extent to which desensitization to the violence in the films might spill over to the victim of violence portrayed in a videotaped reenactment of a rape trial.

The experiment was conducted in four phases: an initial pre-screening, a film-viewing session, a simulated rape trial, and an extended debriefing. Fifty-two males recruited from the engineering, computer sciences, and psychology departments at the University of Wisconsin-Madison completed the Symptom Checklist-90[42] in the Psychology Department. SCL-90 is a 90-item self-report symptom inventory designed to reflect the psychological symptom patterns of psychiatric and medical patients. Scores on the hostility and psychoticism subscales were used as screening variables to eliminate from the sample anyone suspected of a predisposition to aggression. Because the second phase of the study involved prolonged exposure to violent materials over several days with no debriefing until the final day, the experimenters feared that overly aggressive subjects might be inclined to ruminate over and perhaps imitate certain scenes from the films. As we noted in the research discussed in the last chapter, Malamuth and Check[43] found that a stated willingness "to rape if assured of not being caught" is correlated with a predisposition toward psychoticism and general hostility. In addition, experimental studies have demonstrated that individuals scoring high in psychoticism are also more likely to both self-report and reveal greater sexual excitement in response to sexual violence than subjects scoring low in psychoticism.[44]

The screening procedure is important for two reasons. First, because Linz et al.[40] had an ethical responsibility to their subjects and to the community, it was critical that they always be cognizant of the possibility that there may be some people who might be inclined to imitate the violence portrayed in the films. Second, by eliminating the most susceptible individuals from the sample, the findings are more compelling than if they had been left in. One would expect that it would be precisely those persons who score high on psychoticism and hostility who would be most affected by depictions of sexual violence. Because these people are perhaps already predisposed toward some level of aggression, and are sexually aroused by sexual violence, they might become rapidly desensitized to depictions of violence against women. By removing them from this and subsequent studies, the experimenters left themselves with those people who are least likely to become desensitized. Therefore, any effects that were obtained were *in spite of* the screening procedure.

Eligible males were contacted by phone and told that a film evaluation study was being conducted in the Communication Arts Department. They were informed that they would be required to view six films over 5 consecutive days (two films on the last day) and would receive a cash payment after all films had been viewed and the debriefing session completed. Those who indicated that their schedules permitted them to attend all sessions were then informed that they would be viewing commercially released R-rated films that might contain explicit sex and/or violence. At that point they were again given the opportunity to decline participation. It is important to note that in all cases, subjects who declined to participate did so when first informed about the time commitment involved *rather* than when informed about the content of the films.

Twelve subjects were randomly assigned to view the R-rated violent films.[45] An additional 12 males were recruited as control subjects from among those who declined to participate because of scheduling difficulties. The control subjects were asked to report to the Communication Arts Department for a single hour session, which involved viewing a videotape and completing a questionnaire.

The men viewed five films, one per day, for 5 consecutive days. Because the experimenters were interested in making comparisons between first-and last-day reactions to the films, the film-viewing subjects were further divided into two groups. One group saw the films in a forward order; the other group saw the films in the reverse order. The films viewed in the R-rated violent condition — *Texas Chainsaw Massacre, Maniac, I Split on Your Grave, Vice Squad,* and *Toolbox Murders*—have been commercially released, and some have been shown on cable television. Each film contains explicit scenes of violence in which the victims are nearly always female, and the films often juxtapose a violent scene with a sensual or erotic scene (e.g., a woman masturbating in the bath is suddenly and brutally attacked).

After viewing each film, the men completed the Multiple Affect Adjective Checklist (MAACL)[46] which yields anxiety, depression, and hostility or annoyance subscale scores. Next, the men completed a questionnaire on which they rated, on several scales, the extent to which the film they had viewed combined sex and violence, was violent (i.e., bloody, gory without being sexually violent), was degrading to women, and was enjoyable. They were also asked to record the number of scenes they found offensive.

On the last day, after viewing the fifth film, the men were informed that the sixth and final film had not arrived. They were then introduced to a "representative from the law school" who told them that the law school was pretesting a rape trial documentary. Because the film to be viewed by the subjects had not arrived, would they agree to watch the law school documentary? At that point the control subjects were brought into the room and were seated with the experimental subjects.

All the men watched a videotaped reenactment of a complete rape trial derived from the transcript of an actual rape trial, involving a man and a woman who meet in a bar. The victim asserts that the defendant followed her from the bar in his car, pulled her over on the road by impersonating a police officer, persuaded her to get into his car, and drove to an abandoned factory lot where the sexual assault occurred. After viewing the trial, the men completed a questionnaire on which they indicated their verdict and assessed the defendant's intentions, and the victim's resistance, responsibility, sympathy, unattractiveness, injury, and worthlessness.

The results of the experiment revealed changes in judgments about the films and in mood while watching them, between the first and last days of film viewing. There were significant differences between subjects' scores on the first and last days for the depression and anxiety subscales of the MAACL.

Table 6–1 presents the items comprising each of the film evaluation scales. There were significant differences between subjects' scores on the first and last days for perceptions of violence and degradation of women, and a marginally significant difference between their first- and last-days' scores for enjoyment, and number of offensive scenes. Surprisingly, there was no significant difference between their first- and last-day scores for perceptions of sex plus violence. It appeared that subjects were estimating that there were just as many scenes pairing sex and violence on the last day as there were on the first. What appeared to change was their evaluation of how violent offensive and degrading those scenes were.

We expected that, compared with the control subjects, the sub-

TABLE 6-1

Postfilm Evaluation Scales: Desensitization to Violence Against Women

Scale	First Day	Last Day
	(Values on 7-Point Scale)	
Perceptions of sex and violence		
1. Overall, to what extent did sex and violence occur together in this film?	2.58	1.97
2. Of the violent scenes (if any), how many also contained sexual content? (This may include intercourse, rape, simple nudity, or other suggestive scenes)	2.45	1.92
3. How many scenes involved the rape (sexual assault) of a woman?	1.16	1.25
4. Did this film portray violence toward women in a sexual context?	2.08	2.50
Perception of violence		
1. Overall, how much violent behavior was portrayed in this film?	6.91	6.16
2. Thinking about the movie as a whole, how many violent scenes did the film contain?	4.42	3.91
3. How graphic was the violence in this film?	6.90	5.45
4. How bloody or gory was the violence in this film?	6.66	4.83
5. To what extent do you think the violence will come to mind in the next 48 hours?	4.17	3.00
6. To what extent did the scenes of violence in the film make you look away from the screen?	3.67	3.16
7. Did this film portray violence toward women but not in a sexual context?	6.58	6.16
8. Did this film portray violence toward men but not in a sexual context?	4.92	4.83
Degrading to women		
1. How degrading is this film to women?	4.50	2.41
2. This movie was: (1) uplifting, . . . , (9) debasing.	5.75	5.66
Enjoyment		
1. This movie was: (1) not entertaining, . . . , (9) entertaining	2.25	3.08
2. Overall, do you enjoy this type of film?	1.64	2.36

jects exposed to the filmed violence against women would judge the rape victim to be less injured. There might also be consistent trends on several other trial evaluation variables. The subjects who had viewed the films might come to assign greater responsibility to the victim for her sexual assault and to judge her as having resisted her assailant less. They might also indicate less sympathy for the rape victim than control subjects.

So far the results of the study revealed a significant relationship between the enjoyment ratings of the films and anxiety and depression scores: Subjects who were less anxious and less depressed at the conclusion of the last film also rated the material as more enjoyable. Prolonged exposure to filmed violence lowered emotional reactions to the material, with subjects significantly less depressed and anxious on the final day of viewing and more likely to enjoy the films. Subjects' perceptions of the violence portrayed in the films also changed over the 5 days. The films were perceived to be significantly less violent by the last day of viewing (although not significantly less sexually violent). Ratings of how degrading the films were to women and of their offensiveness were also significantly lower by the last day. But these were reactions to the films themselves; what about judgments about other victims?

We also found a tendency for the desensitization to the filmed violence against women to spill over into subjects' judgments of a female victim in another context. Men who were exposed to the large doses of filmed violence against women judged the victim of a violent assault and rape to be significantly less injured, and evaluated her as generally less worthy than did the control group of subjects who saw no films. Finally, subjects who rated the material as less offensive or violent and more enjoyable by the last day of viewing were much more likely to judge the victim more responsible for her own sexual assault and the defendant as less responsible. Subjects who reported seeing fewer offensive and violent scenes on the last day also judged the victim as offering less resistance to her assailant, and felt less sympathy for her. Greater enjoyment of the material on the final day was also correlated with attributions of greater victim responsibility and less defendant intention, with a significant tendency to rate the victim as a less attractive and less worthy individual. These findings add strength to the mounting evidence that sustained exposure to filmed violence may lower sensitivity to victims of violence in other contexts.

The second study[47] was designed to extend the generalizability of the previous study in several ways. First, the study was an attempt to replicate the findings of the previous study using a completely different rape trial (to make sure that the effects generalized across different rape trials and different victims). In the previous study, subjects were exposed to five films on consecutive days, with no "recovery period" between viewings. Also, the victim ratings were made in the same physical setting in which films were viewed, and the measures of sympathy concerned only the specific rape trial victim and not victims in general. Linz now employed a set of procedures that (1) would determine how many movies were necessary for the effect to be evident; (2) provided rest periods between violence exposure sessions; (3) dissociated the violence-viewing phase of the experiment from the rape-trial phase of the experiment; and (4) obtained an additional measure of general empathy for rape victims.

For the most part, the original findings concerning subjects reactions to violence were replicated in the second study. When subjects are exposed to large amounts of graphically depicted film violence against women, initial feelings of anxiety and depression begin to dissipate. As in the first study, material that was once anxiety provoking and depressing became less so with prolonged exposure. The perceptual changes found in the first study also appeared to be robust ones. The men reported seeing less violence with continued exposure. They also evaluated the material differently after continued exposure. Material once found somewhat degrading to women was judged to be less so after prolonged exposure. The marginally significant increase in enjoyment found in the first study was not detected in the second study. However, it is important to note that enjoyment did not decline with continued exposure.

The Linz investigation also suggested that two movies (the equivalent of about 3 hours of viewing time and approximately 20–25 violent acts) was sufficient to obtain a desensitization effect similar to that obtained after five movies. These findings suggest that desensitization to filmed violence may occur rather rapidly. The implication is that once the viewer has reached a certain level of comfort in the face of violence, continued exposure may not further inure him to the material to any significant degree. The results indicated that men exposed to R-rated filmed violence against women were less sympathetic to the victim of rape portrayed in the trial and less able to empathize with rape victims in general compared with no-exposure control subjects and men exposed to other types of films. Level of film exposure, however, affected specific sympathy and general empathy differently—longer film exposure was necessary to diminish the general empathic response.

In sum, the research of Linz and his colleagues supports the conclusion that exposure to R-rated fantasy film depictions of extremely brutal violence against women affects men's responses to a victim in other more realistic contexts.

DO WOMEN ALSO BECOME DESENSITIZED TO SLASHER FILMS?

One of the most serious shortcomings of mass media research is the lack of investigations into the effects of exposure to pornography and violence on women. Hans,[48] in a critique of the research undertaken by the 1970 Presidential Commission on Pornography, suggests that the focus of the Commission may have reflected the predominately male composition of the panel. Research on aggressive behavior and the effects of exposure to media violence have also focused principally on males. Frodi, Macauley, and Thome[49] note that of 314 experimental studies on aggression dated 1967 to 1974, only 24% studied male *and* female subjects and only 8% studied females, the majority of whom were children rather than adults. Those that did include women largely focused on variables such as guilt and reparation among harm doers, traits and concerns that are stereotypically associated with women.

Krafka[50] wondered if women, like men, would become emotionally desensitized when exposed to the slasher films. Or since the victims portrayed in slasher films are predominately female, would women react very differently? Perhaps exposure increases women's empathy toward victims. The study conducted by Malamuth and Check,[51] discussed early in this chapter, suggested that greater rather than less empathy for victims of sexual aggression might be expected from women who have viewed sexually violent films. In that study, as the reader will recall, men and women participated in a film-rating study in which they watched either two feature-length nonexplicit films depicting women as the object of sexual violence or control films depicting a couple in love. Several days later, subjects completed scales assessing rape myths and acceptance of interpersonal violence. The results indicated that exposure to the films portraying the myth that women benefit from sexual violence significantly increased males' but *not* females' acceptance of interpersonal violence. In fact, there was some indication of an opposite effect for women. They appeared to have a greater sensitivity to rape myths and acceptance of interpersonal violence after exposure to sexually violent films than they did before exposure.

Krafka's study was conducted in four stages. First was a pretest stage in which the experimenter measured beliefs about rape and asked subjects to complete a questionnaire about their sexual history. Several weeks after the pretest the women viewed one full-length film a day for 4 days. These films were of the following types: sexually explicit and degrading to women; sexually explicit, sexually degrading, and sexually violent to women; graphically violent toward women; and sexually nonexplicit, but tending to portray the violence within an erotic or sensual context. Like the men in the Linz[41] and Linz et al.[40] studies, the women were asked to complete daily mood measures, and their perceptions and attitudes toward violence were measured after each of the films. Following 4 days of film viewing, the women participated as mock jurors by watching a videotaped reenactment of a sexual assault trial and rendering judgments about the victim and the circumstances surrounding the assault. In addition, the women were asked about their own feelings of victimization.

The results of the study revealed that relative to baseline measures, women, like men, become desensitized to depictions of sexual violence. According to Krafka: "Material that evoked hostility in subjects or material that elicited a high degree of anxiety and depression at initial exposure lost its ability to elicit extreme mood changes by the end of the weeks' viewing."[52] Interestingly, however, the perceptual changes that Linz and his colleagues[40] found as part of the desensitization process for males did not occur for females. Women viewers of slasher films did *not* report seeing less violence. Nevertheless, although women in the study did not have altered perceptions of violence in the films, with repeated exposure their judgments of violence in another setting—the rape trial—were affected. The slasher film subjects were higher than other film groups on a global measure of trial outcome where high scores reflected a tendency to return a verdict of acquittal, to excuse the conduct of the defendant, to place responsibility for the events on the victim, to hold a restrictive definition of sexual assault, and to impeach both the victim's resistance attempts and her credibility.

When considering the work of Linz and his colleagues[40] and Krafka,[50] it appears that with repeated exposure, both men and women desensitize emotionally to graphic violence against women. The process of desensitization, at least at the *emotional* level, may be inevitable regardless of viewer gender. Where men and women appear to differ is in the other components of desensitization: specifically, changes in perceptions and attitudes about the material. This suggests that viewer cognitions take a different course for males and females. It is possible that women develop strategies that help them cope with feelings of vulnerability that might arise as they watch the female victims portrayed in these films. As Krafka points out, Lazarus and Alfert[53] have shown that certain strategies for viewing and interpreting stressful film events help to "short-circuit" stress reactions to the films. When women are exposed to sexually violent material in which the victims of violence are often women, they might engage in a short-circuiting strategy that helps them disassociate themselves from the victims portrayed in the films. This strategy might carry over to victims they encounter in subsequent situations, at least temporarily.

Krafka's findings are congruent with the predictions from theories about the self-protective reactions people may have to descriptions of crime or misfortune. Several researchers have speculated that our reactions to victims are motivated by a need to maintain a sense of personal security. These motives, such as the desire to believe one has control over the aversive events in one's life,[54] or the belief in a just world (the idea that ultimately we all get what we deserve),[55] appear to operate when people are confronted with serious accidents or traumatic life events. The need for the observer to feel safe from a similar calamity apparently motivates him or her to view victims as responsible for their misfortunes and promotes negative evaluations of victims. If casuality for a negative outcome is assigned to an unpredictable or uncontrollable set of circumstances, people are forced to concede that a similar event might happen to them. This might be what happened to the slasher film group — the only group that derogated the rape trial victim and blamed her for her plight. Exposure to a large number of randomly inflicted acts of violence against women through film may threaten both women's sense of control over negative events and their belief that only just things happen in their world.

THE IMPACT OF DESENSITIZATION ON AGGRESSIVE BEHAVIOR

Are viewers likely to become more aggressive after continued exposure to media violence? The answer to this question might, at first, appear to be obvious. Naturally, the more violence a viewer is exposed, to the greater the chances that viewer will be violent. However, there is reason to believe that this will not always be the case. Berkowitz[56] and others[57] have speculated that frequent viewing of mass media aggression could theoretically result in increases *or* decreases in the probability of an open display of aggression.

It might be the case that continued exposure to media violence will reduce aggression because continued exposure leads to lower levels of arousal. Theoretically, any treatment that reduces arousal should reduce aggression. As we discussed in Chapter 3, an experiment by Zillmann and Bryant[58] in which individuals were exposed to depictions of sex for relatively long periods of time suggests that such a habituation or satiation effect might occur with repeated exposures to these stimuli. Massive exposure to exciting pornography resulted in sharply reduced aggressiveness. Other experiments[59] have demonstrated that continued exposure to violence, while initially physiologically arousing, will eventually become less so. Thus, we might be left with the paradox that aggressive behavior in response to violent media might diminish with continued exposure to the material.

On the other hand, repeated exposure to violent scenes might lead to increases in aggression. Repeated viewing of violence might diminish concerns and anxieties about aggression. This might be due to the activation of aggression-approving thoughts. This would seem particularly likely when people see typical instances of televised or movie violence. These depictions often portray morally justified or sanctioned aggression as the normal state of affairs. On the televised series *The A Team,* for example, it is the hero who is responsible for the bulk of the physical and verbal violence against morally inferior or bad characters. The typical John Wayne Western or World War II saga contains similar instances of morally "correct" or justifiable violence. It is also reasonable to assume that continued exposure to aggression of this sort might result, as Berkowitz has maintained, in reduced internal conflict or decreased anxiety about aggression. Such reductions in this form of anxiety should also lead to increased rather than decreased aggressive behavior.

Two laboratory experiments shed light on the question of whether increases or decreases in aggressive behavior follow desensitization to violence. The results of these studies were mixed. Thomas[60] found that men who watched a violent movie subsequently had lower arousal levels and tended to give more electric shocks to a confederate of the experimenter. Angered individuals who had previously seen a lengthy aggressive television program exhibited higher levels of aggression and lower levels of physiological arousal immediately before behaving aggressively. This provides support to the idea that prolonged exposure to violence may lead to reduced anxiety about aggression and thus a greater likelihood of subsequent aggressive behavior. But the differences in aggressive behavior (i.e., shocks administered to a confederate of the experimenter) between the group exposed to the violence and the control group were extremely small, and when both groups were angered there were no differences in behavior at all. Geen[61] found that while subjects were less aroused by subsequent violence once they had been exposed to prior violence, those who had seen the violent movies did not necessarily behave more violently than those who had not. In his experiment the most aggressive subjects were those who had seen an exciting but nonviolent film scene, then were exposed to an instance of justified aggression taken from another film.

The results of a large-scale longitudinal study conducted in several countries by Eron, Huesmann, and their associates on childrens' aggressiveness and television exposure support the notion that continued exposure to media violence can lead to increased acts of aggression. In this longitudinal study, first and third graders were interviewed and tested in the United States, Australia, Finland, Poland, and Holland. An analysis of the data available from the United States, Finland, and Poland has shown that in each of these countries there are significant correlations between viewing of television violence and reports of aggressive behavior obtained from peers for both boys and girls. The data from these studies speak directly to the issue of long-term exposure, because the best prediction of a child's aggressiveness was obtained when the investigators included only the violence scores for programs the child watched "almost always." This is probably the strongest evidence collected so far for the idea that continued exposure to violence leads to increases in violent behavior. In fact, there is evidence that prolonged exposure to television violence in childhood is related to aggressive behavior in adulthood.[62]

To date, no one has conducted a study that examines adults who have been exposed to media violence for prolonged periods of time outside the laboratory in order to determine if there is an increase in aggressive behavior. Such research must be done before we can be more confident that prolonged exposure to violence in the media is related to greater aggressiveness.

The cautionary statements we made in Chapter 1 concerning the conditions under which aggressive behavior will be manifested should be taken into account here. As we mentioned then, the relationship between exposure to violent media and aggressive behavior is moderated by many factors. Aggressive behavior following exposure to violence is dependent upon the nature of the individual, the features of the situation in which the person finds him or herself following exposure, and the characteristics and availability of victims.

In conclusion, it is possible that the whole genre of movies called slasher films, which graphically depict mutilation of women, may be desensitizing viewers almost as efficiently as if they were patients in our fictious therapy described in the beginning of the chapter, undertaken by a malevolent psychologist and designed to make them more tolerant of blood and gore. This reduced anxiety about violence, particularly violence against women — even if it does not lead to increases in violent behavior — may make viewers less sensitive to female victims of violence. We have shown these effects on judgments about the victim of sexual assault, and it would be reasonable to expect similar effects for judgments about female victims in other situations, such as an incidence of wife battering.

It would also be expected that just as prolonged exposure to nonsexual media violence results in a dampening of physiological responsivity, exposure to sexualized violence would have the same effect. We must then face the possibility that desensitized individuals may be less responsive. For example, lower levels of physiological reaction to subsequent incidents of violence following media exposure may have implications for bystander intervention behavior. Several studies on responses to emergencies have shown increases in GSR and heart rate in bystanders in the presence of a victim in distress.[63] This arousal is highly correlated with the swiftness of bystander intervention. Gaertner and Dovidio,[64] for example, found that subjects' heart rate and the speed of intervention in the presence of a staged emergency situation were substantially correlated with one another. The greater the arousal, the less time it took for the bystander to intervene. Similarly, Sterling[65] found a relatively large correlation between the difference in subjects' baseline heart rate before and after the emergency and speed of intervention. Piliavin, Piliavin, and Trudell[66] revealed an even higher degree of association between GSR and speed of intervention. The research on arousal and helping suggests that any experience that undermines a bystander's arousal to a victim in distress might have a negative effect on the quickness with which a bystander intervenes to assist the victim. It is possible — although there is presently no empirical evidence to support the contention — that prolonged exposure to filmed violence portraying victims being severely physically injured might dampen physiological arousal to situations involving actual victims in distress.

If this proves to be true, we risk the possibility that many members of our society, particularly young viewers, will evolve into less sensitive and responsive individuals as a result, at least partly, of repeated exposure to violent media, particularly sexually violent media. Such a possibility should be alarming, if not to law makers, at least to policy makers responsible for rating motion pictures and thus to limiting young people's access to sexually violent depictions. In the next chapter we discuss some of the policy implications for rating motion pictures of the research findings on desensitization covered in this chapter, as well as the implications of the results of investigations described in the previous chapters.

7 | The Search for Legal Solutions

O<small>N</small> December 30, 1983, the Minneapolis city council amended its civil rights ordinance to include pornography as a practice of sex discrimination.[1] The premise underlying the amendment was that pornography is a discriminatory practice because its effect is to deny women equal opportunities in society. According to the council, pornography promotes bigotry and contempt for women, fosters acts of aggression against women, and harms women's opportunities for equal employment and education, and full participation in society. Introduction of the amendment followed a set of public hearings where testimony from alleged victims of pornography (including former *Deep Throat* actress Linda Lovelace) and the views of University of Minnesota law professor Catherine MacKinnon and feminist author Andrea Dworkin figured prominently. But before the amendment could become law it was vetoed by the mayor of Minneapolis, Donald M. Fraser. It was then reintroduced to the council for further consideration, passed by the council again, and again vetoed by Fraser. His veto was praised by Harvard law professor Alan M. Dershowitz, a well-known champion of many legal causes including freedom of the press. Another Harvard law professor, Lawrence Tribe, expressed disappointment at the veto and pointed out that the mayor had deprived the courts of the opportunity to assess "what may eventually be found to be the first sensible approach to an area which has vexed some of the best legal minds for decades".[2]

Several months later, a nearly identical antipornography ordinance was introduced and *enacted* in the city-county of Indianapolis
under Mayor William Hudnut.[3] The passage of the Indianapolis
ordinance was the result of an unusual political alliance of radical
feminists and conservative Republicans. While the original ordinance was conceived by feminists as a mechanism to further protect
women's rights, it was widely held that the Indianapolis ordinance
was introduced to the city-county council by Republican conservative councilwoman Beulah A. Coughenour because of growing dissatisfaction with the ineffectiveness of traditional criminal obscenity
statutes in curbing the spread of immoral and antireligious
materials.

Less than 90 minutes after the law was signed by the mayor, a
group of publishers, booksellers, and broadcasters, assisted by the
ACLU, challenged the measure in the Southern District Court of
Indiana, charging that the law was an unconstitutional violation of
the First Amendment right to free speech.[4]

The Southern District Court found the law to be unconstitutional. The decision was then appealed by the city of Indianapolis,
and the case moved to the Seventh Circuit Court of Appeals in
Chicago, which likewise found it unconstitutional. In February
1986, the U.S. Supreme Court stayed the decision of the Seventh
Circuit court without hearing arguments in the case.

Originally, the citizens and elected officials of Minneapolis
wanted to create a tougher zoning law to control the growth of adult
establishments in residential neighborhoods. As part of this effort, the Neighborhood Pornography Task Force asked University of Minnesota law professor Catharine MacKinnon and feminist
author Andrea Dworkin to testify at a public hearing on a new
zoning ordinance. At the hearing, MacKinnon and Dworkin testified that zoning laws are generally ineffective but, more importantly, inappropriate for dealing with pornography because they do
not address the *harm* done to women when pornography is made,
distributed, and consumed. According to Dworkin and MacKinnon, pornography is central in creating and maintaining women's
inferior status in society. It is a form of sex discrimination and practice that infringes on the rights of women. They also made suggestions on how the city council might create a new, civil rights – based,
legal approach to controlling pornography. The first step, they
pointed out, would be to establish a legislative record through public testimony to document the types and extent of harm done to
women by pornography.

Two days of public hearings were held on December 12 and 13, 1983. Several types of evidence of pornography's harmful effects were considered at the hearings: testimony from incest and domestic abuse victims who alleged that pornography played a role in their victimization, and testimony from social workers and clinicians who had encountered situations in which pornography had been implicated in the physical abuse of women. The research findings on sexual violence described in Chapter 6 were also entered into the legislative record. One especially notable witness was Linda Marchiano (Linda Lovelace), a former pornography actress who appeared in the film *Deep Throat*. She testified that she was coerced into making that film.

At the conclusion of the hearings, the Minneapolis city council made the following findings:

Pornography is a discriminatory practice based on sex which denies women equal opportunities in society. Pornography is central in creating and maintaining sex as a basis for discrimination. Pornography is a systematic practice of exploitation and subordination based on sex which differentially harms women. The bigotry and contempt it promotes, with the acts of aggression it fosters, harm women's opportunities for equality of rights in employment, education, access to and use of public accommodations, and acquisition of real property; promote rape, battery, child abuse, kidnapping and prostitution and inhibit just enforcement of laws against such acts; and contribute significantly to restricting women in particular from full exercise of citizenship and participation in public life, including in neighborhoods.[5]

Based on these findings, the city council passed a general ordinance that amended the human relations and equal opportunity code of Minneapolis. The ordinance defined pornography as:

The sexually explicit subordination of women, graphically depicted whether in pictures or in words, that also includes one or more of the following:

Women are presented dehumanized as sexual objects, things or commodities; or

Women are presented as sexual objects who enjoy pain or humiliation; or

Women are presented as sexual objects who experience sexual pleasure in being raped; or

Women are presented as sexual objects tied up or cut up or mutilated or bruised or physically hurt; or

Women are presented in postures of sexual submission or sexual servility, including by inviting penetration; or

Women's body parts — including but not limited to vaginas, breasts, and buttocks — are exhibited, such that women are reduced to those parts; or

Women are presented as whores by nature; or

Women are presented being penetrated by objects or animals; or

Women are presented in scenarios of degradation, injury, or torture, shown as filthy or inferior, bleeding, bruised, or hurt in a context that makes these conditions sexual.[6]

The material in question must meet each part of the definition — it must be sexually explicit *and* graphically depicted in pictures or words *and* must contain at least one of the listed characteristics — to be considered pornography. Once the definition is met, the ordinance provided for four claims of discrimination:

1. *Coercion into performing for pornography.* Women who have been forced to make a pornographic film or pose for pornographic photographs would have a cause of action against the makers, sellers, exhibitors, or distributors of pornography.
2. *Forcing pornography on a person.* Women who have been involuntarily exposed to pornography — for example, at the workplace or in some other public place — would have a cause of action against the perpetrator.
3. *Assault or physical attack due to pornography.* Women who are assaulted, attacked, or injured in a way that is caused by a specific example of pornography could seek relief from makers and distributors.
4. *Trafficking in pornography.* Any woman could bring a complaint against traffickers in pornography on behalf of all women.

This ordinance, like any law that prohibits discrimination in a city, county, or state, would make available the full administrative apparatus of the Human Rights Commission and the courts for adjudicating complaints.

What distinguishes this approach from the traditional legal approach to obscenity law, according to feminists, is that it reasserts rather than blurs the distinction between obscenity and pornography, as the Supreme Court has done from *Hicklin* down to *Miller* (two cases we will discuss in the next section). According to MacKinnon, whether or not something is obscene is a social value judgment, whereas the effects wrought on society from pornography are indisputable facts. Obscenity laws suggests that women's bodies are dirty, that thoughts about sex are bad or wrong. To quote MacKinnon:

Obscenity is a moral idea; pornography is a political practice. Obscenity is abstract; pornography is concrete . . . Nudity, explicitness, excess of candor, arousal or excrement, prurience, unnaturalness — these things bother obscenity law when sex is depicted or portrayed . . . Sex forced on real women so that it can be sold at a profit to be forced on other real women; women's bodies trussed and maimed and raped and made into things to be hurt and obtained and accessed and this presented as the nature of women . . . this . . . bothers feminists about pornography. Obscenity as such probably does little harm; pornography causes attitudes and behaviors of violence and discrimination which define the treatment and status of half the population.[7]

As noted earlier, the ordinance was passed by the Minneapolis city council and was vetoed by the mayor, who claimed the city would be endlessly mired in legal battles over its constitutionality. The ordinance was reintroduced and passed again by the council several months later. Again it was vetoed by the mayor. Shortly after the veto in Minneapolis, the ordinance was introduced in another major midwestern city—Indianapolis. On May 1, 1984, testimony given in Minneapolis about the alleged harms of pornography was introduced into the record of the city-county council of Marion County and the city of Indianapolis. On the same evening the ordinance was signed into law, making pornography a violation of women's civil rights. The law was nearly identical to the ordinance devised by MacKinnon and Dworkin in Minneapolis, with the exception of the elimination of language concerning "women presented as dehumanized, as sexual objects, things or commodities" and elimination of the qualification that pornography is present, "if women's body parts—including but not limited to vaginas, breasts, and buttocks—are exhibited, such that women are reduced to these parts."

The fact that the law was passed in Indianapolis would have been extraordinarily only if the conservative Republican city council had been fully convinced of the feminist definition of pornography as a form of discrimination against women. Instead, it is probably the case that the law passed because Mayor Hudnut saw the ordinance as a way to placate religious and conservative citizen groups who oppose pornography on scriptural and moral grounds.[8] In fact, the female legislator who introduced the ordinance to the council had spoken out publicly against the proposed Equal Rights Amendment to the Constitution.[9] Rather than publicly articulating a conservative argument in favor of restrictions on pornography and obscenity, the advocates of the ordinance chose to emphasize the harms done to women by pornography.

The American Booksellers Association and the Association of American Publishers filed suit against the mayor of Indianapolis in the United States Southern District Court of Indiana, claiming that the law would unconstitutionally restrict free speech.[10]

The Southern District Court ruled that, indeed, the Indianapolis ordinance was an unconstitutional restriction of free speech. The court noted that while speech such as "the lewd and obscene,[11] the profane, the libelous and insulting or 'fighting' words,[12] or child pornography,[13]" does not receive First Amendment protection, the ordinance was attempting to restrict speech that falls outside these categories.[14] Consequently, the court ruled the ordinance unconstitutionally vague and overly broad. Furthermore, the court ruled that the establishment of a governmental committee to make findings and conclusions, as well as the authority to require a defendant to cease distributing or publishing while the decision is being arbitrated, is an unconstitutional form of "prior restraint."[15] In September 1985, the United States Court of Appeals for the Seventh Circuit affirmed the Southern District Court's decision, and in February 1986 the Supreme Court stayed the decision of the Seventh Circuit Court.[16]

There is probably no single event, in the seemingly unending public controversy about pornography, that so clearly illustrates the difficulties in defining pornography, assessing its effects, and weighing the pros and cons of legislating against it, than the antipornography laws of Minneapolis and Indianapolis. President Ronald Reagan's view that "it's time to stop pretending that extreme pornography is a victimless crime,"[17] and his administration's June 1984 call for a new national commission on pornography to examine any evidence that might have turned up since the 1970 Presidential Commission, have brought Washington and the Justice Department into the pornography controversy (a matter we discuss in the next chapter). Considered together, these events signal a reemergence of national interest in the question of the role of pornography in our society.

From among the many voices heard in the public debate on pornography over the last three years, several policy positions can be culled: (1) the view that we have just described, that pornography portrays women as sex objects at best, and as the willing victims of violent torture at worst, and thus fosters discrimination and even violence against women; (2) the traditional legal view that pornography (more precisely obscenity) is a form of speech that falls outside the free-speech guarantees of the Constitution primarily because it violates most Americans' sense of decency and morality; and (3) the civil libertarian view, which acknowledges that portrayals of women in pornography may be reprehensible and that pornography may in fact promote bigotry and even violence against women, but counters that all powerful speech is potentially dangerous and at least arguably offensive to one political, racial, or ethnic group, and the benefits we derive as a society from protecting these forms of speech outweighs these harms.

Each of the three perspectives comes with its own set of philosophical assumptions and an implied set of actions, or, as in the case of the civil libertarian view, explicit arguments prohibiting action. Essentially, the proponents of each position can be seen as grappling with four basic questions: (1) What is obscene or pornographic? (2) What effect does exposure to obscenity and pornography have on viewers? (3) Should this material be controlled? (4) If it should be controlled, what form of control is desirable? Of course, proponents of each position do not give equal time to each of these questions. Legal scholars have devoted considerable time to the debate over the definition of obscenity, whereas the effects of exposure to obscene and pornographic material has not been an area of active consideration. In contrast, the alleged harmful effects of pornography have been of paramount concern to the feminists who have challenged traditional obscenity law.

The history of obscenity law in the United States has essentially involved a struggle between the view that obscene materials are immoral because they incite lust or appeal to the prurient interest and the view of the civil libertarians, who admonish the government not to become involved in legislating public morality and who have sometimes advocated lifting criminal sanctions against the purveyors of pornography and obscenity.[18] Those feminists and others whose primary concern is not the underlying assumption in obscenity law that the free portrayal of sex is "dirty" or immoral have nevertheless suggested that even more far-reaching legislation is necessary to counter the harmful effects of *discrimination* arising from pornography. Others deplore the values reflected in pornography but focus more on the evils of censorship. They oppose restrictions on pornography, and argue that laws against pornography imposed today could backfire for women tomorrow in the form of suppression of sex education material or other sexually explicit portrayals by those who consider these materials immoral.

Most attempts to censor movies — from the inception of the motion picture industry to the present — have arisen from the proponents of the viewpoint that public morality is threatened by certain types of film depictions. It is against the backdrop of the continued threat of censorship that the motion picture industry has developed its own set of rules and regulations governing the content and distribution of motion pictures. These rules have changed over the years. As we note later, many films now considered either works of art or, at least, as tolerable facets of American popular culture were once deemed morally unacceptable by conservative religious groups.

Can social science research provide a definitive answer to the question of what materials are pornographic or obscene? Can social scientists say with confidence which materials should be controlled and what form of control is desirable? As individuals we are certainly entitled to our opinions about these matters, but as researchers we would be hard pressed to derive a set of rules for regulating pornographic materials on the basis of the empirical inquiries undertaken so far. At best, we are able to specify which types of materials result in given effects (with some of these effects generally accepted as harmful and others more questionably so) and under what conditions the effects are more likely to occur. In general, the research findings presented in the previous chapters probably speak most readily to concerns about the types of harm that follow exposure to pornography raised by feminists—but with some major qualifications.

As we noted earlier, at this point there is not enough evidence from laboratory experiments to conclude that exposure to nonviolent pornography leads to increases in aggression against women under most circumstances. With regard to negative changes in attitudes about women's roles in society, less sensitivity toward rape victims, or tendencies to be less harsh in evaluations of rapists following long-term exposure to pornography the data are sparse. The data that exist are contradictory. However, we can be fairly confident that exposure to violent pornography may have negative effects on attitudes about women, and appears to increase aggressive behavior against women—at least in the laboratory. We have also seen that normal college-age males become sexually aroused to violent pornography, especially if it contains the message that women enjoy being raped. Most compelling, however, would be the combination of results from laboratory studies with longitudinal studies in which individuals were first assessed for their level of exposure to sexual violence, then followed for several years to determine if these individuals were more involved in sexually violent crimes, antisocial incidents in school, or other antisocial acts. Until these studies are undertaken, it would be prudent to refrain from advocating outright bans on violent pornography.

Social scientists have generally not asked the questions that have been most relevant to the concerns of traditional obscenity law — whether pornography is offensive or immoral — not because these are unimportant questions but because they are exceedingly difficult to pursue given the methods traditionally used by social scientists. Generally, this research has consisted of asking individuals with differing levels of experience with pornographic materials to render opinions about them. Survey research undertaken by the 1970 Pornography Commission and discussed in Chapter 2 indicated that, at least in the late 1960s, few Americans considered pornography to be a significant social problem, and an equally low number were concerned about pornography's harmful effects. This may be changing. A 1986 poll undertaken for *Time*[19] indicated that 60% of men and 70% of women surveyed believe that pornography leads people to become more sexually promiscuous. Thirty-five percent of men and women surveyed believe that female nudity in a movie should be considered pornographic, and nearly 60% of the respondents believed that magazines with nude pictures should be outlawed in local stores. Overall, nearly two-thirds of the poll respondents indicated that they were "very" or "fairly concerned" about the pervasiveness of pornography in the United States. Perhaps this signals the reemergence of the traditional concerns about pornography that have been codified in obscenity law as it has evolved over the years. We turn now to a brief discussion of the major developments in obscenity law in the United States.

THE HISTORY OF OBSCENITY LAW

In his discussion of the history of censorship, Barber[20] observes that the ancient Greeks were largely unperturbed by pornography and did not seek to censor it, although both Plato and Socrates expressed concerns about its effect on children. Pornographic and obscene materials apparently flourished during Roman times, and even the advent of Christian morality did not give rise to attacks on pornography. Sexual vices were low on the Church's agenda, largely because the Church was much more concerned at the time with political challenges to its sovereignty.

In England, the government had undertaken to censor publications as early as 1538 (approximately 60 years after the printing press was introduced), and during the 16th and 17th centuries printers commonly had to obtain a license to print their works from agents of both the government and the church. The objects of censorship were largely political, and as a result pornographic materials were readily licensed while "serious" (especially political) works were given much closer scrutiny. By the end of the 17th century these licensing laws were largely ineffective, but there was a growing interest in controlling pornographic materials. In 1708 there was an unsuccessful effort to prosecute (under the common law of libel) a pornographic work, and two decades later the publisher of *Venus in the Cloister*—a volume detailing sexual debaucheries in a convent—was successfully prosecuted under what was then a new notion of "obscene libel."[21]

By the end of the 18th century, private societies were formed for the purpose of suppressing vice such as obscene and pornographic materials. For the next 150 years these societies proceeded to institute private prosecutions of pornography publishers. In addition to initiating their own suits under English law, these private associations were also active advocates of legislative action, based on an assumption that exposure to erotic materials produced harms. It was assumed that such exposure could deprave or corrupt persons who might otherwise remain morally pure. This idea was enshrined in Anglo-American law in 1868 in the case *Queen* v. *Hicklin*.

The first American common law obscenity prosecution took place in the early 19th century. In that Pennsylvania case, *Commonwealth* v. *Sharpless*,[22] the defendant was charged with showing a picture of a man and woman in an indecent posture. The Connecticut obscenity statute of 1821, the Federal Customs Law of 1842, and the Postal Act of 1865 were all directed at trade in pornographic materials. A more extensive postal act was passed in 1873 as a result of pressures from Anthony Comstock's Society for the Suppression of Vice. Under this act's definition, a work is obscene in "any substantial part" as gauged by its effects on the "most susceptible persons." Until the 1950s, most state courts retained the *Hicklin* test of obscenity. Materials were judged obscene if they depraved and corrupted those minds that are open to immoral influences.

It should be evident that throughout most of the history of American law there have been no clear legal standards governing obscenity and pornography. The First Amendment to the Constitution clearly provides broad protections for speech: "Congress shall make no law . . . abridging the freedom of speech or of the press." Although enacted in 1791, it was more than a century before the Supreme Court began to consider the application of the First Amendment to obscenity and pornography. The Supreme Court sought to answer three essential questions: (1) How should obscenity be defined?; (2) Who should decide what is obscene?; and (3) Who is most likely to be adversely affected by obscene materials?

The development of obscenity law has proceeded with a mixture of moralism and paternalism. Indeed, some[23] have argued that the *only* rationale for most obscenity laws is the belief that the government should protect public morals. Only occasionally has the Supreme Court referred to other justifications and standards, such as a requirement that obscene materials be offensive or produce harmful antisocial effects.

In any discussion of obscenity law it is desirable to differentiate between the terms "obscenity" and "pornography," as have feminists Dworkin and MacKinnon. Up to now we have used the words interchangeably. Indeed, both within and outside the law there has been a confusion of obscenity and pornography. Webster's dictionary[24] indicates that obscene is derived from the Latin *ob*, which means "to" or "before," and *caenum,* which means "filth." In a careful review of the origins of the term, Richards[25] reports that another source might be the Latin *scena,* which refers to "what takes place offstage." Richard's notes that in many ancient plays, acts of violence and moral or sexual perversion took place offstage. He further comments that obscene has traditionally referred to disgusting and filthy acts or depictions that offend people's sense of decency. Obscenity has often been associated with moral corruption and feelings of shame, and obscenities or verbal epithets often refer to excretory and sexual behavior. Richards concludes that obscene captures a sense of the unnatural or abusive exercise of bodily function. He is especially careful to note that different societies are offended by different behaviors.[26]

Webster's reports that "pornography" is derived from the Greek *porngraphos,* which refers to the "writing of harlots" or descriptions of the acts of prostitutes. Richards stresses that pornography is tied to graphic and explicit depictions of sexual intercourse and genitalia. He further argues that pornography traditionally was not viewed as obscene in the sense of shame and filth. He asserts that Catholic canon law initiated a confusion of the two terms, Victorian morality reinforced the confusion, and the U.S. Supreme Court has elevated the confusion to law in its decisions.

When defining obscenity and pornography in legal tests, the Supreme Court speaks of obscenity, though it is clear it actually has in mind pornography.[27] As Feinberg notes, the Court has primarily concerned itself with words, pictures, or other portrayals that cause the reader or viewer to become sexually aroused. The Court has not usually been concerned with what is obscene in the conventional sense—profanity, scatology, impolite language, objects that are disgusting to the senses, or nonsexual conduct that offends higher sensibilities. This point is underscored in Justice Harlan's opinion in *Cohen* v. *California*,[28] in which the defendant had been convicted for disturbing the peace by wearing a jacket enscribed with the words "Fuck the Draft" inscribed on the back. Harlan wrote: "This is not . . . an obscenity case. Whatever else may be necessary to give rise to the States's broader power to prohibit obscene expression, such expression must be, in some significant way erotic."[29]

As early as 1896, in *Swearingen* v. *United States*,[30] the Supreme Court defined obscenity in terms of "sexual impurity," and the emphasis on sexual and pornographic aspects of materials examined by the Supreme Court still permeates the definitions. The *Hicklin* test, discussed earlier, survived in some states until the 1950s, but the decision by Federal Judge Woolsey in the 1933 case of *United States* v. *One Book Entitled "Ulysses"*[31] initiated the reworking of Lord Cockburn's definition. Woolsey insisted that the intent of a work should be considered "in its entirety" (or, in Hand's words, its "dominant effect") and not on the basis of isolated passage. He also substituted an "average man" standard rather than examining effects on the most susceptible persons. The *Ulysses* standard thus called for a balance between literary and scientific value (without which a work loses its First Amendment protection) and a work's tendency to lead to lustful and sexually impure thoughts or impulses.

The 1948 case of *Winters* v. *New York*[32] merits special attention, primarily because the Supreme Court dealt directly with the issue of violence in the media, and secondarily because it illustrates the fate of a state statute directed at publications "devoted . . . to criminal news, police reports, or accounts of criminal deeds, or pictures, or stories of deeds of bloodshed, lust or crime."[33] As Krattenmaker and Powe[34] have noted, the case was a difficult one — it was argued three times before the Supreme Court before the Court overturned the statute for vagueness. Although the New York Court of Appeals had approved a legislative finding that massed collections of criminal deeds and bloodshed could incite "violent and depraved crimes against the person,"[35] the Supreme Court (Justice Reed writing for the majority) decided that the magazine in question[36] merited First Amendment protection because it was not "lewd, indecent, obscene or profane."[37]

It was not until the 1957 *Roth* v. *United States*[38] case that the Supreme Court rendered its first authoritative modern decision on pornography/obscenity. Justice Brennan, writing for the majority, largely followed *Ulysses* in formulating his test: "Whether to the average person, applying contemporary community standards, the dominant theme of the material taken as a whole appeals to prurient interests."[39] The definition of "prurient interest" was ambiguous. In one part of his opinion, Brennan emphasized "the tendency to incite lustful thoughts"; elsewhere, he endorsed the definition of the American Law Institute's Model Penal Code, which, while it used the term "prurient interest," went to great lengths to downplay eroticism and emphasized "exacerbated, morbid, or perverted interest" in nudity, sex, or excretion. Brennan did not note these qualifications. In *Roth*, the Court concluded that obscene materials had traditionally been regarded as utterly without redeeming social value and placed them outside First Amendment protection.

One impact of the *Roth* decision was a rapid growth in appellate litigation.[40] In a short period of time, the Supreme Court decided a number of cases in its efforts to refine the *Roth* standards. Five years after *Roth*, in the *Manual Enterprises* v. *Day*[41] and *Mishkin* v. *New York*[42] cases, the Court added the concept of offensiveness to its original formula. According to Justice Harlan, a publication had to pass a two-fold test before being ajudged obscene: The material must be patently offensive *and* the material must appeal to prurient interests. In 1966, a plurality opinion (Brennan, Warren, and Fortas), in the case of *A Book Named "John Cleland's Memoirs of a Woman of Pleasure"* v. *Attorney General of Massachusetts*[43] (the so-called Fanny Hill case), added the "utterly without redeeming social value" test to the *Roth* standard. This produced a "three-pronged test" for obscenity: appeal to prurient interest, patent offensiveness, and utter absence of redeeming value. For the record, another case decided in the same period, *Jacobellis* v. *Ohio*,[44] produced a notable quote illustrating the difficulties inherent in defining obscenity. It was this in case that Justice Stewart acknowledged that although he might have trouble specifying an intelligible definition of pornography, "I know it when I see it."[45]

The next landmark obscenity case was *Stanley* v. *Georgia*.[46] The issue was whether mere possession of a pornographic film in one's own home, with no intention to sell or distribute the film, was grounds for prosecution. The Court unanimously agreed that it was not. In Justice Marshall's words: "If the First Amendment means anything, it means that a State has no business telling a man sitting alone in his own house, what books he may read or what films he may watch."[47]

Contemporary standards governing obscene and pornographic materials arise from several 1973 obscenity cases, the most important of which are *Miller* v. *California*[48] and *Paris Adult Theatre I* v. *Slaton.*[49] In *Miller,* Chief Justice Burger, a politically conservative appointee of the Nixon administration, wrote for the five-member majority and announced a new and stricter obscenity test. The Court took the three-prong test laid down in the Fanny Hill case and modified it. Now, according to the Court:

The basic guideline for the trier of fact must be: (a) whether "the average person, applying contemporary community standards" would find that the work, taken as a whole, appeals to the prurient interest . . . ; (b) whether the work depicts or describes, in a patently offensive way, sexual conduct specifically defined by the applicable state law; and (c) whether the work, taken as a whole, lacks serious literary, artistic, political, or scientific value.[50]

The *Miller* decision modified prior thinking on obscenity law in two basic ways: First, it moved the test from a national standard to a local standard. Second, it replaced the "utterly without redeeming social value" test with a standard requiring only that the work lack "serious" literary, artistic, political, or scientific value. The intention of the new standard was clearly to permit more aggressive prosecution of pornographers. The obscene materials could now be judged by local standards, and as Feinberg notes:

Recourse to a local community norm rather than a national standard . . . permits local courts to find persons guilty for distributing materials that could not plausibly be found obscene in other, more sophisticated jurisdictions. . . . The substitution of local community standards in effect makes it difficult to publish anywhere materials that would violate the most puritanical standards in the country. Publishers will have to screen out-of-state orders more carefully than Larry C. Flynt did when he routinely mailed a copy of his publication *Hustler* to a person who had ordered it by mail from a town in Ohio. [51]

Flynt was later tried for violation of the Ohio obscenity statutes (patterned after the standards in *Miller*) and sentenced to 7 to 25 years in prison. Replacing the "utterly without redeeming social value" test with the requirement that only "serious" works deserve First Amendment protection appears to limit constitutional protection to artistically good novels or movies or seriously valuable political commentary. If this modification were to be taken literally by publishers and writers, many preconceptions about what has been traditionally protected by the First Amendment would be invalidated. According to Feinberg:

The Court's message to writers is a discouraging one: If you plan to write a novel that contains explicitly sexual scenes that the average person in a remote community would judge to be titillating or shocking, you had better make sure that it has important literary value; if it turns out to be merely mediocre on literary grounds, your publisher may end up in jail.[52]

In the *Paris Adult Theater* case, Chief Justice Burger provided some insights into the majority's thinking. The Court seemed prepared to reach the sweeping conclusion that pornographic materials could pose sufficient threat to a community or even the nation that it might be banned entirely. The Chief Justice asserted:

The States have the power to make a morally neutral judgment that public exhibition of obscene material, or commerce in such material, has a tendency to injure the community as a whole, to endanger the public safety (emphasis added), or to jeopardize, in Mr. Chief Justice Warren's words, the States' right . . . to maintain a decent society.[53]

To further bolster the language concerning possible harms, Burger cited the 1970 Minority Report of the Commission on Obscenity and Pornography as support for the proposition that "there is at least an arguable correlation between obscene material and crime."[54] Although the Court's willingness to turn to empirical research is laudable, the Court somehow ignored the majority report, which concluded that there was "no evidence to date that exposure to explicit sexual materials plays a significant role in the causation of delinquent of criminal behavior among youth or adults."[55]

As the law stands today, three basic questions must be answered by juries in an obscenity case: (1) Would the average person applying community standards find that this material, as a whole, appeals to prurient interest?; (2) Does the material offensively depict sexual conduct as defined by state law?; and (3) Does the work lack literary, artistic, political, or scientific value?

Under the *Miller* standards, if a state statute prohibiting the distribution of obscene materials were used as the basis for a prosecution, and the local jury is prepared to convict the defendant, it would be possible to stem the flow of obscene materials to a community. However, such a scenario clearly requires assertive district attorneys and juries. For example, a few years ago an aggressive prosecutor and supportive juries in Atlanta, Georgia, were able to close nearly all X-rated movie houses and adult bookstores.[56] However, the Atlanta experience is unusual. One post-*Miller* survey of prosecutors found fewer jurisdictions prosecuting for obscenity after *Miller,* and that there was a drop in the total number of prosecutions.[57] At the same time, the majority of prosecutors indicated that obscene materials were increasingly available in their communities.

Ironically, Justice Brennan, who devised the *Roth* test, had by the time of the *Miller* and *Paris Adult Theater* rulings come to mistrust the notion of government regulation of so-called obscene materials. In his dissent in the *Paris Adult Theater* case he urged the Court to seriously consider abandoning the approach he had initiated 16 years earlier. In recommending a new beginning, Brennan argued that obscenity laws fail to "provide adequate notice to persons who are engaged in the type of conduct that [obscenity laws] could be thought to proscribe."[58] It has long been argued that no citizen can be responsible for conduct that he or she could not reasonably have understood to be against the law.[59] Since no one can reasonably predict how the Supreme Court is going to decide close obscenity cases, obscenity law, as it now stands, makes publishing and bookselling a somewhat hazardous profession. This state of uncertainty, according to Brennan, is bound to create a chilling effect on all writing that deals with sex. Writers and publishers wary of ending up on the wrong side of the law may choose not to write or publish at all.

WHAT HARMS IS SOCIETY WILLING TO TOLERATE?

As we mentioned earlier, the social science research evidence collected to date seems to speak most directly to the concerns of feminists about the harms following exposure to certain images of women rather than to the concerns about morality and prurient interest that dominate traditional obscenity law. At this point, though, the evidence for the effects of exposure to violent pornography, rather than all forms of pornography, seems most compelling. Interestingly, when considering the legality of the Indianapolis ordinance, neither the Southern District Court nor the Seventh Circuit Court disagreed with the premise of the legislation, founded partly on evidence from social psychological experiments on sexual violence, that pornographic depictions of violence toward women and depictions of subordination of women tend to perpetuate subordination. In fact, as the Seventh Circuit Court noted, "this subordination [may in turn lead] to lower pay at work, insult and injury at home or even battery and rape on the streets."[60] In this regard, they likened pornography to other forms of speech that promote hatred and bigotry, such as manifestos by the Ku Klux Klan or even violent programming on TV.

Though the courts recognized that harmful effects are likely to arise from materials such as these, they concluded that the materials are nonetheless all protected by the First Amendment. According to the Seventh Circuit Court:

Racial bigotry, anti-semitism, violence on television, reporters' biases — these and many more influence the culture and shape our socialization. None is directly answerable by more speech, unless that speech too finds its place in the popular culture. Yet all is protected speech, however insidious. Any other answer leaves the government in control of all of the institutions of culture, the great censor and director of which thoughts are good for us.[61]

In other words, the harm done to society as a whole by restricting certain forms of speech is greater than the harms to the individual groups of persons who are suffering the discrimination. The harms resulting from exposure to pornography, defined by feminists, are not, in the Court's opinion, as devastating to society as harms that might be incurred if the government were to attempt to regulate it in any manner other than through existing obscenity laws.

The danger, according to the courts, of accepting sex discrimination as a more compelling state interest than First Amendment protections, is that it may open the door for any legislative body to regulate speech concerning nearly any group in society. If the court were to accept the defendants' argument — that the state's interest in protecting women from the humiliation and degradation that comes from being depicted in a sexually subordinate context is so compelling as to warrant the regulation of otherwise free speech — there is nothing to prevent the city-county council (or any other legislative body) from enacting protections for other equally compelling claims against exploitation and discrimination. To set such a legal precedent would encourage legislative bodies to enact legislation prohibiting other unfair expression, such as the publication and distribution of racist material, for example, on the grounds that it causes racial discrimination. It would also encourage legislation prohibiting ethnic or religious slurs on the grounds that they cause discrimination against particular ethnic or religious groups; legislation barring literary depictions that are uncomplimentary or oppressive to handicapped persons on the grounds that they cause discrimination against that group of people, and so on.[62]

The courts seem to be saying that no matter how compelling the data linking violent pornography to antisocial attitudes and behavior, the question is a legal and political-moral one, and only tangentially an empirical one. The Southern District Court makes this point quite clearly in its discussion of the social-psychological evidence entered as evidence in the Indianapolis hearings:

> The defendants argue that there is more than enough "empirical" evidence in the case at bar to support the City-County Council's conclusion that "pornography" harms women . . . it is not the Court's function to question the City-County Council's legislative finding. The Court's solitary duty is to ensure that the ordinance accomplishes its purpose without violating constitutional standards or impinging upon constitutionally protected rights.[63]

Even if there were unequivocal empirical evidence that exposure to particular forms of pornography would result in a recognizable harm, United States courts may still not decide that additional regulation beyond the traditional restraints contained in the criminal obscenity statutes are permissible.

It is interesting to note that a significant contingent of feminists would subscribe to an argument much like the one constructed by the courts. Not all feminists support the idea of creating laws to regulate pornography. Recently, a group of feminists working against violence have published an anthology entitled *Women Against Censorship,* edited by Varda Burstyn.[64] In it the contributors outline alternatives to legal censorship of pornography. Burstyn asserts that the attempts by some feminists to isolate pornography as "*the* culprit, *the* demon, the very *cause* of sexism and violence against women," rather than one of the more obvious manifestations of a larger sexist culture, are misguided.[65] According to Burstyn, the political ramification of this narrow focus on pornography and the creation of laws banning it is the possibility that state censorship initially brought about by feminists will eventually be used against them. The same laws that would be used to prohibit the sale of *Hustler* magazine could be used to ban *Our Bodies Ourselves* or similar information on birth control, or to censor information on homosexuality.

Burstyn cites examples involving the Ontario Board of Censors, who have deemed films as unacceptable when, in the opinion of some feminists, these materials have been important critiques of pornography. Films like *The Tin Drum* and *Pretty Baby* were banned because they involved children, despite the fact that these films were critical of societies treatment of women and children. "Most frightening of all," according to Burstyn, has been the Boards' insistence that films by feminists themselves, such as *Not a Love Story,* only be shown in relatively inaccessible galleries instead of local neighborhood theaters that show "films like *Emmanuelle, Dressed to Kill,* and *Porky's,* which all pass without difficulty through the censors hands."[66] The central problem is that there is no guarantee that people who work on censorship boards will be feminists; in fact, it is quite likely that they will not be. Those persons who end up on governmental censorship boards do so because they are interested in maintaining the status quo. They do not see feminists as their constituency, but may "feel a much greater affinity for social forces with conservative and reactionary values that thinks sex itself is bad."[67] Rather than working to legislate against certain depictions, feminists should instead work to demand access for their views and work to replace sexists pornography with alternative material that presents sexuality in a positive nonsexist manner. Burstyn warns: "Progressive people simply cannot afford to play around with democratic principles."[68]

DEMONSTRATING INCITEMENT AND INSTRUCTIONAL EFFECTS IN A CIVIL CASE

The primary legal problem with civil ordinances such as the Indianapolis ordinance in the United States is that they operate on the premise of a "sociological harm"—that pornography harms *all* women as a class—rather than on the premise of individual tangible harms. The Indianapolis ordinance sought to protect women as a group from discrimination and from diminished social status. The courts have concluded that to rule in favor of this approach would encourage other legislative bodies to create laws limiting unfair expressions such as racial and ethnic slurs. Governmental bodies, thus unrestrained, would ultimately come to limit many forms of expression now protected by the First Amendment. On the other hand, the Supreme Court and state supreme courts have repeatedly confirmed the constitutional acceptability of state obscenity statutes as long as they are patterned after the *Miller* prototype.

These arguments suggest that (1) if harm is limited to an individual woman and is physical in nature (rather than predicated on the proposition that all women are harmed through discriminatory practices), and (2) if the material implicated in the harmful act is unprotected by the First Amendment because it is legally judged to be obscene, then some form of civil liability might attach to the producers and/or distributors of the material, and the recovery of damages by the victim might be possible.

In order to initiate such a suit, several major legal hurdles would have to be overcome. First, the victim or plaintiff (for example, a woman who has been the victim of a violent rape ostensibly modeled after a rape depicted in a motion picture viewed by the assailant shortly before the assault) would have to establish that a harm (tort) has occurred.[69] This might not be a significant problem, especially if there has been a criminal trial in which it was proved that the victim was raped and the defendant was found guilty. Presumably, this is a type of harm that society wishes to redress. Next, a defendant must be named. While it would be possible to name the rapist himself as a defendant in a civil suit, the primary defendants in the suit might more appropriately be the creators, producers, and distributors of the film in question.

Any tort suit would require that the plaintiff demonstrate a causal connection between an "individual instance (depiction) of damage and an individual instance of damage-causing behavior."[70] For a particular case, it would be necessary to demonstrate a relationship between a particular portrayal, message, or movie scene and the harm to the victim. It would not be sufficient merely to allege that such materials are widely available, that they promote an aggressive tendency in people generally, and that the rapist's act was a reflection of this process. This argument would imply that all film producers, directors, and so forth involved with such materials are potentially liable. Instead, tort liability is most compellingly established when an identifiable message associated with the tortious behavior can be located in a particular film and that a specific film and persons associated with this material be named in the suit.[71]

In other words, it may be necessary (and sufficient) for the plaintiff to demonstrate that the injury resembled in some unique detail a similar rape enacted in materials viewed by the rapist. Such demonstrations are clearly difficult, but, as Spak[72] has noted, the uniqueness of the act is probably the pivotal point for establishing media liability. In Spak's words, "a relatively commonplace punch in the nose — a generally violent act"[73] — can never be directly linked to a specific media presentation. But unusual, rare, or distinctive acts may be traceable. For example, "murder by means of a magnum gun rather than an ordinary gun, assault with a karate blow rather than the more usual fisted punch, or a stabbing with a machete instead of a more mundane knife"[74] may all be acts that can be linked to specific media events. One example of a traceable act is an incident in which Boston youths soaked a woman with gasoline and set her on fire two days after the TV movie *Fuzz*, which contained scene in which a wino was similarly set afire[75]. Of course, demonstrating that a rape contained no unusual characteristics or peculiarities was caused by a film depiction would be a significantly more difficult task.

Hilker[76] has observed that the claim that a particular harmful act is traceable to a particular depiction asserts what may be termed an "instructional" effect. The claim would be that the rapist learned his particular method from the film depiction. In addition, the victim might claim a more general "incitement" effect, predicated on the assertion that the rapist was motivated by the depiction to reenact what he had learned. Hilker has noted that it would be difficult to prove an incitement effect without first establishing an instructional effect. In any case, it would probably be difficult to persuade a jury that a rapist derived his inspiration to commit a rape from viewing particular materials unless the rape resembled, in some unique way, the rape portrayed in the film materials.

If an appropriate causal groundwork is laid by an attorney, and a jury is prepared to believe that the harmful act and the film depiction were related to one another, a social psychologist might be called by a plaintiff to help demonstrate an instructional effect, an incitement effect, or both. The social psychologist is probably best situated to assist the jury in ascertaining whether an incitement effect was present. This is because none of the existing data on the effects of violent pornography or nonpornographic violent depictions have directly demonstrated that exposure to these materials produces learning or mimicking of the specific behaviors portrayed in films. In other words, social psychologists have not conducted a study whereby one group of persons is exposed to sexually violent materials and another is not, then waited to see if subjects in the exposed group committed crimes closely resembling the depictions to which they were exposed. These studies obviously cannot be done for ethical reasons. Consequently, we have no experimental data on specific imitation effects.

What the research has demonstrated is that exposure may foster a motivation to aggress against women more generally, and may provide the viewer with the psychological means or justification for such aggression. Furthermore, research on the effects of violent pornography[77] indicate that a positive victim response will facilitate aggressive behavior against females by male laboratory subjects. Using these research findings, we can begin to construct a profile of what may constitute the most "risky" set of materials — that is, the type of film or magazine portrayal that may inspire or instigate an imitation effect.

What type of materials pose the greatest risk? Research conducted by Malamuth and his colleagues described in preceding chapters indicated that when the victim was portrayed as becoming involuntarily sexually aroused by the assault, male subjects' own sexual arousal, as indexed both by self-reports and penile tumescence measures, becomes as high, and is sometimes higher, than sexual arousal resulting from mutually consenting depictions. In other studies, males who watched or listened to rape depictions that supposedly had positive consequences for the victim thought the victim had suffered less, and believed that a larger percentage of women in general would find forced sex or rape pleasurable, compared with males exposed to materials depicting a negative consequence for the victim.

Studies by Donnerstein and his colleagues have provided evidence that a positive victim response will facilitate aggressive behavior against females by male laboratory subjects. Even when male subjects were not angered, the positive-outcome aggressive-pornographic films significantly increased aggression against females. These results are only obtained when the target of aggression is a female. When the experimenters' confederate is a male, male subjects shock the confederate significantly less in both positive- and negative-outcome conditions.

A profile of what may constitute the most risky set of materials would have to include portrayals of rapes or other forms of sexual assault that show the female victim becoming involuntarily aroused or otherwise responding positively to sexual aggression. There is some indication that the film or other materials need not necessarily be hard-core explicitly detailed portrayals to have effects on viewers attitudes. But because behavioral effects have been demonstrated only for material that is both sexually explicit and explicitly violent, it may be best to limit our definition of what is most risky — to materials that contain explicit sex and violence.

Who is most likely to be influenced by these materials? The experimental evidence collected to date indicates that rapists appear to become sexually aroused by material that stresses the rape victim's abhorrence of the attack. For a sizable portion of the normal male population, which might be identified via instruments such as the Likelihood of Raping Scale (LR) devised by Malamuth and Check (see Chapter 5), depictions of rape in which the victim seems to experience a positive outcome are sexually arousing. There are also data to suggest that men who score high on psychological scales measuring power as a motivation for sexual acts, men who report lower levels of actual sexual experience, and men who score low on love and affection as a motivation for sex are likely to perceive an ambiguous rape experience as having a positive outcome for the victim.

While there may be certain individuals who are drawn to violent pornography more than others, and there may be those predisposed to aggression who are more likely to immitate these depictions, it may not be the case that only when a person is angry does violent pornography have a facilitative effect. Research has demonstrated that even when subjects are not angered, films depicting a positive outcome for the victim result in increased aggression against females by males. These findings lead the researchers to conclude that whereas depictions that emphasize the pain and suffering of the victim have their effect only with male subjects who are predisposed toward aggression, the more common story line in aggressive pornography—of a willing and positive-reacting victim—influences all subjects.

Who is most likely to be the victim of the individual incited by these materials? The research presented in the preceding chapters can also help us answer this question. Donnerstein and his colleagues have shown that exposure to aggressive pornographic materials results in little increase in aggression against a male target. Exposure to the aggressive pornographic material did increase male aggression against a female target, however, and this effect occurred regardless of whether or not the males were angered before exposure. The most obvious targets of aggression incited by these materials will be females. But, an interesting question not addressed by the research conducted to date is the impact of materials depicting homosexual rape on aggression toward male victims. The effect of positive versus negative male victim reactions on subsequent aggressive behavior toward males by males is unknown. It may be that exposure to these materials results in a pattern of responses similar to male/female rape with victim depictions resulting in greater male-to-male aggressiveness. Defining this risk must await further empirical research.

On the basis of what we know so far, we have to assert that the kind of film that is most dangerous would be that which depicts sexual violence against women in either a sexually explicit or non-explicit manner, where the victim(s) are shown enjoying or some-how benefiting from this treatment. Furthermore, we might expect that young male adolescents who are in the process of exploring their own sexuality or beginning to date members of the opposite sex might be most affected by this material. This group might be more inclined than others to turn to the media for ideas about the appropriateness of certain sexual behaviors.

Ironically, attempts by film industry to protect young people from these depictions may have helped as much as hurt, in our opinion. On the positive side, by encouraging film makers and dis-tributors to clearly label films that include explicit depictions of sex and restrict those under the age of 18 from viewing them, they may have helped to protect those most impressionable from exposure to sexually explicit depictions of rape and sexual violence. But by no means are sexually violent materials the only ones with these restric-tions. In general, this category is comprised of films that are sexually explicit but nonviolent, and of the two types of X-rated materials it is this type of film to which the young person is much more likely to be exposed. In contrast, films with far less restrictive ratings often contain a great deal of violence against women and more than a few sexually nonexplicit depictions of rape and other forms of sexual violence. The message to young people in our society may be that sexual violence is permissible, but nonviolent sexual relations are not.

The film industry has succeeded over the years in devising nu-merous systems that have imposed self-censorship while avoiding excessive interference from the government or other groups. But it may have failed to restrict the more impressionable members of their audience from viewing the most dangerous material by not specifically encouraging limited access to depictions of sexual violence.

FILM INDUSTRY REGULATION BOARDS AND RATING SYSTEMS

If you are a teenager or the parent of a child of any age, you are aware that movies are rated either G, PG, PG-13, R, or X. But few of us probably know why movies are rated this way. In fact, as *New York Times* film critic Vincent Canby has remarked: "Even those of us who are paid to watch movies are frequently baffled."[78] For example, since April 1986 the Motion Picture Association of America (MPAA) and the National Association of Theater Owners (NATO) have had an official policy of being tougher on movies that depict or refer to the use of illegal drugs or that use sexually graphic language. In addition to the usual criteria, any reference to the use of illegal drugs in a film results in a rating of PG-13 (special parental guidance suggested for those younger than 13) by the MPAA. It is also the policy of the board that one use of "the harsher, sexually derived words" will earn a film a PG-13 rating, and that two or more such words will automatically result in an R (children under 17 not permitted unless accompanied by parent or adult guardian).

It is unlikely that most people realize the board takes these matters into consideration. In fact, the MPAA has often been criticized for its refusal to announce the specific reasons for giving a film a particular rating. But these same critics are quick to agree that the film board has ultimately succeeded in keeping calls for censorship in check by monitoring movies and attempting through its lettering system to give the public at least a rough idea of the content of particular films. In fact, film historians have asserted that if it were not for the fact that the producers and distributors of films in the United States had joined to form their own regulation board, some form of government censorship of movies might well have been created to placate city and state officials and various religious and political groups. (See Table 7–1 for a partial list of movies involved in litigation or censored in various regions of the country throughout this century.)

It is estimated that in 1907, 1.5 million New Yorkers went to the movies per week.[79] On Christmas Eve 1908, the mayor of New York closed every movie house in the city—over 600 theaters. Officially, the theaters were to be closed because they were thought to be a safety hazard but, DeGrazia and Newman report, the mayor also threatened to revoke the licenses of all theater owners who showed movies that were degrading or injurious to the morals of the community. The city's theater owners baned together and obtained an injunction to stop the closings, but the city's board of aldermen did manage to pass an ordinance prohibiting children under 16 from attending movies unless accompanied by an adult. By 1909, the New York State Association of Motion Picture Exhibitors called for the creation of a citizens committee to preview all movies to stave off

TABLE 7-1

List of Well-known Films and Censorship Activities Associated with Them

Film	Censorship Activity or Legal Importance
The Man with the Golden Arm	Banned in Maryland, 1956. The case has importance because of the distinction between constitutionally protected discussion and constitutionally unprotected advocacy of such ideas as the use of narcotics. The film was viewed as "discussing," not "advocating" such use.
And God Created Woman	Banned in Philadelphia, 1958.
The Anatomy of a Murder	The Chicago censorship board refused to grant the distributor of this film a permit for its exhibition in the city, evidently because of a rape scene and the use of the words "rape" and "contraceptive"; the mayor approved the denial.
Desire Under the Elms	After the Chicago censorship board granted the distributor of this film a permit to exhibit it only to persons over 21, the distributor brought suit for an injunction to prevent the city from interfering with its general exhibition. The U.S. District Court for the Northern District of Illinois issued the injunction requested by the distributor.
Where Eagles Dare	The Sheriff of Rutherford County, North Carolina, undertook a campaign to stop the exhibition within the county of all films not recommended by the Motion Picture Association of America "for general audiences."
The Exorcist	The corporate owner of a theater in Hattiesburg, Mississippi, was tried and convicted for publicly exhibiting "an obscene, indecent and immoral motion picture."
Woodstock	Several persons under 18 years of age in the company of two adults who were parents of some of them were denied entrance to a movie theater showing this film because a City of Kenosha, Wisconsin, ordinance forbade the entrance of minors at theaters showing movies classified by the Motion Picture Association of America as R or X. The adults, on their children's behalf, asked

162

TABLE 7–1 *(continued)*

List of Well-known Films and Censorship Activities Associated with Them

Film	Censorship Activity or Legal Importance
	a federal district court to enjoin enforcement of the ordinance because it denied to children their rights of freedom of expression. The court issued the injunction.
Last Tango in Paris	The Montgomery, Alabama, chief of police wrote the exhibitor that his showing the film, prior to a judicial declaration that it was not obscene, "might result in [criminal] prosecution" under state law. The distributor went into federal district court to have the statute declared unconstitutional and to restrain enforcement.
The Last Picture Show	After receiving "several complaints from citizens" concerning this film, which had shown for a week at a Phoenix, Arizona, drive-in theater and which apparently could be seen by neighboring residents and travelers upon the public way," the city attorney wrote the theater manager that "it was [his] opinion" the film violated both the "explicit terms" and "spirit as well" of a state criminal obscenity statute.
I Am Curious—Yellow	When the distributor of Grove Press sought to bring this Swedish film into the United States, the U.S. Customs Service seized it as obscene and went into federal district court for a judicial determination of the issue. The government requested a jury trial, and the jury found the film obscene. On review, the U.S. Court of Appeals for the Second Circuit reversed, holding the movie was not obscene "under the standards established by the Supreme Court" and "the showing of the picture cannot be inhibited."
Deep Throat	This film was involved in litigation in a great number of cities and states because of its alleged obscenity. One such case, which reached the U.S. Supreme Court, arose when the landlord of a theater operator who was exhibiting the movie notified the operator that his lease would be terminated because the county attorney had threatened

continued on page 164

TABLE 7–1 (continued)
List of Well-known Films and Censorship Activities Associated with Them

Film	Censorship Activity or Legal Importance
	to "abate the theater as a public nuisance in order to prevent the future showing of allegedly obscene motion pictures."
Behind the Green Door	The prosecutor argued that the film was "unqualifiedly worthless" and therefore obscene, and that if it was not obscene to devote almost an entire film to a sexual orgy of the sort depicted in this film, then "nothing is obscene."
The Devil in Miss Jones	This film was involved in litigation in numerous cities and states because of its alleged obscenity. The Wayne County, Michigan, prosecutor brought civil actions against several theaters as "public nuisances" because they had exhibited "lewd" films, including this one as well as *Deep Throat* and two others. The nuisance statute was in its terms applicable to "any building, vehicle, boat, aircraft, or place" used for the purpose of "lewdness," prostitution, gambling, etc.
Caligula	By May 15, 1981, according to the Federal District Court in the Northern District of Georgia that tried this case, the movie had been shown in over 100 cities in the United States. In Atlanta, the film's distributor asked the court to declare *Caligula* not obscene but, rather, protected by the First Amendment, and to enjoin the Solicitor General of Fulton County from arresting or prosecuting anyone concerned with the film's distribution or exhibition. The court issued the requested declaration but declined to enjoin any criminal prosecution.

SOURCE: Adapted from DeGrazia and Newman (1982).

further government intervention. This committee evolved into a nationwide nongovernmental organization, The National Board of Censorship of Motion Pictures. By 1915, according to DeGrazia and Newman, "virtually the entire output of the country's movie industry was being reviewed prior to exhibition by 250 affiliated local organizations nationwide."[80] Later the board changed its name to the National Board of Review of Motion Pictures, claiming that it was opposed to censorship, and encouraged the public to view its role as a movie classifier rather than a censor. The board had eight standards by which it classified movies: It prohibited obscenity and vulgarity; representation of crime that might teach methods of committing crime; "morbid" scenes of crime; prolonged scenes of suffering, brutality, and violence; religious blasphemy offending any large group of people in the country; malicious libel; any "scenes of films which, because of elements frequently very subtle which they contain, have a deteriorating tendency on the basic moralities or necessary social standards."

Despite the efforts of the National Board of Review to curb government censorship before 1920, several state and local boards continued to exert influence largely because of dissatisfaction with what they perceived to be the liberal standards of the national board. DeGrazia and Newman[81] note that censorship activities of the state and local boards mirrored developing moral conflicts in American society. The movie Birth Control, a biographical film portraying Margaret Sanger advising poor women on methods of birth control, was suppressed by the New York City theater licensing commissioner because he felt the film did not display proper respect for law enforcement officials (Sanger was depicted as defying state law that prohibited the dissemination of birth control information). The commissioner said the film also "sought to teach immorality and was entirely opposed to the public welfare."[81] In addition, the commissioner claimed that disseminating birth control information would cause young women to engage in promiscuous sexual behavior from which they might otherwise refrain if threatened with the shame of unwanted pregnancy.

After World War I, several religious organizations, including Episcopalian, Presbyterian, Methodist, and Baptist groups and the Central Conference of American Rabbis, passed resolutions criticizing the movie industry for its immoral influence in American society. In an attempt to avoid not only local but perhaps federal censorship, movie producers and distributors formed the National Association of the Motion Picture Industry (NAMPI), which adopted a 13-point list of taboo subjects that included "exploiting interest in sex in an improper and suggestive manner," "prolonged passionate love," and "vulgar scenes, improper gestures, and salacious titles." Political problems and internal dissent caused the association to disband shortly after its formation, however, and it was replaced in 1922 by the Motion Picture Producers and Distributors Association of America. Under the leadership of William Hays, a prominent Republican and friend of Warren G. Harding, a self-governing organization of producers, distributors, and exhibitors was created that sought advice from and representatives from civic, religious, and educational organizations. DeGrazia and Newman[79] report that from 1922 to 1927, 48 separate bills designed to impose statewide censorship were considered by state legislatures. In 1926, the U.S. House of Representatives held hearings on a proposal to create a federal motion picture commission in the Department of the Interior. According to DeGrazia and Newman,[79] only 17 persons or organizations opposed the formation of the national commission. But one of those in opposition was the President of the United States, Calvin Coolidge, who declared he was against the bill on constitutional grounds. Besides, as a spokesman for Coolidge pointed out, the producers themselves under the direction of Hays had made "long strides in the right direction."

Under the direction of the Hays office, the Motion Picture Production Code was established. The code, officially established in 1931, imposed three general principles on the film industry, the first of which stated:

No picture shall be produced which will lower the moral standards of those who see it. Hence the sympathy of the audience shall never be thrown to the side of crime, wrongdoing, evil or, sin.

By 1932, the code was already being challenged by films such as *Scarface*, produced by Howard Hughes. The Hays office demanded that Hughes reduce the level of violence in the film and see to it that the gangster portrayed in the movie was punished by the law rather than gunned down by fellow gangsters. Other films either denied a seal of approval by the board, fined, or modified after initial production to accommodate the board included the 1935 film *Ecstasy* starring Hedy Lamarr; the 1939 film *Gone With the Wind;* and the 1941 film *The Outlaw,* starring Jane Russell.

Interestingly, due to concern with portrayals of crime and violence, a number of empirical (interview) studies of the influence of violence on children were initiated in the 1930s and early 1940s.[82] Spurred on by the writings of psychiatrist Frederic Wertham,[83] pressure mounted against post–World War II "horror" comic books that depicted sadistic violence, sex crimes, and the use of deadly weapons. Although several state statutes were passed to curtail the sale of these comics, the statutes were struck down by the courts (one such case is discussed later).

In the 1950s and 1960s, the Motion Picture Association of America (MPAA), as it was now called (a title still retained today), denied a seal of approval to Otto Preminger's 1955 *The Man with the Golden Arm,* a film about a heroin addict (a role for which Frank Sinatra later won an Academy Award). The MPAA also forced modifications in the screen adaptation of Edward Albee's play *Who's Afraid of Virginia Woolf?* The latter carried the advisory warning "suggested for mature audiences" (SMA). All contracts with exhibitors required that no one under the age of 18 be allowed to see the film unless accompanied by a parent. This was the first time the association had imposed a restriction that excluded a portion of its customers.

By 1968, the New York State Legislature had already began work on an age-classification system, and legislation was also proposed in California to create a state board to review films and make age classifications. The MPAA, under the direction of Jack Valenti, took a similar course, devising a rating system that it hoped would distinguish between adult entertainment and films suitable for all ages. Originally the classification categories were: G — suggested for general audiences; M — for adults and mature young people; R — restricted to those 17 or older unless accompanied by parent or guardian; and X — those under 18 not admitted. This classification system was revised in 1970. The M category was dropped and replaced by PG or "parental guidance suggested" (all ages admitted), and the age limits for R and X rated categories were raised from 16 to 17 years. By 1984, the PG-13 category had been added — "special parental guidance suggested for those under 13." All films produced or distributed by MPAA — and this constitutes most films in the United States — are submitted to the Code and Rating Administration before completion. Films are given an initial "probable" rating, and suggestions are made for "improvements" that will result in a less restrictive rating. The standards used to determine the rating include:

Upholding the dignity of life, exercising restraint in portraying juvenile crime, not demeaning religion, and prohibiting extreme violence brutality, as well as obscene speech, gestures or movements. Finally, sexual content and nudity are to be limited.[84]

A film rated G, PG, PG-13, or R can receive an MPAA seal of approval; an X-rated film cannot. The rating must appear on all prints of the film distributed in the United States.

Looking back over the history of film regulation in the United States, we see a steady movement toward greater tolerance of sexual explicitness and the portrayal of all forms of behavior, including violence, deemed unacceptable in past eras. The MPAA takes pains to assert that in reality it is nothing more than a voluntary classification board. Producers and distributors voluntarily choose to bring films to the association for ratings, then choose to accept and to use the rating. According to Richard Heffner, the association's current director: "We do not intend to impinge upon the right of any adult American to decide for himself or herself what to see or to hear or to read or to say or to believe. Our premium is upon freedom . . . in the belief that in the area of creative expression, ultimately the only truly responsible society is built upon freedom, not control."[85]

Has the association focused its attention on materials that are appear to be most harmful—at least harmful in terms of the research findings reported in this volume? We find it curious that under the present system, the whole genre of slasher films, which graphically depict mutilation of women and which may be desensitizing viewers, fall into the same rating category as films that may contain no sex or violence but that have two or more instances of the "harsher sexually derived words." In this regard it is interesting to contrast the policies of the MPAA in the United States with film rating policies in Great Britain, the nation from whom we have adopted most of our cultural and legal traditions. The comparison is useful, not because we advocate a system whereby films are censored as they are by the film rating board in England if they do not meet with its approval, but because the rationale for censoring seems more closely tied to the harms elucidated by the research.

Most films seen in England have first been approved by the British Board of Film Censors (BBFC), a governmental agency that oversees the importation and distribution of motion pictures. Like the MPAA ratings in the United States, acceptance of the BBFC's rating is purely voluntary. (When the BBFC was formed it was thought inappropriate for an unofficial body to have the last word on what could or could not be shown in the cinema, and democratically elected local authorities are free to revise any decision of the BBFC, either banning films that have already been certified by the BBFC or permitting films the BBFC has refused to certify.) But unlike the MPAA, the British board, as its name implies, does cut scenes from films. It is interesting to note the evolution of the BBFC's policies over the years, particularly in light of the research findings on the combination of sex and violence we have cited in previous chapters. During the 1950s and early 1960s, the BBFC was primarily censoring nudity and premarital or extramarital sex. In 1967, the BBFC approved for the first time a film containing pubic hair, and by 1970 the BBFC had formulated an informal checklist of acceptable sexual positions and genital displays. By the middle of the 1970s, the BBFC was less concerned with nudity and genitalia and more concerned with the increasing levels of violence in films from America, Italy, and Hong Kong. According to Lord Harlech, the BBFC's president:

The combination of sex and violence was a new and alarming trend in films made merely as sensational entertainment for the young male audience of 16–24 who were beginning to dominate the box office . . . Some film-makers no longer treated rape as a reprehensible crime, but were turning it into an erotic spectacle.[86]

Gradually, the BBFC's focus shifted from explicit sex to concern for the combination of sex and violence. For example, in 1974 the BBFC cut a small number of scenes from the French film *Emmanuelle* and forced the film to comply with the current checklist of acceptable displays and positions. At the time, the BBFC was not concerned with the causal treatment of rape in the last segment of the film. According to Harlech:

This French money-spinner represented the apotheosis of the male chauvinist view that women are not subjects, but objects for the sexual gratification of men. The Board in 1979 called in the film Emmanuelle and required the cutting of the whole of the violent rape which takes place in an opium den in the last reel.
    The reason for cutting this scene had nothing to do with its visual explicitness. The Board had passed rape scenes far more detailed than this one, and has done so since. It was the intention of this scene which was unacceptable, since its aim was to persuade the audience that the rape of this woman, despite her resistance, was sexually beneficial rather than harmful.[87]

One of the primary concerns within the BBFC in recent years has been the proliferation of films that pair sex and violence. The implicit concern is that such films may make the audience (particularly men) more callous in their attitudes toward women and perhaps more likely to engage in aggressive behavior against women. For the BBFC, these possibilities constitute the principal rationale for censorship:

We believe . . . that films can influence people's behaviour, and that some people may be influenced more than others. For that reason, we believe that society has the right to set some limits. . . . In recent years, many have seen the cinema as the vehicle for promoting and normalizing the use of violent solutions to problems which we as a people have attempted to solve through other means. It is right that we should be concerned about such trends, just as we think it is right to be concerned about the degradation of women for male enjoyment and other activities which can desensitise and brutalise our society.[88]

We recommend that policy and film makers in the United States show greater sensitivity to the portrayal of sexual violence in films, as have the members of the BBFC. We do not recommend that films be censored as they are in Great Britain, but we encourage debate concerning the possibility of prohibiting children and young adolescents from viewing films that may either lead to desensitization to violence against women or result in greater acceptance of the idea that women enjoy or secretly desire to be the victims of sexual violence. It appears to us that the research findings cited in this and other chapters justify a special category of film warnings accompanied by audience age restrictions. Materials that portray rape or other forms of sexual violence, whether sexually explicit or not, in ways that suggest that women deserve, want, or benefit from such treatment should be clearly labeled. Parents should be advised of the content of such films and also of the scientific research that suggests that their children might be adversely affected.

8

Alternatives for the Future

IN light of the scientific literature reviewed in the previous chapters, we can conclude that some forms of pornography, under some conditions, promote certain antisocial attitudes and behavior. Specifically, we should be most concerned about the detrimental effects of exposure to violent images in pornography and elsewhere, particularly material that portrays the myth that women enjoy or in some way benefit from rape, torture, or other forms of sexual violence. It is important to remember, however, that the portrayal of this theme is not limited to pornography. Many mass media depictions that either contain little explicit sex or are only mildly sexually explicit portray the same myth.

To date, the evidence supporting the contention that so-called degrading pornographic materials, as long as they are not violent, are harmful is sparse and inconsistent. The few studies that have been done on these materials, including our own, have yielded contradictory findings, and the question of the effects of these materials awaits further research. Brief exposure to less degrading materials or simple nudity appears to result in few, if any, antisocial effects.

On the basis of these findings, we may ask: Where do we go from here? First, additional research is needed to replicate current findings and reconcile the inconsistencies we have alluded to in the previous chapters. But is there anything we might do to counter the effects of material for which there is less doubt about its negative

171

effects, namely the violent material? Should harsher penalties be leveled against persons who traffic in pornography, particularly violent pornography? We do not believe so. Rather, it is our opinion that the most prudent course of action would be the development of educational programs that would teach viewers to become more critical consumers of the mass media. We believe it is premature to advocate either more zealous enforcement of existing obscenity laws or the creation of new laws to curb the distribution of pornography because existing research leaves too many questions unanswered. Educational programs and stricter obscenity laws are not mutually exclusive, but the legal course of action is more restrictive of personal freedoms than an educational approach. And, as we have noted, the existing research probably does not justify this approach. It seems wise at this point to refrain from putting additional restrictions on any portrayals until more research evidence is obtained.

There are many who disagree. The Attorney General's Commission on Pornography has recommended an expansion of existing obscenity statutes (for example, by amending the federal obscenity laws to prohibit the transmission of obscene material through the telephone, and eliminating the "utterly without redeeming social value" clause still retained in some state obscenity statutes). These recommendations supposedly stem in part from the commission's reading of the social science literature.

The remainder of this chapter is devoted to two topics: first, a discussion of the conclusions drawn by the 1986 Attorney General's commission and its call for more strident enforcement of obscenity law; second, our own call, not for stricter controls, but for educational programs to mitigate the effects of sexual violence in the media. We find the Attorney General's conclusions and subsequent recommendations for social policy unwarranted extrapolations from the available research data as we interpret it. Instead, greater emphasis should be placed on educational programs that provide young consumers with the insight necessary to make informed choices among various media portrayals.

DO THE COMMISSION'S CONCLUSIONS FIT THE DATA?

Chapter 5 of the commission's report, entitled "The Question of Harm," sets forth its conclusions regarding the impact of exposure to pornography. While this report makes it clear that some of its conclusions are based on evidence beyond that supplied by research in the social sciences, it maintains that "these conclusions rest on findings from the social sciences . . . to a significant extent."[1] The commission subdivided pornographic materials into four categories: (1) sexually violent material; (2) nonviolent materials depicting degradation, domination, subordination, or humiliation; (3) nonviolent and nondegrading materials; and (4) nudity. We will discuss each of these in turn. Our analysis of their findings with regard to each of these categories will draw upon the discussion of research in Chapters 2 through 6 of this book.

Sexually Violent Pornography

This was defined by the commission as that which features actual or simulated violence within a sexually explicit context. In Chapter 5 we termed this material "violent" or "aggressive" pornography. In its discussion of legal remedies, the commission places its highest priority on sexually violent materials:

In light of our conclusions . . . we would urge that prosecution of obscene materials that portray sexual violence be treated as a matter of special urgency. With respect to sexually violent materials, the evidence is strongest, societal consensus is greatest and the consequences of rape and other forms of sexual violence are hardly ones that this or any other society can take lightly. In light of this, we would urge that the prosecution of legally obscene material that contains violence be placed at the top of both state and federal priorities in enforcing the obscenity laws.[2]

Why did the commission come to these conclusions about sexually violent pornographic materials? First, it considered these materials to be "increasingly, the most prevalent forms of pornography."[3] But is this true? Is violent pornography really becoming the most prevalent form of pornography? As we discussed in Chapter 5, while it has often been assumed that the amount of sexually violent pornography has increased over the years, the evidence for this assumption is not supported by available research. The few studies that have been conducted suggest that violent images in mainstream publications such as *Playboy* have actually decreased after peaking several years earlier. Content analysis of X-rated versus R-rated films showed far more violence against women in the R-rated films. This is not to say that future research involving a broader sample of materials over a longer period of time would reveal an increase in the prevalence of violent pornography relative to other forms. We can say only that the available evidence does not support this contention.

Second, the commission stated that there is a "causal relationship" between exposure to sexually violent materials and aggression toward women. As we have seen, this is an accurate statement as long as we are referring to laboratory studies of aggression in which men are asked to administer electric shocks or other forms of "punishment" to a female victim. The research to date clearly indicates that when males are exposed to violent pornography they will display heightened levels of aggression against a woman in a laboratory setting. Whether this laboratory aggression is representative of real-world aggression, such as rape, is still a matter for considerable debate. As we noted in Chapter 1, we must be careful when generalizing the results of laboratory experiments in aggression to real-world situations. Only when we have both experimental evidence obtained from the laboratory in which exposure to sexual violence has been manipulated as an independent variable, and evidence collected from field studies (e.g., longitudinal studies in which consumption of sexually violent material is correlated with later arrest rates for sexual assault or a similar variable), are we completely justified in coming to the conclusion that there may be a robust effect. So far, there have been no field studies measuring naturally occurring levels of exposure to sexual violence and later sexually violent behavior that would allow us to assess the external validity of the laboratory work in this area.

Third, the commission notes that even if there is only tentative evidence of effects on subjects' aggressive behavior, a number of attitudinal and perceptual changes result from exposure to violent pornography. These include (1) changes in the perception of a rape victim (e.g., seeing her as less injured and more responsible for her assault); (2) seeing a rapist as less responsible for his actions and less deserving of punishment; and (3) increasing the acceptance of rape myths such as women enjoy being raped. While we certainly agree that these perceptual and attitudinal changes can and do occur, the question of whether they are a function of exposure to pornography per se (i.e., sexually explicit images) or to certain messages or images of violence is crucial. As we noted in both Chapters 5 and 6, depictions of women "enjoying" force are pervasive throughout the media. Many of the studies finding the effects reported by the commission have employed films or audio depictions of rape or other forms of violence against women that would certainly not be classified as pornography. These have included both R-rated commercially available films as well as movies seen on network television. This is not to say that violent pornography does not have a similar effect. Quite the contrary. The important point is that much of the evidence for stating that sexually violent pornography is harmful (i.e., leads to calloused attitudes and perceptions) is based upon materials that probably are not sexually explicit enough to be judged obscene by most standards.

Interestingly, in its discussion of the effects of exposure to sexually violent pornography, the commission noted that once a certain level of sexual content is reached, increases in this variable are not as important as increases in violence. In other words, increasing violence results in more harmful consequences than increasing sexual explicitness. In order to find certain harmful effects, the level of sexual explicitness need not be pornographic (i.e., X-rated). The commission noted this in discussing the effects of slasher films. According to the commission:

the so-called "slasher" films, which depict a great deal of violence connected with an undeniably sexual theme but less sexual explicitness than materials that are truly pornographic, are likely to produce the consequences discussed here to a greater extent than most materials available in "adults only" pornographic outlets.[4]

Since these films are R-rated and would not be legally defined as obscene, it is somewhat misleading to consider them as evidence for the general conclusion that some forms of pornography can be harmful. In fact, the most reasonable conclusion that one can reach from the commission's own statement is that depictions of violence against women, whether or not in a sexually explicit context, should be the focus of concern.

Nonviolent Materials Depicting Degradation,
Domination, Subordination, or Humiliation

This category of material, according to the commission, includes images that are nonviolent but depict either: (1) women in subordinate roles; (2) women existing just for the sexual satisfaction of others; or (3) sexual practices that most people would consider humiliating. Our discussions of research in Chapters 3 and 4 would include materials of this sort. With respect to the harmful effects of these materials, the commission asserts that the results of viewing this material are similar to those obtained from exposure to sexually violent depictions. To its credit, the commission draws these conclusions with "less confidence" because, as it points out, the scientific evidence is more tentative. We are compelled to say not only tentative, but very inconsistent.

The commission stated that substantial exposure to this material will lead individuals to (1) view rape as less serious, (2) view rape victims as more responsible for their plight, and (3) increase the likelihood that men will say they would force a woman into sexual practices. Based upon the research we reviewed in Chapter 4, we can find no convincing evidence for these specific conclusions. Only one study, a pilot experiment conducted by us in 1986,[5] has shown that long-term exposure to this type of material changes an individual's perceptions of the level of injury sustained by a rape victim in a subsequent depiction. But later studies, with both male and female viewers, have not replicated these findings. Furthermore, only one study has found changes in subjects' willingness to say they would use force with a woman in order to have sex. This study, conducted by Check,[6] involved some methodological procedures that prevent us from placing as much confidence in the outcome of the experiments we would like. To conclude, on the basis of existing research, that exposure to these types of materials has the effects noted is certainly premature.

The commission also concluded that substantial exposure to this type of material bears some causal relationship to sexual violence. This conclusion is apparently based upon data reported by Malamuth[7] indicating a relationship between certain rape-related attitudes and self-reported acts of sexual aggression (discussed in Chapter 5) and on research reported by Zillmann and Bryant[8] (discussed in Chapter 4) suggesting that exposure to degrading pornography results in calloused attitudes about rape. There are several problems with combining the results of these two independently conducted studies to arrive at the conclusion that sexually degrading pornography causes sexual violence.

While there are data suggesting that certain calloused attitudes about rape, sexual arousal to rape depictions, and other antisocial characteristics are predictive of self-reported sexual aggression,[7] research has not consistently demonstrated that these calloused attitudes about rape are the result of exposure to degrading but nonviolent sexual material. However, even if there were an unequivocal relationship between exposure to degrading pornography and negative attitudes about women in one study and evidence for a relationship between similar attitudes and self-reported sexual violence in another study, we still could not conclude that degrading pornography increases violent behavior. Ideally, to conclude that degrading pornography influences negative attitudes, which then, in turn, affect behavior, we would need to show these relationships in the same experimental study on a single sample of subjects. Such an experimental study is, of course, ethically impossible to conduct. Barring this approach, at least a longitudinal study in which both attitudes and violent behaviors are measured in the same individuals, or experimental studies of interventions designed to reduce violence against women that would have implications for understanding the causes of violent behavior, should be undertaken before any scientifically valid conclusions can be reached. These studies have not been conducted to date. (For a further discussion of these issues see Malamuth and Briere.[8]) Finally, the commission appears to have attended selectively to the results of the study on long-term exposure to degrading pornography (conducted by Zillmann and Bryant[9]; described in Chapter 4), which examined *both* attitudes and behavior. This study revealed that while exposure to degrading pornography did result in more calloused beliefs about rape, it also resulted in *less* rather than more aggressive behavior.

Nonviolent and Nondegrading Materials

The material in this category depicts explicit sexual behavior that is not considered degrading, humiliating, or subordinating to women. The commission report admitted that there were differences in opinion regarding the effects of this form of pornography. However, it did conclude that, in general, the scientific evidence shows no causal relationship between exposure to these depictions and acts of sexual violence. Our view of the scientific literature (see Chapters 2, 3, and 4) is in agreement with this conclusion. The commission noted, however, that making sex public and commercial, depicting sex outside of marriage and love, and depicting certain acts of sex that may be condemned by society could be harmful to the moral environment of our society. It should be noted that this is not a consensus conclusion, and that the commission was in disagreement about these potential harms.

Nudity

Overall, the commission concluded, depictions of nudity are not harmful. But there was even some disagreement about this. Although not stating that harms could arise from exposure to nudity, there was concern about materials that were intended to "maximize" sexual impact due to the context of the depiction. At one point, the commission report states:

Consider a woman shown in a reclining position with genitals displayed, wearing only red feathers and high heeled shoes, holding a gun and accompanied by a caption offering a direct invitation to sexual activity. With respect to such more explicit materials, we are unable to reach complete agreement. We are concerned about the impact of such material on children, on attitudes toward women, on the relationship between the sexes, and on attitudes towards sex in general, but the extent of the harms was the subject of some difference of opinion.[10]

Based upon the research we reviewed in Chapters 2–4, we would have to conclude that here is no evidence that exposure to nudity has any detrimental effects. In fact, on the basis of evidence cited in this book and collected by social scientists over the years, we are more inclined to be concerned about the weapon included in the portrayal, and the combination of both sexual and violent images and the ramifications of this combination on children, than the sexuality or nudity involved in such an example.

Relying partly on its interpretation of the social science research and partly on testimony from individuals who claimed to be victimized in some fashion by pornography, the commission made 92 recommendations. Primarily, these involved changes in existing federal, state and local obscenity laws, although some recommendations for mental health agencies and suggestions for future research were also included. Universally, the recommendations for legal changes were for greater restrictions on sexually explicit material and on broader interpretations of current obscenity law.

It seems to us that the legal recommendations made by the commission for strengthening obscenity laws do not follow from the data. It should be obvious to anyone with a television set that the mass media contain an abundance of violent nonsexually explicit (and thus nonobscene) images and messages. These ideas about rape and sexual violence may be so pervasive in our culture that it is myopic to call them the exclusive domain of violent pornography, much less the domain of the broader category of legally obscene materials. In fact, one would not have to search farther than a local bookstore to find numerous bloody murder mysteries that reinforce this point. And this is where we have our strongest disagreement with the commission. Granted, the charter of the group was to examine the pernicious effects of pornography on society. Granted also that time, money, and other resources of the commission were limited. But it seems appropriate to note that if the commissioners were looking for ways to curb the most nefarious media threat to public welfare, they missed them. The most well-documented finding in the social science literature is that all sexually violent material in our society, whether sexually *explicit* or not, tends to promote aggression against women. Unfortunately, legal remedies directed at suppressing these materials would extend into every form of communication, and any laws devised to curb messages of violence against women could be used to suppress other messages of questionable interpretation. Rather than calling for stricter laws, we call for a more-informed public. Our own inclination has been to explore the possibility of developing educational programs that enable viewers to make wiser choices about the media to which they expose themselves.

AN ALTERNATIVE APPROACH TO LEGAL REMEDIES

As a basis for educational interventions, we would rely upon the empirical research conducted during the last few years on methods of countering or mitigating the impact of exposure to sexual violence in the media. This research has not reached the point where we can say with certainty that a given message, educational program, or label on a particular media product is effective in reducing the impact of exposure. We are, however, able to identify some promising procedures developed independently by several researchers that may counter the effects of exposure to sexual violence. Nor are we naive about the impact such interventions may have — we realize that there are a number of cultural actors operating against any intervention program. Zillmann and his colleagues,[11] for example, have conducted an experiment that suggests that women who watch slasher films with men who display a fearless macho image in the face of the violence find the films themselves to be more enjoyable and their male companion more attractive than when watching with men who appear to be distressed by the blood and gore. Equally disturbing is the fact that males seemed to enjoy the slasher films more when their female companions evidenced distress rather than indifference at the violence. This study suggests that there may be strong social reinforcers present for teenagers who watch these films. These will be difficult for any intervention program to overcome.

The intent of this section of the chapter is to review the findings on mitigating the effects of exposure to violent pornography and mass-released (R-rated) sexually violent media presentations. Several of our suggestions for intervention programs for consumers of sexual violence are derived from the results of investigations of programs to counter the effects of exposure to milder forms of violence contained in network television portrayals among grade-school children.

We might add that while programs designed to mitigate the effects of sexual violence on young adults are certainly worth undertaking, waiting until late adolescence or early adulthood to teach critical viewing skills may, in fact, be waiting too long. A recent report on the viewing patterns of a sample of 4,500 children in England and Wales (countries that have declared many of the sexually violent films that receive an R-rating in the United States to be obscene) indicates that by the ages of 7 and 8, 6.5% of boys in those countries have seen the movie *I Spit on Your Grave*. The percentage climbs to nearly 20% by ages 13 to 14.[12] Comparable data for the United States are not currently available. One can probably safely assume that if 20% of preadolescent males have seen a film declared liable for prosecution, and thus relatively scarce in Great Britain, a much larger number of preadolescents have probably been exposed to such films in the United States. In addition, with the current availability of home videocassette players, and cable television services devoted to adult entertainment, much of which may include sexual violence, we should expect that an even greater number of young children will be exposed to these materials in the future.

RESEARCH ON MITIGATING THE EFFECTS OF MASS-MEDIA SEXUAL VIOLENCE

At the end of all the experiments we discussed in Chapters 5 and 6 on violent pornography and R-rated sexual violence, subjects were debriefed. These debriefings generally concentrated on the *unre-*

ality of the media depiction. Subjects were cautioned that pornographic and nonpornographic portrayals of women desiring, enjoying, or sexually aroused to forced sexual relations were fictitious.
Material was also presented that tried to dispel common rape
myths,[13] especially any myths that were portrayed in the stimulus
materials used in the experiment.

Over the last few years, several follow-up studies of the effectiveness of these debriefings have been undertaken. Donnerstein and
Berkowitz[14] compared the responses of debriefed subjects who had
been exposed to violent and nonviolent pornography with subjects
exposed to a neutral film who received no debriefing, on seven
items taken from the Rape Myth Acceptance Scale and the Acceptance of Interpersonal Violence Scale.[15] Subjects in this study were
followed up anywhere from 2 weeks to 4 months after participation
and asked to complete the seven-item questionnaire. The results of
this follow-up showed that those subjects who viewed aggressive and
nonaggressive pornography who were debriefed showed less acceptance of rape myths than nondebriefed subjects (who had been
exposed to nonaggressive pornography or neutral films).

More recently, Malamuth and Check[16] conducted a study in
which male and female subjects were exposed to sexually explicit
stories depicting either rape or mutually consenting intercourse.
Afterward, subjects exposed to the rape version were given statements emphasizing that the depictions of rape in the stories they
read were complete fantasy, and that in reality rape is a serious
crime punishable by law and that victims of rape usually suffer
severe psychological and physical damage after the assault. Subjects
were also given specific examples of rape myths and assurance that
these commonly held beliefs are indeed completely fictitious. Ten
days later, subjects received a "public survey" in their classes. As
part of the survey, subjects were asked to read newspaper articles
and give their opinions, one of which was an article about rape. In
addition, subjects were asked questions regarding the police's decision to bring charges, the victim's responsibility for her own rape,
the recommended sentence for the man if convicted, and whether
they thought they themselves might rape a woman if they could be
assured of not being caught and punished. Subjects were also asked
to what extent victim, rapist, and societal factors contribute to rape.
The debriefing had no effects for subjects' evaluation of the newspaper article on rape. Subjects who were exposed to the rape stories
and then debriefed were, however, less inclined to see women as

wanting to be raped and to see victim behavior generally as a cause of rape, compared with subjects who read the consenting story and received no debriefing. Debriefed subjects were also less likely to see rape as the result of a normal sexual tendency among males.

In another experiment, Check and Malamuth,[17] using basically the same procedures, had subjects first read rape depictions in which the victim and assailant were either acquainted or unacquainted with one another. As in the previous study, subjects were later (2 to 3 days) presented with several newspaper stories with a story about rape embedded among them. Subjects, when exposed to the rape debriefing, gave the rapist in the newspaper report a higher sentence and saw the rape victim as less responsible for her own assault. However, these effects only happened if subjects had been exposed to an example of a rape depiction that was relevant both to the rape myths discussed in the rape debriefing and the newspaper report of the rape. Specifically, only when subjects were exposed to an acquaintance rape scenario and given a debriefing that emphasized rape myths pertinent to that acquaintance situation (e.g., a woman who goes to a man's apartment deserves to be raped) was the debriefing effective. Further, there were no effects for participation in the debriefing if it was preceded by a nonviolent mutually consenting scenario instead of a rape scenario.

The effectiveness has also been assessed of debriefings used in studies of long-term exposure to movies that are nonpornographic but portray violence against women in an extremely graphic manner (R-rated slasher films). One aspect of these studies that is particularly noteworthy is the long-term nature of these follow-ups. Subjects who are surveyed as long as 7 – 8 months after participation in debriefings show significant increases in their sensitivity toward rape victims. In a study designed to assess effectiveness of the debriefing used in a study on long-term exposure to R-rated slasher films,[18] subjects were assessed several weeks before participation in the study, 1 – 3 days after participation in the study and receipt of the debriefing, and again 6 weeks later. At each point in time, subjects completed the entire Rape Myth Acceptance Scale.

The debriefing used in this study was a videotaped message that cautioned subjects that "constant exposure to violence can desensitize or harden and make people callous to violence." The part of the message particularly relevant to the rape myths portrayed in the films used in the study emphasized that "one problem with some of the scenes in the films that you saw this week is that they tend to reinforce certain myths about rape, such as the notion that women who wear provocative clothing are asking for or deserve sexual assault, or that women who put themselves in a risky situation are setting themselves up to be raped and hence are responsible for what happens." The subjects were told that research has shown that films of this type tend to reinforce and maintain these common but fictitious beliefs about rape. The results of the follow-up showed that immediately after participation in the study and debriefing, subjects' average scores on the Rape Myth Acceptance Scale declined relative to the prestudy participation score by a few points (although the decrement was not statistically significant). The scores obtained 6 weeks later were nearly identical to the immediate postparticipation level scores (and still a few points lower than those obtained before the study).

More compelling is a follow-up study done by Linz,[19] which tried to assess the effectiveness of debriefings given to subjects who received either high doses (five movies) or low doses (two movies) of graphic filmed violence against women. As in the previous study, subjects' scores on the Rape Myth Acceptance Scale were obtained before exposure to the violent films (in this case, nearly 2 months) and again after participation in the study and debriefing. The films used in this study did not portray rape behavior per se, although the films could be interpreted as propagating several myths about blaming the victim for her assault if she places herself in certain situations. Consequently, subjects were told:

Although there were no rape scenes in these films, these films tend to reinforce certain myths about rape and other forms of sexual assault. Some examples of the types of rape myths that these films may have reinforced are that "only certain types of women get raped," or that "if a woman really wanted to fend off an attacker, she could," or that "women who dress provocatively are asking to be sexually assaulted."[20]

After receiving this message (conveyed by videotape), subjects were told they would be contacted later and were dismissed from the laboratory.

As in the previous study, the effectiveness of the debriefing was assessed, but instead of surveying subjects 6 weeks after participation, the subjects were requested to complete the Rape Myth Acceptance Scale 6–7 *months* after participation in the study and debriefing. The results of this follow-up showed that subjects experienced a statistically significant decline in rape myth acceptance relative to their prestudy levels. Further, the decline in this index was equal in size for both the large dosage and small dosage film exposure groups.

Similar decreases in rape myth acceptance after a proper debriefing can also be found among female participants in studies involving exposure to sexually violent media. Previous research on female subjects' sexual responsiveness to rape depictions indicates a tendency for women to become sexually aroused to rape depictions if the depiction emphasizes the women victims of rape becoming sexually aroused by the experience.[21] More recently, Krafka[22] has found that females exposed to R-rated nonpornographic sexual violence (slasher films) become emotionally desensitized (less anxious and depressed) to these depictions with repeated exposure. Later, when asked to evaluate a videotaped reenactment of a physical assault-rape trial, they were more likely than females exposed to other types on film to evaluate the victim of sexual assault harshly.

As with studies involving males, females exposed to sexual violence were thoroughly debriefed after participation in these studies. They were warned about the possibility of becoming desensitized to the violence in the film stimuli used in the study, and were also debriefed about the portrayal of various rape myths in sexually violent movies. In addition to pointing out these concerns, females in the study by Krafka[22] also received an additional message concerning the more general belief prevalent in our society that women are sexually aroused by force:

The sum total of rape-myth says that women enjoy rape, will be sexually aroused by force, and that they ask to be raped in subtle, if not direct, ways. One of the most common sexual fantasies for women, in fact, involves rape — a point that is not lost on the writers of best-selling romance novels. A common theme of the romance trade is that a handsome devil-hero ravishes the novel's heroine in a fit of uncontrolled passion; she later falls in love with her ravisher. The popularity of the romance novel is due in part, I think, to their ability to play on our fantasies. But important distinctions must be made between the fantasy and the fact of rape. First of all, fantasy does not typically involve violence or pain. The typical rape fantasy involves being overwhelmed gently by a man who considers one so desirable that he quote "simply cannot control himself." Second, fantasy is safe. Lots of people, male and female alike, experience things through fantasy that they would never want to experience in real life.

Fantasy is okay — and yet we know that the typical real-world rape bears little resemblance to either rape as it is depicted most often in film or to the kind of pseudo-rape which might play out in a woman's fantasy. Rape is a crime, and it is a crime of violence that has little to do with the satisfying of sexual urges. It involves coercion or threat in some form, and in a large percentage of cases, requires physical force to subdue the victim. This may result in pain or serious injury to a woman, and most women who have been assaulted respond with extreme emotional trauma. Film-depicted rape tends to gloss over unpleasantries, so consequently, it doesn't reflect reality.

Follow-up evaluations of the effectiveness of a debriefing containing this type of message have been undertaken immediately, 6 weeks, and 6 months after participation in the study and debriefing.[23] The results of these evaluations indicate that exposure to sexually violent materials coupled with debriefings will produce significant reductions in rape-myth acceptance (compared with a baseline measure taken several weeks before participation in the study) not only immediately, but the effects will remain 6 months later.

WHAT FACTORS MEDIATE THE EFFECTS OF DEBRIEFINGS?

As we have seen, subjects participating in studies using violent pornographic depictions, as well as in studies using nonviolent pornographic depictions of violence against women who have received a proper debriefing, emerge from this experience more sensitive to cultural stereotypes about violence against women. Further, these effects have been found in studies in which subjects have been exposed to relatively large or relatively small doses of sexual violence during the experimental phase of the study, for male subjects as well as female subjects, immediately after participation in the debriefings, and 6–8 months after participation.

What is it about the debriefings and/or participation in the studies themselves that lead to these changes? The results of two of the studies that we have reviewed[24] suggest factors about participation in sexual violence experiments and debriefings that may be of great importance. First, as Check and Malamuth[25] note, it is probably necessary to specifically tailor the debriefings to the types of myths portrayed in the material used during the experimental phase of the study. Debriefings that focused on rape myths not specifically portrayed in the experimental phase of the Check and Malamuth study,[25] for example, were not effective in reducing rape myth acceptance. This finding seems congruent with the research by others,[27] where debriefings were presented in a videotaped format that was interspersed with specific examples from the material presented to subjects during the preceding phase of the experiment.

Second, messages dispelling rape myths might be most effective for subjects who had first been exposed both to the rape scenarios in the experimental portion of the study and to the debriefing. Debriefings coupled with preexposure to consenting sex scenarios in the Malamuth and Check[28] study were relatively ineffective in changing attitudes about rape. These findings imply that it may be necessary for subjects to first become aware of increased levels of sexual arousal in response to the rape passages, or experience desensitization in the face of violent portrayals, then to receive a debriefing that addresses these processes. As Malamuth, Heim, and Feshbach[29] point out, the debriefing might provide the subject with a certain kind of insight comparable to that experienced by students who might become aware of racist feelings during a study on social prejudice. This may also be the case for subjects who have participated in studies using nonpornographic materials that portray rape myths.

Finally, a word of caution. As the research currently stands, it is difficult to tell from any of the studies reviewed if *any* aspect of the debriefings actually accounts for changes in subjects' rape-myth acceptance or, if given enough time, subjects would naturally experience a change in these beliefs. Those debriefings that have been effective in changing subjects' beliefs have always been confounded by exposure to the rape-depiction phase of the experiment. That is, there has been no experiment in which subjects were exposed to sexually violent materials and not debriefed. Consequently, it is impossible to rule out the possibility that exposure to the rape materials alone and participation in some other activity besides the debriefing, or even sufficient time for subjects to reflect or rest, might result in lowered rape-myth acceptance or at least a return of rape-myth acceptance to prestudy participation levels. From a study by Malamuth and Ceniti,[30] for example, we suggest the possibility that a rest period might result in greater sensitivity toward rape victims. These authors have found that subjects exposed to violent pornography who are asked 1 week later to participate in an ostensibly unrelated experiment involving the administration of aversive noise showed no increases in aggression. The findings of this study stand in apparent contradiction to the results of previous studies.[31]

As Malamuth and Ceniti[31] themselves point out, the important difference between past studies and this study is that earlier investigations examined aggressive behavior immediately after subjects were exposed to violent pornography rather than testing for relatively long-term effects. These findings suggest that with time, subjects exposed to sexual violence might return to baseline levels of hostility and aggression toward women, or even dip below baseline once subjects were given time to reflect on the sexually violent portrayal. Rape-myth acceptance among subjects exposed to violent pornography might well decline naturally with the passage of time also. (It is also possible that subjects' attitudes concerning sexual violence were changed in a negative direction, but that their behavior, for one reason or another, did not reflect this change.) However, examining the possibility of this decrement with time experimentally would involve exposing subjects to sexually violent depictions and *not* debriefing them—a procedure that would be unethical.

DESIGNING INTERVENTIONS TO COUNTER SEXUAL VIOLENCE IN THE MEDIA

One way to test the idea that providing subjects with knowledge about psychological processes they may be experiencing while viewing sexual violence might counter the effects of these depictions would be to design an experiment directed at reducing acceptance of rape myths and aggressive behavior toward women in the laboratory through the use of *pre*briefings. Messages could be constructed that inform subjects about the effects of exposure to violent pornography and other forms of aggression against women administered before participation in experiments.

Recently, Bross[33] has examined the effectiveness of a prefilm message informing male viewers, who were later exposed to large doses of R-rated slasher films, about the psychological processes that might be operating. These prefilm messages explained to subjects what psychological effects might result from viewing sexually violent media. The message was similar to the videotaped debriefing presented after participation in experiments involving sexually violent materials.[34] Clips of scenes from slasher films were interspersed throughout the filmed message to assist subjects in understanding the effects that can be caused by viewing slasher films. Of special interest were the subjects' awareness of desensitization to violence, and the possibility that viewers might come to view violent scenes less critically when they are juxtaposed with sexual ones.

Thirty-three male college students took part in the experiment. Eleven subjects were exposed to the manipulation, while the other 22 were examined for comparison purposes. Subjects were informed that they had been chosen to take part in a film evaluation study and were to view six full-length feature motion pictures (all R-rated slasher films) over a period of 2 weeks. Subjects in the experimental condition saw the prefilm message before viewing the first film. The control group saw only the first motion picture after signing the consent form. All subjects viewed four more slasher films over the next 2 weeks. After each film, subjects indicated how much violence they perceived in the films, how degrading the films were to women, the realistic nature of the violence, and self-reported psychological arousal. On the final day of the experiment, all subjects were contacted by phone and told that the last film they were originally scheduled to see had not arrived and were asked if they would take part in a study being run by the university's law school. All agreed, and reported the next day to the law school courtroom, where they viewed a videotaped reenactment of a mock rape trial. Following the viewing, subjects evaluated a number of aspects of the trial (to determine if there were any "spill over" effects into decision-making in a more realistic context).

The prefilm message is a videotaped presentation with clips from slasher films edited into the tape. The message stated:

During the next 2 weeks we will show you six full-length feature films and then we will ask for your reaction to these films. The six films you will see during the next 2 weeks have one thing in common. They are all R-rated, which means they all contain scenes of explicit aggressive behavior. In addition, the films may contain scenes of a sexual and/or erotic nature. I would now like to discuss with you the effect that this type of material can have on viewers.

One major problem with these films is that constant exposure to violence can desensitize or harden and callous people to violence in general. As an example, we will show you some scenes from these films. [Film Clip]

While you may initially find some of the violence in these films disturbing, it will perhaps become a little easier to tolerate the violence after continued exposure. This is a normal reaction. You should, however, be aware that this type of film can make people less sensitive to violent acts.

Another concern we have in reference to desensitization to violence is that many of the films that you will see are particularly violent in regard to women. For example, the following scenes are among those you will see.

We are particularly concerned about the issue of violence against women. Just as you may experience desensitization to violence after viewing these types of films, you may experience the same effect with regard to violence against women. Again, you should be aware of this issue and sensitive to this problem.

A second major problem is that in many of the films, an erotic or sexual scene is combined or juxtaposed with a violent scene. As an example of this type of combination, here is a scene from one of the films. [Film Clip]

This type of scene may quicken the process of desensitization that makes one more tolerant of violence. Also, such a combination places the violence in a very positive context because it occurs while the viewer is aroused or in a very positive state. Many of the violent scenes you will see are preceded by sexual, sensual, or erotic content. One potential problem with this combination is that some individuals who become sexually aroused to the sexual portion of the scene also become sexually aroused to the violent portion of the scene. Again, this is a normal reaction for some individuals, but you should be aware that this type of conditioning can occur. Further, you should be aware that some individuals become less sensitive to this type of violence, especially violence against women when the violence is placed in an erotic context. You should be aware that films like these can condition people to become sexually aroused during violent scenes.[33]

It should be noted that this message tries primarily to increase subjects' awareness of the psychological processes that might be the result of continued exposure to slasher films, instead of a direct attempt to persuade subjects that viewing sexual violence is wrong or harmful.

The results indicated that, overall, subjects exposed to the prefilm message were less susceptible to the effects of the slasher films on the first day of the study than were those who were not exposed to the message. Although the differences were not statistically significant, subjects in the message condition reported seeing more violent scenes (number of scenes) and more violent scenes directed at women than did subjects in the no-message condition. Subjects exposed to the prefilm message also reported seeing more combinations of erotic and violent scenes than the nonexposure subjects on Day 1 of the experiment. Subjects in the message condition found the Day 1 film to be significantly more degrading to women than the no-message subjects. There was no discernible pattern of differences between prebriefed and control subjects' responses to the mock rape-trial questionnaire.

Another finding that should be noted was the high dropout rate of subjects who had been exposed to the prefilm message. Eleven subjects were originally shown the message on Day 1 of the study. One subject decided not to continue his participation in the study immediately after viewing the message. Over the 2-week experimental period, four more subjects dropped out of the study (over 45% of those originally shown the message). The no-message group had only a 32% dropout rate. Comparisons between subjects who discontinued participation in the experiment and those who decided to stay throughout indicate some interesting trends. Those who dropped out of the study reported seeing more scenes of violence, more combinations of erotic and violent scenes, and found the film to be more degrading to both men and women on Day 1 than those who stayed for the duration. Subjects who dropped out of the study also reported more physiological arousal to the first film than those who completed the entire study. The message might have convinced subjects to leave the study. In fact, the one subject who decided to discontinue his participation immediately after viewing the prefilm message stated that he did not want to be exposed to the slasher films because of the possible effects mentioned in the videotaped message.

The findings from this small-scale study are, of course, only suggestive. The effects, for the most part, are only trends, and even these manifested themselves immediately after the first film viewing in a 2-week study. More effective may be an intervention program that assists young adults in making critical evaluations of sexual violence in the media based on what has been learned from research on mitigating the effects of TV violence on school children.

MITIGATING THE EFFECTS OF TELEVISION VIOLENCE

Recently, there has been interest among mass-media violence researchers in teaching children skills to enable them to understand and evaluate what is being presented on television.[35] The underlying premise has been, in general, that the media can teach behaviors, but the behaviors can also be unlearned.[36] Of the studies undertaken, the majority have been directed at modifying children's beliefs about television, particularly beliefs about the unrealistic nature of much of what is presented.[37] Most successful of these attempts has been an intervention designed by Huesmann et al[38] to change attitudes about aggression. The program relied upon some of the major empirical developments in the area of aggression and television violence, including: the notion that children learn through the observation of aggressive models that violence can sometimes be rewarding or an effective solution to problems: that increased identification with aggressors may facilitate aggressive behavior in viewers; and that viewing violence that is portrayed as socially acceptable or permissible may increase behavior. Hues-

mann et al. reasoned that even if children learned the violent prob-
lem-solving strategies they viewed on television, they might be less
likely to enact these strategies if they could be convinced that they
are unrealistic, inappropriate, and unrepresentative of most people's behaviors.

In their study, Huesmann et al. chose a sample of 169 first- and
third-grade boys and girls who had a history of high exposure to
television violence, randomly divided into control and experimental groups, both of which received three training sessions over a 6 – 8
week period. Before the intervention the children were pretested
for the degree to which they considered the behavior of television
characters as realistic. In the first study, children in the experimental condition were taught, through a series of discussions and lec-
tures, three principles: (1) the behavior of the characters on shows
such as Starsky and Hutch and Charlie's Angels does not represent the
behavior of most people; (2) the camera techniques and special
effects give the illusion that characters are actually performing
highly aggressive and unrealistic feats; (3) the average person uses
other methods to solve problems. This technique resulted in little
change in the children's aggressiveness, as measured through a peer
nomination technique,[39] or as measured by frequency of violence
viewing, judgments of television realism, or television character
identification. Consequently, Huesmann et al. made a more direct
attempt to motivate the children not to enact aggressive behaviors.
This new approach was based on "counter attitudinal advocacy"
research that has been found to be effective in producing enduring
behavioral changes in other domains.[39] Social psychologists have
noted that generally people are motivated to align their behaviors
with public expressions of their attitudes. In other words, if subjects
in a laboratory who are smokers can be induced to say that they
think smoking is bad for their health and can't attribute this statement to any coercion or reward on the part of the experimenter, the
subjects may very well reduce their smoking in order to maintain
some degree of consistency between their attitudes and their behavior. The same might be true of children and their attitudes toward
violence in the media. In the Huesmann et al. experimental group's
training sessions, children were first credited with the attitudes that
the experimenters wished them to adopt. The children were then
asked to make videotapes for other children who had been "fooled"
by television and "got into trouble by imitating it," even though
they themselves knew better. Finally, the children composed per-

suasive essays explaining how television is unlike real life and why it would be harmful for other children to watch too much television and imitate the violent characters. A videotape of each child reading his or her essay was then played before the entire group.

This second intervention was successful both in changing children's attitudes about television and in modifying aggressive behavior. Four months after the intervention there was a significant decline in peer-nominated aggression and attitudes about the harmfulness of television violence for the experimental group. Further, analysis revealed that the strongest predictor of decreases in aggressive behavior and attitude changes about the harmfulness of television violence occurred for subjects who had a tendency to identify less with television characters. However, the intervention did not significantly reduce violence viewing or the judgments of the realism of television violence. As the reader will recall, Huesmann et al.[41] reasoned that there may be three factors contributing to the likelihood that a child would behave more aggressively as a result of viewing violence: (1) its perception of the violence as realistic; (2) its identification with the TV character; and (3) its beliefs about society's acceptance of aggression. Huesmann et al.[41] have devised a successful intervention program based on these three factors. A similar set of factors may account for the young male adult's acceptance of sexual violence against women and predisposition toward aggressive behavior following exposure to violent pornographic depictions. It is possible that an intervention designed to (1) change males' perceptions that the portrayal of sexual violence or rape in the typical violent-pornographic film are realistic; (2) reduce the likelihood of males identifying with the aggressor in the pornographic film and change males' beliefs about the acceptability of aggression against women; and (3) provide subjects with descriptions of the possible psychological effects of prolonged exposure to violence against women may result in less acceptance of violence against women and lowered predispositions to aggress after exposure to violent pornographic films.

Such an attitude-change program as Huesmann et al. point out may be most effective if based on prior research on cognitive consistency and the persistence of attitude change.[43] As Cook and Flay[44] note, programs of attitude change that involve making salient inconsistencies between attitudes and behavior (emotional role playing, behavioral rehearsal, modeling) or inconsistencies with cognitions about the self seem to produce persistent attitude change. For example, observing one's own behavior usually causes greater and more persistent change than observing others behave in some counternormal way;[45] an attribution manipulation (in which the subject can only justify his or her counterattitudinal behavior by referring to an internal disposition or motivation rather than some external motivation) results in greater attitude persistence than the simple receipt of a persuasive message;[46] and writing one's own counterattitudinal message will produce more persistent change than passively reading a message.[47] Examples of some of the long-term changes caused by consistency approaches include: teaching children self-control and honesty—with effects persisting for periods up to 6 weeks;[48] and reducing smoking for up to 18 months.[49] These approaches have also produced decreases in ethnocentrism (directed toward the physically handicapped) that have persisted over 4 months,[50] and reduced phobic behavior of many kinds for periods as long as 2 years.[51]

Operationalization of the consistency approach for changing attitudes about sexual violence might include: (1) crediting adolescent males for possession of the attitudes we wish them to adopt; (2) inducing behaviors that would lead to the self-attribution of these attitudes; (3) inducing perceptions of personal responsibility for an outcome related to the attitudes; (4) inducing the perception of participation out of free choice, and (5) promoting the perception that the consequences of their behaviors are important. The subjects could be asked (in exchange for a small payment) to help prepare a videotape on sexual violence. This film, they would be told, will be used in area high schools to inform male adolescents who have been fooled by mass-media depictions into thinking that women desire sexual violence. The subjects could then be informed by the experimenter that he or she assumes that the subjects do not really believe the message being advocated, but a younger adolescent male might, and therefore get himself into trouble for imitating such behavior. Subjects would then spend time composing essays on "myths about sexual violence," which will be read and evaluated by the experimenter, then rewritten by subjects. These essays will then be read before a videocamera. Subjects could be instructed to focus on the unreality of sexual aggression as presented in the media, and why it is harmful to adopt attitudes that trivialize rape and sexual violence. These instructions will be presented only as rough guides because the experimenter will emphasize the need for subjects to contribute their own ideas. Each subject's videotaped reading will then be played before the entire group of subjects so that the group may evaluate the product.

This intervention procedure could be tested against a direct persuasion approach designed to teach subjects: (1) that women do not enjoy, desire, or become sexually aroused by violence and rape; (2) that repeated exposure to violence against women may desensitize subjects to violence, not only in the films, but perhaps to the plight of other actual victims of violence. This intervention would essentially be comprised of debriefing tapes and scripts we have used in previous studies. After subjects have participated in the interventions, several measures of intervention effectiveness could be taken, including (1) self-reported sexual violence viewing (in a follow-up assessment); (2) ratings of realism in portrayals of sexual violence (i.e., portrayals of the myth that women desire sexual violence.); (3) general attitudes toward rape and rape victims; and (4) identification with sexual aggressors.

MASS-AUDIENCE INTERVENTIONS

The interventions suggested are only practical with relatively small groups in a classroom or other controlled setting. Probably the most well-known efforts at educating the general public about sexual violence in the media has involved large-scale projects. As Malamuth[52] notes, there have been several large-scale educational efforts directed at large audiences concerning subjects such as rape and rape myths (e.g., the films *Cry Rape, Why Men Rape, A Scream of Silence*) and pornography (e.g., *Not a Love Story*). These documentaries were expressly created to make the general public more aware of these issues.

If the effectiveness of other mass-media campaigns are taken as an indication, there can be little doubt that documentaries about rape or sexual violence have great potential for informing the public about these issues *if* they are seen by enough people. Research evaluating the effectiveness of antismoking television information spots, for example, has demonstrated that these programs have been successful in increasing public awareness about the negative health consequences of smoking.[53] But this success has probably been the result of the large number of antismoking messages delivered during prime viewing times. Most public service announcement campaigns do not produce significant effects because they consist of a small number of spots, often of questionable quality delivered at unpopular viewing hours.[54] In order for informational programs on rape and sexual violence to be effective, they must be viewed by a large proportion of the population. Even then, the most effective program for altering viewing patterns or changing attitudes about sexual violence would include a mass-media information campaign conducted in conjunction with small more focused workshop interventions, such as the program suggested earlier, in schools or the home. Programs that have combined mass-media campaigns with individualized skills-training sessions have proven to be quite successful in delaying the onset of adolescent smoking behavior, alcohol, and drug abuse.[55]

A preliminary investigation by Bart, Freeman, and Kimball[56] into the effectiveness of the film *Not a Love Story* to change attitudes about pornography and sexual violence suggests that viewers may benefit from exposure to this film. Bart et al. surveyed a group of 332 males and 318 females after they had viewed this film in an art film house in the Chicago area. The findings indicated that exposure to the film resulted in changes in beliefs and attitudes about pornography (e.g., "I didn't know pornography was that violent" and "The film made me angrier about pornography"). Unfortunately, because audience members were not randomly assigned to view the film, only self-reported attitude-change data were collected by the investigators (i.e., subjects were asked if their attitudes about pornography changed after viewing the film). No attempt was made to assess prefilm viewing attitudes or compare the film viewers' attitudes with a matched sample of control subjects.

It should be noted that programs concerning rape and sexual violence aimed at large audiences may also result in serious unintended consequences.[52] These films may contain explicit sexual depictions and rape scenes that would be sexually arousing to some members of the audience. This arousal may interfere with the attitude changes sought by the films' producers. In addition, the films often contain interviews with convicted rapists or other persons who may express rape myths. Certain audience members may process only information that supports their preconceptions about rape and rape victims.

Even with these problems, we are sufficiently encouraged by the research on debriefings and the work with children and television violence cited here to call for large- and small-scale educational interventions aimed at grade schoolers, adolescents, and young and older aged adults. Public service announcements should precede and/or follow television programs that even hint at the justification of violence against women. Grade schools should structure their sex education curriculums so that a significant segment of instruction is devoted to sexual portrayals in the media, with specific attention focused on aggression against women. These programs could range from prepackaged instruction materials that explored and specifically denounced myths about sexual violence, to more elaborate classroom exercises in which young males in particular are made aware not only of myths in the media, but the degree to which their fellow female students find offense and pain at these portrayals.

Parents also could forestall the onset of calloused attitudes about rape and violence by prohibiting young children from viewing depictions of violence against women. The research described in this volume suggests that the process of desensitization of media violence may be inevitable with repeated exposure. One way to maintain sensitivity to victims of violence (certainly to those portrayed in the media and perhaps to those encountered elsewhere) is to delay exposure to these materials as long as possible in the hope that when children are exposed to graphic depictions of violence, they will have reached a level of emotional maturity that will enable them to be appalled or at least taken aback by depictions commonly found in mass-released movies. This requires that parents themselves become educated about the content of the movies and television programs their children may be watching. Parents should be advised that the so-called slasher films are shown with great frequency on cable television, and the the horror movies of today are significantly different from the films they may have viewed when they were young.

Throughout this book we have attempted to approach the topic of violence against women in the media as objectively as possible. But as men, husbands, significant others, and fathers, let us leave the reader with no doubt that we are personally and morally deeply offended by many of the media depictions of women we have described in this book. We have undertaken our investigations both because we are intellectually curious about the effects of exposure to pornography and other images of women in the media, and because we are concerned about the negative impact of these materials on the members of our society — particularly our fellow male members. Our utopian and perhaps naive hope is that in the end the truth revealed through good science will prevail and the public will be convinced that these images not only demean those portrayed but also those who view them.

Notes

Chapter 1. Studying the Effects of Pornography *(pp. 1–22)*

1. Kilpatrick, 1975.
2. Falwell, 1980; Gould, 1977.
3. Longino, 1980.
4. Steinem, 1980.
5. Steinem, 1980, p. 37.
6. Steinem, 1980, p. 37.
7. Commission on Obscenity and Pornography, 1970.
8. *Attorney General's Commission on Pornography,* 1986.
9. Maslin, 1982.
10. *Olivia* v. *National Broadcasting Co., Inc.,* 1978.
11. *Schenck* v. *United States,* 1919.
12. *Schenck,* p. 52.
13. *Whitney* v. *California,* 1927.
14. *Whitney,* p. 376.
15. *Brandenburg* v. *Ohio,* 1969.
16. *Brandenburg,* p. 447.
17. *Bridges* v. *California,* 1941.
18. Krattenmaker & Powe, 1978.
19. Defendants' memorandum, 1984, p. 8.
20. Defendants' memorandum, 1984, pp. 4–5.
21. Brief *Amici Curiae,* 1985.
22. Kirkpatrick, 1984, pp. 2–3.
23. Pomeroy, 1984, pp. 3–4.

24. Money, 1984, p. 4.
25. Krattenmaker & Powe, 1978.
26. Donnerstein, 1980a, 1980b; Donnerstein & Berkowitz, 1981; Malamuth, 1978.
27. Malamuth, 1983.
28. Berkowitz & Donnerstein, 1982.
29. Turner & Simons, 1974.
30. Turner & Simons, 1974.
31. Berkowitz & Donnerstein, p. 252.
32. Hindelang, 1981.
33. Sears, 1986.
34. Orne, 1969.
35. Rosenthal, 1976.
36. Donnerstein, 1980a, 1980b; Donnerstein & Berkowitz, 1981.
37. Krattenmaker & Powe, 1978, p. 1155.
38. Krattenmaker & Powe, 1978, p. 1156.
39. Baron, 1977.
40. Baron, 1977, p. 7.
41. Berkowitz & Donnerstein, 1982.
42. Berkowitz & Donnerstein, 1982.
43. Berkowitz, 1986.
44. Liebert, Sprafkin, & Davidson, 1982.
45. Wakshlag, Vial, & Tambori, 1983; Zillmann, 1980, 1984; Zillmann & Wakshlag, 1985.
46. Grusec, 1973; Hicks, 1968.
47. Berkowitz & Geen, 1967; Donnerstein & Berkowitz, 1983; Geen & Berkowitz, 1966a, 1966b, 1967a, 1967b.
48. Geen & Thomas, 1986.
49. Berkowitz & Alioto, 1973; Feshbach, 1972; Geen, 1975.
50. Geen & Thomas, 1986.
51. Geen & Thomas, 1986.
52. Collins, Sobol, & Westby, 1981.
53. Cantor, Zillmann, & Einsidel, 1978.

Chapter 2. Research of the 1970 Presidential Commission *(pp. 23–37)*

1. Commission on Obscenity and Pornography, 1970.
2. Cairns, Paul, & Wishner, 1962; Cairns, Paul, & Wishner, 1970.
3. Cline, 1974a; Wilson, 1974.
4. *Attorney General's Commission on Pornography*, 1986.

5. *Attorney General's Commission on Pornography,* 1986, p. 224.

6. Commission on Obscenity and Pornography, 1970, p. 142.

7. Gagnon & Simon, 1967.

8. Kilpatrick, 1967.

9. Kubie, 1967.

10. van den Haag, 1967.

11. Egan, 1955.

12. Karpman, 1954, p. 274.

13. Cairns et al., 1962, p. 1036.

14. Hyman, 1970.

15. Howard, Reifler, & Liptzin, 1970.

16. Byrne & Lamberth, 1970; Davis & Braucht, 1970; Kutchinsky, 1970a, 1970b; Mann, Sidman, & Starr, 1970; Mosher, 1970.

17. Mann et al., 1970; Mosher, 1970.

18. Commission on Obscenity and Pornography, 1970, p. 194.

19. Howard, Reifler, & Liptzin, 1970; Mosher, 1970; Mann, Sidman, & Starr, 1970; Kutchinsky, 1970a, 1970b.

20. Mosher, 1970.

21. Mosher, 1970.

22. Byrne & Lamberth, 1970.

23. Amoroso, Brown, Pruesse, Ware, & Pilkey, 1970.

24. Tannenbaum, 1970.

25. Tannenbaum, 1970.

26. Commission on Obscenity and Pornography, 1970, p. 225.

27. Kupperstein & Wilson, 1970.

28. Commission on Obscenity and Pornography, 1970, p. 229.

29. Ben-Veniste, 1970.

30. Kutchinsky, 1970a.

31. Goldstein, Kant, Judd, Rice, & Green, 1970.

32. Walker, 1970.

33. Johnson, Kupperstein, & Peters, 1970.

34. Cook & Fossen, 1970.

35. Commission on Obscenity and Pornography, 1970, p. 243.

36. Commission on Obscenity and Pornography, 1970, p. 139.

37. Rist, 1975.

38. Berkowitz, 1971; Cline, 1974a, 1974b; Wills, 1977; Wilson, 1974.

39. Cline, 1974.

40. Lederer, 1980.

41. Cline, 1974b.

42. Bart & Jozsa, 1980.

43. Dienstbier, 1977.

Chapter 3. Nonviolent Pornography and Aggressive Behavior *(pp. 38–73)*

1. Fisher & Harris, 1976; Sapolsky, 1977; Zillmann, 1971; Zillmann, Hoyt, & Day, 1974; Rosene, 1971; Meyer, 1972a; Jaffe, 1975.
2. Zillmann, 1971.
3. Zillmann, Katcher, & Milavsky, 1972.
4. Donnerstein & Wilson, 1976.
5. Mueller & Donnerstein, 1977.
6. Mueller & Donnerstein, 1981.
7. Baron, 1974a, 1974b; Baron & Bell, 1973, 1977; Donnerstein, Donnerstein, & Evans, 1975; White, 1979; Frodi, 1977; Zillmann & Sapolsky, 1977.
8. Baron, 1974b.
9. Baron, 1983a, p. 187.
10. Baron, 1977; Baron 1983a, 1983b.
11. Donnerstein, Donnerstein, & Evans, 1975.
12. McConahay, 1974; Sanford, 1974.
13. Bandura, 1973.
14. Zillmann & Johnson, 1973; Donnerstein, Donnerstein, & Barrett, 1976.
15. Zillmann & Johnson, 1973.
16. Donnerstein, Donnerstein, & Evans, 1975.
17. Baron, 1977.
18. Sapolsky & Zillmann, 1981; Zillmann, Bryant, Comisky, & Medoff, 1981; Zillmann & Sapolsky, 1977.
19. Sapolsky, 1984.
20. Zillmann, Bryant, Comisky, & Medoff, 1981.
21. Zillmann et al., p. 249.
22. Jaffe, Malamuth, Feingold, & Feshbach, 1974; Baron, 1979; Fisher & Harris, 1976; Cantor, Zillmann, & Einsidel, 1978.
23. Baron, 1979.
24. Zillmann & Bryant, 1984.
25. Morgan, 1978b.
26. Brownmiller, 1975.
27. Eysenck & Nias, 1978.
28. Mosher, 1970.
29. Cline, 1974a, 1974b.
30. Howitt, 1982, p. 113.
31. Jaffe, Malamuth, Feingold, & Feshbach, 1974.
32. Baron & Bell, 1973.
33. Taylor & Epstein, 1967.

34. Donnerstein & Barrett, 1978.
35. Dengerink, 1976; Taylor & Epstein, 1967.
36. Donnerstein & Hallam, 1978.
37. Bandura, 1973.
38. Baron, 1977.
39. Donnerstein & Hallam, 1978.
40. Eysenck & Nias, 1978.
41. Check & Malamuth, 1983a.
42. Spence & Helmreich, 1978.
43. Malamuth & Ceniti, 1986.
44. Donnerstein & Hallam, 1978.
45. Geen, Stonner, & Shope, 1975.
46. Quanty, 1976.
47. Leonard & Taylor, 1983.
48. Leonard & Taylor, p. 292.
49. Taylor, 1967.
50. Kutchinsky, 1970a.
51. Court, 1976, 1984.
52. Kutchinsky, 1985.
53. Court, 1984.
54. Kutchinsky, 1985.
55. Kutchinsky, 1985.
56. Court, 1976, 1979, 1980, 1981, 1982, 1984.
57. Court, 1984, p. 149.
58. Court, 1984.
59. Abramson & Hayashi, 1984.
60. Court, 1984, p. 166.
61. Kutchinsky, 1985.
62. Check & Malamuth, 1986; Malamuth & Billings, 1986.
63. Nelson, 1982; Check & Malamuth, 1986.
64. Nelson, 1982.
65. Cochrane, 1978.
66. Committee on Obscenity and Film Censorship, 1979.
67. Committee on Obscenity and Film Censorship, 1979, p. 80.
68. Kupperstein & Wilson, 1970.
69. Baron & Straus, 1984, 1985, 1986.
70. Baron & Straus, 1984.
71. Baron & Straus, 1985.
72. Baron & Straus, 1986.
73. Baron & Straus, 1984, p. 206.
74. Baron & Straus, 1986, p. 11.

75. Davis & Smith, 1982.
76. Baron & Straus, 1986.
77. Mosher & Anderson, 1986.
78. Scott, 1985.
79. Kant & Goldstein, 1978.
80. Cook, Fosen, & Pacht, 1971.
81. Abel, Mittelman, & Becker, 1985.
82. Check & Malamuth, 1986.
83. Nelson, 1982.
84. Groth & Hobson, 1983, p. 168–169.
85. Nelson, 1982.
86. Dietz, Harry, & Hazelwood, 1986, p. 197.
87. Abel et al., 1978; Abel, Barlow, Blanchard, & Guild, 1977; Abel, Barlow, Blanchard, & Mavissakalian, 1975; Abel, Blanchard, & Barlow, 1981; Barbaree, Marshall, & Lanthier, 1979; Hinton, O'Neill, & Webster, 1980; Kolarsky, Madlafousek, & Novotna, 1978; Laws & Holmen, 1978; Quinsey & Carrigan, 1978.
88. Cox, 1979, p. 308.
89. Groth, 1979, p. 9.

Chapter 4. Changes in Viewers' Attitudes and Beliefs *(pp. 74–85)*

1. Zillmann & Bryant, 1986.
2. Kutchinsky, 1970b.
3. Mosher, 1970.
4. Howard, Reifler, & Liptzin, 1970.
5. Zillmann & Bryant, 1982, 1984, 1986.
6. Mann, Sidman, & Starr, 1970.
7. Zillmann & Bryant, 1984.
8. Berkowitz, 1984; Berkowitz & Rogers, 1985.
9. Wyer & Srull, 1980.
10. Kahnemann & Tversky, 1981.
11. Zillmann & Bryant, 1982.
12. Check, 1985b.
13. Zillmann & Bryant, 1982.
14. Check, 1985b, p. 116.
15. Zillmann & Bryant, 1982.
16. Linz, 1985.
17. Malamuth & Ceniti, 1986.
18. Krafka, 1985.
19. Check, 1985b.

20. Zillmann & Bryant, 1986.
21. Zillmann & Bryant, 1986, p. 18.
22. Kenrick, Gutierres, and Goldberg, in press.
23. Rubin, 1970.
24. Kenrick et al., in press.
25. Zillmann & Bryant, 1986.
26. Kenrick & Gutierres, 1980.
27. Cash, Cash, & Butters, 1983.
28. Dermer & Pyszczynski, 1978.
29. Yaffe & Nelson, 1982.
30. Wilson, 1978.
31. Wilson cited in Malamuth and Billings, p. 96.
32. Zillmann & Bryant, 1986.
33. Einsiedel, 1986.

Chapter 5. The Impact of Violent Pornography *(pp. 86 – 107)*

1. Morgan, 1978b.
2. Malamuth & Donnerstein, 1984.
3. *Attorney General's Commission on Pornography,* 1986, pp. 324 – 326.
4. Malamuth & Check, 1980a.
5. *Attorney General's Commission on Pornography,* 1986, p. 323, emphasis added by authors.
6. Malamuth & Donnerstein, 1984.
7. Smith, 1976b.
8. Malamuth & Spinner, 1980.
9. Scott, in press.
10. Dietz & Evans, 1982.
11. Dietz, Harry, & Hazelwood, 1986.
12. Slade, 1984.
13. Palys, 1986.
14. Palys, 1986, p. 33.
15. Malamuth, 1984; Malamuth & Donnerstein, 1984; Check & Malamuth, 1986.
16. National Institute of Mental Health, 1982.
17. Abel, Blanchard, & Becker, 1978.
18. Carroll, 1978.
19. Check & Malamuth, 1986.
20. Malamuth, 1978.
21. Donnerstein, 1980a, 1980b.
22. Donnerstein & Berkowitz, 1981.

23. Baron, 1977.
24. Donnerstein, 1980a, 1980b.
25. Malamuth, 1978.
26. Baron, 1977.
27. Malamuth & Ceniti, 1986.
28. Berkowitz, 1984.
29. Malamuth & Ceniti, 1986, p. 136.
30. Brownmiller, 1975.
31. Bandura, 1973.
32. Malamuth, 1981a, 1981b; Malamuth, 1984.
33. Malamuth, Haber, & Feshbach, 1980.
34. Briere & Malamuth, 1983.
35. Malamuth & Ceniti, 1986.
36. Malamuth, 1984.
37. Malamuth & Check, 1980a.
38. Malamuth, Reisin, & Spinner, 1979.
39. Malamuth, 1984.
40. Malamuth, 1984.
41. Malamuth & Check, 1985.
42. Abel, Barlow, Blanchard, & Guild, 1977.
43. Malamuth, 1981a, 1981b, 1984; Malamuth & Check, 1983; Malamuth & Donnerstein, 1982; Malamuth, Haber, & Feshbach, 1980; Malamuth, Heim, & Feshbach, 1980.
44. Abel & Blanchard, 1976; Abel, Blanchard, & Becker, 1976, 1978.
45. Abel, Barlow, Blanchard, & Guild, 1977; Malamuth, 1981a, 1981b, 1984.
46. Malamuth, 1981a, 1981b, 1984.
47. Malamuth, 1981b.
48. Malamuth, 1983, 1986.
49. Malamuth, 1983.
50. Burt, 1980.
51. Malamuth, 1986.
52. Check & Malamuth, 1983c; Check, 1985c.
53. Koss & Oros, 1982.

Chapter 6. Is It the Sex or Is It the Violence? *(pp. 108–136)*

1. Friday, 1980.
2. Malamuth & Check, 1981a.
3. Malamuth & Check, 1981a.

4. Donnerstein, Berkowitz, & Linz, 1986.
5. Berkowitz, 1974.
6. National Institute of Mental Health, 1982.
7. Abel, Barlow, Blanchard, & Guild, 1977.
8. Malamuth, Check, & Briere, 1986.
9. Maslin, 1982.
10. *Filmgore,* 1983.
11. Maslin, 1982, p. 2.
12. Koop, 1983.
13. McCutcheon & Adams, 1975.
14. Wolpe & Lang, 1964.
15. Zillmann & Bryant, 1984.
16. Paul & Bernstein, 1973.
17. Wilkins, 1971.
18. Bandura, 1969; Davidson & Wilson, 1973; Reid, 1973.
19. Kazdin & Wilcoxin, 1976.
20. Lader & Mathews, 1968.
21. Lang, 1977; Lang, 1984.
22. Lazarus & Alfert, 1964; Lazarus, Speisman, Mordkoff, & Davison, 1962.
23. National Commission on the Causes and Prevention of Violence, 1969.
24. Surgeon General's Scientific Advisory Committee on Television and Social Behavior, 1972.
25. American Medical Association, 1976.
26. National Institute of Mental Health, 1982, p. 6.
27. Andison, 1977.
28. Freedman, 1984.
29. Belson, 1978; Huesmann, Lagerspetz, & Eron, 1984.
30. Schwartz, 1982.
31. Milavsky, Kessler, Stipp, & Rubens, 1982a, 1982b.
32. Corry, 1983.
33. Freedman, 1984.
34. Lazarus, Speisman, Mordkoff, & Davison, 1962.
35. Cline, Croft, & Courrier, 1973.
36. Thomas, Horton, Lippencott, & Drabman, 1977.
37. Thomas et al., 1977.
38. Thomas et al., 1977.
39. Thomas et al., 1977, p. 455.
40. Linz, Donnerstein, & Penrod, 1984.
41. Linz, 1985.

42. Derogatis, 1977.
43. Malamuth & Check, 1983.
44. Barnes, Malamuth, & Check, 1984b.
45. Two additional conditions were also included in this study — one in which eight subjects viewed nonviolent pornographic X-rated films, and another in which ten subjects viewed X-rated pornographic films portraying rape and sexual violence. The latter films, while depicting violence against women, did not portray the violence in a particularly graphic or gory fashion. In addition the outcomes of rape depictions were also sometimes ambiguous (the victim did not always express abhorrence or experience trauma as a result of being raped). Because the theoretical focus of the present study is desensitization to graphic presentations of violence against women (with no ambiguity about the victim's abhorrence of the experience), results from these experimental conditions are not reported here.
46. Zuckerman & Lubin, 1965.
47. Linz, 1985.
48. Hans, 1980.
49. Frodi, Macauley, & Thome, 1977.
50. Krafka, 1985.
51. Malamuth & Check, 1981a.
52. Krafka, 1985, p. 39.
53. Lazarus & Alfert, 1964.
54. Kelley, 1971; Walster, 1966.
55. Lerner, 1965; Lerner, 1971.
56. Berkowitz, 1984.
57. Geen, 1981.
58. Zillmann & Bryant, 1984.
59. Thomas, Horton, Lippencott, & Drabman, 1977.
60. Thomas, 1982.
61. Geen, 1981.
62. Eron & Huesmann, 1980; Huesmann, Eron, Klein, Brice, & Fischer, 1981.
63. Byeff, 1970; Piliavin, & Trudell, 1974, Gaertner & Dovidio, 1977.
64. Gaertner & Dovidio, 1977.
65. Sterling, 1977.
66. Piliavin, Piliavin, & Trudell, 1974.

Chapter 7. The Search for Legal Solutions *(pp. 137–170)*

1. *Public Hearings on Ordinances,* 1983.
2. Shipp, 1984.

3. Indianapolis and Marion County, Ind., 1984.
4. *American Booksellers Association* v. *Hudnut*, 1984.
5. *Public Hearings on Ordinances*, 1983.
6. *Public Hearings on Ordinances*, 1983.
7. MacKinnon, 1985.
8. Duggan, 1984.
9. Duggan, 1984.
10. *American Booksellers Association* v. *Hudnut*, 1984.
11. *Miller* v. *California*, 1973.
12. *Chaplinsky* v. *New Hampshire*, 1942.
13. *New York* v. *Ferber*, 1982.
14. *American Booksellers Association* v. *Hudnut*, 1984.
15. *Freedman* v. *State of Maryland*, 1965.
16. *American Booksellers Association* v. *Hudnut*, 1985.
17. Goodman, 1984.
18. Penrod & Linz, 1984.
19. Shulman, 1986.
20. Barber, 1972.
21. Barber, 1972.
22. *Commonwealth* v. *Sharpless*, 1815.
23. Feinberg, 1983.
24. *Webster's Third New International Dictionary*, 1965.
25. Richards, 1974–1975.
26. LaBarre's 1955 observation that Tahitians, at least at one point in time, were offended by eating in public but not by public sexual intercourse.
27. Feinberg, 1979.
28. *Cohen* v. *California*, 1971.
29. p. 20.
30. *Swearingen* v. *United States*, 1896.
31. *A Book Named "John Cleland's Memoirs of a Woman of Pleasure"* v. *Attorney General of Massachusetts*, 1966.
32. *Winters* v. *New York*, 1948.
33. *Winters*, p. 508.
34. Krattenmaker & Powe, 1978.
35. *People* v. *Winters*, 1945, p. 100.
36. *Headquarters Detective*, cited in *Winters* v. *New York*, 1948.
37. *Winters*, p. 510.
38. *Roth* v. *United States*, 1957.
39. *Roth*, p. 489.
40. Clor, 1969.

41. *Manual Enterprises* v. *Day*, 1962.
42. *Mishkin* v. *New York*, 1965.
43. *A Book Named "John Cleland's Memoirs of a Woman of Pleasure"* v. *Attorney General of Massachusetts*, 1966.
44. *Jacobellis* v. *Ohio*, 1964.
45. *Jacobellis*, p. 197.
46. *Stanley* v. *Georgia*, 1969.
47. *Stanley* v. *Georgia*, 1969.
48. *Miller* v. *California*, 1973.
49. *Paris Adult Theatre I.* v. *Slaton*, 1973.
50. *Paris Adult Theatre I*, p. 24.
51. Feinberg, 1979, p. 130.
52. Feinberg, 1979, p. 131.
53. Feinberg, 1979, p. 69.
54. *Paris Adult Theater I.* v. *Slaton*, 1973, p. 58.
55. Commission on Obscenity and Pornography, 1970, p. 32.
56. Beck & Smith, 1981.
57. Leventhal, 1977.
58. *Paris Adult Theater I* v. *Slaton*, 1973.
59. *United States* v. *Harriss*, 1954.
60. *American Booksellers Association* v. *Hudnut*, 1985, p. 8.
61. *American Booksellers Association* , 1985, p. 9.
62. *American Booksellers Association* v. *Hudnut*, 1984, p. 43.
63. *American Booksellers Association*, 1984, p. 46.
64. Burstyn, 1985.
65. Burstyn, 1984.
66. Burstyn, 1984, p. 29.
67. Burstyn, 1984, p. 29.
68. Burstyn, 1984, p. 44.
69. Hilker, 1979; Wade, 1973.
70. Hilker, 1979, p. 531.
71. Prosser & Wade, 1971.
72. Spak, 1981.
73. Spak, 1981, p. 672.
74. Spak, 1981, p. 672.
75. *New York Times*, 1973.
76. Hilker, 1979.
77. Donnerstein & Berkowitz, 1981; Malamuth, Heim, & Feshbach, 1980; Malamuth & Check, 1980a, 1980b.
78. Canby, 1986.
79. DeGrazia & Newman, 1982.

80. DeGrazia & Newman, 1982, p. 11.
81. Quoted in DeGrazia & Newman, 1982, pp. 16–17.
82. Krattenmaker & Powe, 1978.
83. Wertham, 1948.
84. DeGrazia & Newman, 1982, p. 120.
85. Heffner, 1984.
86. Harlech, 1982, pp. 9–10.
87. Harlech, 1982, pp. 10–14.
88. Harlech, 1982, pp. 16, 19.

Chapter 8. Alternatives for the Future *(pp. 171–196)*

1. *Attorney General's Commission on Pornography*, 1986, p. 322.
2. *Commission on Pornography*, 1986, pp. 376–377.
3. *Commission on Pornography*, 1986, p. 323.
4. *Commission on Pornography*, 1986, p. 329.
5. Linz, Krafka, Donnerstein, & Penrod, 1986.
6. Check, 1985b.
7. Malamuth, 1986.
8. Malamuth & Briere, 1986.
9. Zillmann & Bryant, 1982.
10. *Commission on Pornography*, 1986, p. 348.
11. Zillmann, Weaver, Mundorf, & Aust, 1986.
12. Nelson, 1985.
13. Burt, 1980.
14. Donnerstein & Berkowitz, 1981.
15. Burt, 1980.
16. Malamuth & Check, 1984.
17. Check & Malamuth, 1984b.
18. Donnerstein, Penrod, & Linz, 1984.
19. Linz, 1985.
20. Stock, 1983.
21. Krafka, 1985.
22. Krafka, 1985.
23. Chapin, 1985; Krafka, 1985.
24. Check & Malamuth, 1984b; Malamuth & Check, 1984.
25. Check & Malamuth, 1984b.
26. Check & Malamuth, 1984b.
27. Donnerstein et al., 1984; Linz, 1985; Krafka, 1985; Chapin, 1985.
28. Malamuth & Check, 1984.

29. Malamuth, Heim, & Feshbach, 1980.
30. Malamuth & Ceniti, 1986.
31. Donnerstein, 1980a, 1980b, 1984; Donnerstein & Berkowitz, 1981; Malamuth, 1978.
32. Malamuth & Ceniti, 1986.
33. Bross, 1985, pp. 104–105.
34. Linz, 1985; Linz, Donnerstein, & Penrod, 1984.
35. Anderson, 1980; Corder-Bolz, 1982.
36. Eron, 1980.
37. Dorr, Graves, & Phelps, 1980; Huesmann, Eron, Klein, Brice, & Fischer, 1983.
38. Huesmann, Eron, Klein, Brice, & Fischer, 1983.
39. Eron & Huesmann, 1980.
40. Cook & Flay, 1978.
41. Huesmann, Eron, Klein, Brice, & Fischer, 1983.
42. Huesmann et al., 1983.
43. Cook & Flay, 1978.
44. Cook & Flay, 1978.
45. Bandura, Blanchard, & Ritter, 1969; Mann & Janis, 1968.
46. Miller, Brickman, & Bolan, 1975.
47. Watts, 1967.
48. Freedman, 1965; Lepper, 1973.
49. Mann & Janis, 1968.
50. Clore & Jeffrey, 1972.
51. Cook & Flay, 1978.
52. Malamuth, 1984.
53. Flay, 1986.
54. Flay & Sobel, 1983.
55. Flay & Sobel, 1983.
56. Bart, Freeman, & Kimball, 1984.

Bibliography

ABC is KO'd on violence. (1983, July). *Access*, p. 1.

A Book Named "John Cleland's Memoirs of a Woman of Pleasure" v. *Attorney General of Massachusetts*, 383 U.S., at 451, 86 S. Ct., at 993 (1966).

AGETON, S. S. (1983). *Sexual assault among adolescents*. Lexington, MA: Lexington Books.

ALSCHULER, M. (1970). Origins of the law of obscenity. In *Presidential Commission on Obscenity and Pornography* (Vol. 2). Washington, D.C.: U.S. Government Printing Office.

ABEL, G. G., BARLOW, D. H., BLANCHARD, E. B., & GUILD, D. (1977). The components of rapists' sexual arousal. *Archives of General Psychiatry, 34*, 395–403; 895–903.

ABEL, G. G., BARLOW, D. H., BLANCHARD, E. B., & MAVISSAKALIAN, M. (1975). Measurement of sexual arousal in male homosexuals: Effects of instructions and stimulus modality. *Archives of Sexual Behavior, 4*(6), 623–629.

ABEL, G. G., BECKER, J. V., MURPHY, W., & FLANAGAN, B. (1981). Identifying dangerous child molesters. In R. B. Stuart (Ed.), *Violent behavior: Social learning approaches to prediction management and treatment*. New York: Brunner-Mazel.

ABEL, G. G., BECKER, J. V., & SKINNER, L. J. (1980). Aggressive behavior and sex. *Psychiatric Clinics of North America, 3*(1), 133–151.

ABEL, G. G., & BLANCHARD, E. B. (1976). The measurement and generation of sexual arousal in male deviates. In M. Hersen, R. M. Eisler, & P. M. Miller (Eds.), *Progress in behavior modification* (Vol. 2). New York: Academic Press.

ABEL, G. G., BLANCHARD, E. B., & BARLOW, D. H. (1981). Measurement of sexual arousal in several paraphilias: The effects of stimulus modality, instructional set, and stimulus content on the objective. *Behaviour Research and Therapy, 19*(1), 25–33.

ABEL, G. G., BLANCHARD, E. B., BARLOW, D. H., & MAVISSAKALIAN, M. (1975). Identifying specific erotic cues in sexual deviations by audio-taped descriptions. *Journal of Applied Behavior Analysis, 8*, 247–260.

ABEL, G. G., BLANCHARD, E. B., & BECKER, J. V. (1976). Psychological treatment of rapists. In M. Walker & S. Brody (Eds.), *Sexual assault: The victim and the rapist.* Lexington, MA: Lexington.

———(1978). An integrated treatment program for rapists. In R. Rada (Ed.), *Clinical aspects of the rapist.* New York: Grune & Stratton.

ABEL, G. G., BLANCHARD, E. B., BECKER, J. V., & DJENDEREDJIAN, A. (1978). Differentiating sexual aggressiveness with penile measure. *Criminal Justice and Behavior, 5*, 315–332.

ABEL, G. G., MITTELMAN, & BECKER, J. V. (1985). *The effects of erotica on paraphiliacs' behavior.* Unpublished manuscript, Emory University.

ABRAMSON, P. R., & HAYASHI, H. (1984). Pornography in Japan: Cross-cultural and theoretical considerations. In N. M. Malamuth & E. Donnerstein (Eds.), *Pornography and sexual aggression.* Orlando, FL: Academic Press.

ABRAMSON, P. R., & MECHANIC, M. B. (1983). Sex and the media: Three decades of best-selling books and major motion pictures. *Archives of Sexual Behavior, 12*, 185–206.

ADAMSON, J. D., ROMANO, K. R., BURDICK, J. A., CORMAN, C. L., & CHEBIB, F. S. (1972). Physiological responses to sexual and unpleasant film stimuli. *Journal of Psychosomatic Research, 16*, 153–162.

ALDER, C. (1984). The convicted rapist: A sexual or a violent offender? *Criminal Justice and Behavior, 11*, 157–177.

———An exploration of self-reported sexually aggressive behavior. *Crime and Delinquency, 31*, 306–311.

American Booksellers Association v. *Hudnut,* 598 F. Supp. 1316 (S.D. Ind. 1984).

American Booksellers Association v. *Hudnut,* 771 F.2d 323 (7th Cir. 1985).

American Medical Association Policy, No. 38, *Violence on TV: An Environmental Hazard,* Reference Committee E, 367, 1976.

AMIR, M. (1971). *Patterns of forcible rape.* Chicago: University of Chicago Press.

AMOROSO, D., & BROWN, M. (1973). Problems in studying the effects of erotic material. *Journal of Sex Research, 9*, 187–195.

AMOROSO, D. M., BROWN, M., PRUESSE, M., WARE, E. E., & PILKEY, D. W.

BIBLIOGRAPHY **213**

(1970). An investigation of behavioral, psychological, and physiological reactions to pornographic stimuli. *Technical Reports of the Commission on Obscenity and Pornography* (Vol. 8). Washington, D.C.: U.S. Government Printing Office.

———(1972). The effects of physiological measurement and presence of others on ratings of erotic stimuli. *Canadian Journal of Behavioral Science, 4,* 191–203.

ANDERSON, J. (1980). The theoretical lineage of critical viewing curricula. *Journal of Communication, 30,* 64–70.

ANDISON, F. S. (1977). TV violence and viewer aggression: A cumulation of study results 1956–1976. *Public Opinion Quarterly, 41,* 314–331.

ARMENTROUT, J. A., & HAUER, A. I. (1978). MMPIs of rapists of adults, rapists of children, and nonrapist sexual offenders. *Journal of Clinical Psychology, 34,* 330–332.

ATHANASIOU, R., & SHAVER, P. (1971). Correlates of heterosexuals' reactions to pornography. *Journal of Sex Research, 7,* 298–311.

Attorney General's Commission on Pornography: Final Report. (1986, July). Washington, D.C.: U.S. Department of Justice.

AVERILL, J. R., MALSTROM, E. J., KORIAT, A., & LAZARUS, R. S. (1972). Habituation to complex emotional stimuli. *Journal of Abnormal Psychology, 80,* 20–28.

BANDURA, A. (1963, October 22). What TV violence can do to your child. *Look,* pp. 46–52.

———(1969). *Principles of behavior modification.* New York: Holt, Rinehart & Winston.

———(1973). *Aggression: A social learning process.* New York: Prentice-Hall.

———(1977). *Social learning theory.* New York: Prentice-Hall

———(1983). Psychological Mechanisms of Aggression. In R. G. Geen & E. I. Donnerstein (Eds.), *Aggression: Theoretical and Empirical Reviews.* New York: Academic Press.

BANDURA, A., BLANCHARD, E. B., & RITTER, B. (1969). The relative efficacy of desensitization and modeling approaches for inducing behavioral, affective, and attitudinal changes. *Journal of Personality and Social Psychology, 13,* 173–199.

BANDURA, A., & MENLOVE F. L. (1968). Factors determining vicarious extinction of avoidance behavior through symbolic modeling. *Journal of Personality and Social Psychology, 8,* 99–108.

BARBAREE, H. E., MARSHALL, W. L., & LANTHIER, R. D. (1979). Deviant sexual arousal in rapists. *Behavior Research and Therapy, 17,* 215–222.

BARBER, D. F. (1972). *Pornography and society.* London: Charles Skilton.

BARCLAY, A. M. (1971). Linking sexual and aggressive motives: Contributions of "irrelevant" arousals. *Journal of Personality, 39,* 481 – 492.

BARCLAY, A. M., & HABER, R. N. (1965). The relation of aggressive to sexual motivation. *Journal of Personality, 33,* 462 – 475.

BARNES, G. E., MALAMUTH, N. M., & CHECK, J. V. P. (1984a). Personality and sexuality. *Personality and Individual Differences, 5*(2), 159 – 172.

———(1984b). Psychoticism and Sexual Arousal to Rape Depictions. *Personality and Individual Differences, 5*(3), 273 – 279.

BARON, J. N., & REISS, P. C. (1985). Same time, next year: Aggregate analyses of the mass media and violent behavior. *American Sociological Review, 50,* 347 – 363.

BARON, L., & STRAUS, M. A. (1984). Sexual stratification, pornography, and rape in the United States. In N. M. Malamuth & E. Donnerstein (Eds.), *Pornography and sexual aggression* (pp. 185 – 209). Orlando, FL: Academic Press.

———(1985). *Legitimate violence, pornography, and sexual inequality as explanations for state and regional differences in rape.* Unpublished manuscript, Yale University, New Haven, CT.

———(1986). *Rape and its relation to social disorganization, pornography, and sexual inequality in the United States.* Unpublished manuscript, Yale University.

BARON, R. A. (1974a). Sexual arousal and physical aggression: The inhibiting influence of "cheesecake" and nudes. *Bulletin of the Psychonomic Society, 3,* 337 – 339.

———(1974b). The aggression-inhibiting influence of heightened sexual arousal. *Journal of Personality and Social Psychology, 30*(3), 318 – 322.

———(1974c). Aggression as a function of victim's pain cues, level of prior anger arousal, and exposure to an aggressive model. *Journal of Personality and Social Psychology, 29,* 117 – 124.

———(1977). *Human Aggression.* New York: Plenum.

———(1978). Aggression-inhibiting influence of sexual humor. *Journal of Personality and Social Psychology, 36,* 189 – 198.

———(1979). Heightened sexual arousal and physical aggression: An extension to females. *Journal of Research in Personality, 13,* 91 – 102.

———(1983a). The control of human aggression: A strategy based on incompatible responses. In R. G. Geen & E. Donnerstein (Eds.), *Aggression: Theoretical and empirical reviews.* New York: Academic Press.

———(1983b). The control of human aggression: An optimistic perspective. *Journal of Social and Clinical Psychology, 1,* 97 – 119.

———(1984). The control of human aggression: A strategy based on incompatible responses. In R. Geen & E. Donnerstein (Eds.), *Aggression: Theoretical and Empirical Reviews* (Vol. 2). New York: Academic Press.

BARON, R. A., & BELL, P. A. (1973). Effects of heightened sexual arousal on physical aggression. *Proceedings of the 81st Annual Convention of the American Psychological Association, 8,* 171–172.

———(1977). Sexual arousal and aggression by males: Effects of type of erotic stimuli and prior provocation. *Journal of Personality and Social Psychology, 35*(2), 79–87.

BARON, R. A., & EGGLESTON, R. J. (1972). Performance on the "Aggression Machine": Motivation to help or harm? *Psychonomic Science, 26,* 321–322.

BARRY, K. (1979). *Female sexual slavery.* Englewood Cliffs, NJ: Prentice-Hall.

BART, P. B., FREEMAN, L., & KIMBALL, P. (1984). *The different worlds of women and men: Attitudes toward pornography and responses to "Not a love story—A film about pornography".* Paper presented at the Second International Interdisciplinary Conference on Women, Groningen, The Netherlands.

BART, P. B., & JOZSA, M. (1980). Dirty books, dirty films and dirty data. In C. Lederer (Ed.), *Take back the night: Women on pornography.* New York: William Morrow.

BECK, M., & SMITH, V. E. (1981, May 25). How to make it hot for porn. *Newsweek.*

BELSON, W. A. (1978). *Television violence and the adolescent boy.* London: Saxon House.

BENEKE, T. (1982). *Men on rape.* New York: St. Martin's.

BEN-VENISTE, R. (1970). Pornography and sex crime — the Danish experience. *Technical reports of the Commission on Obscenity and Pornography* (Vol. 7). Washington, D.C.: U.S. Government Printing Office.

BERGER, A. S., SIMON, W., & GAGNON, J. H. (1973). Youth and pornography in social context. *Archives of Sexual Behavior, 2*(4), 279–308.

BERGER, S. (1962). Conditioning through vicarious instigation. *Psychological Review, 69,* 405–456.

BERKOWITZ, L. (1971). Sex and violence: We can't have it both ways. *Psychology Today, 5*(7), 14–23.

———(1974). Some determinants of impulsive aggression: Role of mediated associations with reinforcements for aggression. *Psychological Review, 81,* 165–179.

———(1984). Some effects of thoughts on anti- and pro-social influences of media events: A cognitive-neoassociation analysis. *Psychological Bulletin, 95,* 410–427.

———(1986). Situational influences on reactions to observed violence. *Journal of Social Issues, 42*(3).

BERKOWITZ, L., & ALIOTO, J. (1973). The meaning of an observed event as a determinant of its aggressive consequences. *Journal of Personality and Social Psychology, 28*, 206–217.

BERKOWITZ, L., & DONNERSTEIN, E. (1982). External validity is more than skin deep. *American Psychologist, 37*, 245–257.

BERKOWITZ, L., & GEEN, R. G. (1967). Stimulus qualities of the target of aggression: A further study. *Journal of Personality and Social Psychology, 5*, 364–368.

BERKOWITZ, L., & ROGERS, K. H. (1985). A priming effect analysis of media influences. In D. Zillmann (Ed.), *Advances in media effects research.* Hillsdale, NJ: Erlbaum.

BERNS, W. (1971). Pornography vs. democracy — A case for censorship. *The Public Interest, 22*, 3–24.

BOGART, L. (1980). After the Surgeon General's report: Another look backward. In S. B. Withey & R. P. Abeles (Eds.), *Television and social behavior: Beyond violence and children.* Hillsdale, NJ: Erlbaum.

BOTTO, R. W., GALBRAITH, G. G., & STERN, R. M. (1974). Effects of false heart rate feedback and sex-guilt upon attitudes toward sexual stimuli. *Psychological Reports, 35*, 267–264.

BRADY, J. P., & LEVITT, E. E. (1965). The relation of sexual preferences to sexual experiences. *Psychological Record, 15*, 377–384.

Brandenburg v. *Ohio,* 395 U.S. 444 (1969).

BRICKMAN, J. R. (1979). Erotica: Sex differences in stimulus preferences and fantasy content. *Dissertation Abstracts International, 39(7-B)*, 3500–3501E.

BRIDDEL, D. W., RIMM, D. C., CADDY, G. R., KRAWITZ, G., SHOLIS, D., & WUNDERLIN, R. J. (1978). Effects of alcohol and cognitive set on sexual arousal to deviant stimuli. *Journal of Abnormal Psychology, 87*, 418–430.

Bridges v. *California,* 314 U.S. 252 (1941).

Brief *Amici Curiae* of the American Civil Liberties Union, the Indiana Civil Liberties Union and the American Civil Liberties Union of Illinois, Cause No. IP 84-3147 (7th Circuit Court, April 8, 1985).

BRIERE, J., CORNE, S., & RUNTZ, M. (1984). *The rape arousal inventory: Predicting actual and potential sexual aggression in a university population.* Paper presented at the annual meeting of the American Psychological Association, Toronto.

BRIERE, J., & MALAMUTH, N. (1983). Self-reported likelihood of sexually aggressive behavior: Attitudinal versus sexual explanations. *Journal of Research in Personality, 17*, 315–323.

BRIERE, J., MALAMUTH, N., & CHECK, J. V. P. (1981). Sexuality and rape-supportive beliefs. In P. Caplan (Ed.), *Sex roles II: Feminist psychology in transition.* Toronto: Eden.

BRITTAIN, R. P. (1970). The sadistic murderer. *Medicine, Science and Law, 10,* 198–207.

BRODSKY, S. L. (1976). Sexual assault: Prespectives on prevention and assailants. In M. J. Walker & S. L. Brodsky (Eds.), *Sexual assault.* Lexington, MA: D.C. Heath.

BROSS, M. (1985). *Mitigating the effects of mass media sexual violence.* Unpublished master's thesis, University of Wisconsin, Madison.

BROWN, C., ANDERSON, J., BURGGRAF, L., & THOMPSON, N. (1978). Community standards, conservatism, and judgments of pornography. *Journal of Sex Research, 14*(2), 81–95.

BROWN, M. (1979). Viewing time of pornography. *Journal of Psychology, 102,* 83–95.

BROWN, M., AMOROSO, D. M., & WARE, E. E. (1976). Behavioral effects of viewing pornography. *Journal of Social Psychology, 98,* 235–245.

BROWN, M., AMOROSO, D. M., WARE, E. E., PRUESSE, M., & PILKEY, D. W. (1973). Factors affecting viewing time of pornography. *Journal of Social Psychology, 90,* 125–135.

BROWNELL, K. D., HAYES, S. C., & BARLOW, D. H. (1977). Patterns of appropriate and deviant sexual arousal: The behavioral treatment of multiple sexual deviations. *Journal of Consulting and Clinical Psychology, 45,* 1144–1155.

BROWNMILLER, S. (1975). *Against our will: Men, women and rape.* New York: Simon & Schuster.

———(1980). Let's put pornography back in the closet. In L. Lederer (Ed.), *Take back the night: Women on pornography.* New York: William Morrow.

BURDICK, J. A. (1978). The relationship between cardiac variability and the evaluation of pictorial sexual stimuli. *Dissertation Abstracts International, 38(12-B),* 6188–6189.

BURSTYN, V. (1984, November). Censoring who? Why state censorship backfires. *Our Times,* pp. 27–44.

———(1985). In V. Burstyn (Ed.), *Women against censorship.* Vancouver: Douglas McIntyre.

BURT, M. E. H. (1976, September). Use of pornography by women: A critical review of the literature. *Case Western Reserve Journal of Sociology, 8,* 1–16.

BURT, M. R. (1980). Cultural myths and supports for rape. *Journal of Personality and Social Psychology, 38,* 217–230.

———(1983). Justifying personal violence: A comparison of rapists and the general public. *Victimology: An International Journal, 8,* 131–150.

BURT, M. R., & ALBIN, R. S. (1981). Rape myths, rape definitions, and probability of conviction. *Journal of Applied Social Psychology, 11,* 212–230.

BYEFF, P. (1970). *Helping behavior in audio and audio-visual conditions.* Senior honors thesis, University of Pennsylvania.

BYERLY, G., & RUBIN, R. (1980). *Pornography: The conflict over sexually explicit materials in the United States—An annotated bibliography.* New York: Garland.

BYRNE, D. (1977a). Social Psychology and the study of sexual behavior. *Personality and Social Psychology Bulletin, 3,* 3–30.

———(1977b). The imagery of sex. In J. Money & L. Musaph (Eds.), *Handbook of sexology.* Amsterdam: Elsevier/North-Holland Biomedical Press.

BYRNE, D., CHERRY, F., LAMBERTH, J., & MITCHELL, H. E. (1973). Husband-wife similarity in response to erotic stimuli. *Journal of Personality, 4,* 385–394.

BYRNE, D., FISHER, J. D., LAMBERTH, J., & MITCHELL, H. E. (1974). Evaluations of erotica: Facts or feelings. *Journal of Personality and Social Psychology, 29,* 111–116.

BYRNE, D., & LAMBERTH, J. (1970). The effect of erotic stimuli on sex arousal, evaluative responses, and subsequent behavior. *Technical reports of the Commission on Obscenity and Pornography* (Vol. 8). Washington, D.C.: U.S. Government Printing Office.

BYRNE, D., & SHEFFIELD, J. (1965). Response to sexually arousing stimuli as a function of repressing and sensitizing defenses. *Journal of Abnormal Psychology, 70,* 114–118.

CAIRNS, R. B., PAUL, J. C. N., & WISHNER, J. (1962). Sex censorship: The assumptions of anti-obscenity laws and the empirical evidence. *Minnesota Law Review, 46,* 1009–1041.

———(1970). Psychological assumptions in sex censorship: An evaluative review of recent research (1961–1968). In *Technical reports of the Commission on Obscenity and Pornography* (Vol. 1). Washington, D.C.: U.S. Government Printing Office.

CALLWOOD, J. (1985). Feminist debates and civil liberties. In V. Burstyn (Ed.), *Women against censorship.* Vancouver: Douglas McIntyre.

CANBY, V. (1986, April 20). Are the ratings just alphabet soup? *New York Times.*

CANTOR, J., ZILLMANN, D., & BRYANT, J. (1975). Enhancement of experienced sexual arousal in response to erotic stimuli through misattribution of unrelated residual excitation. *Journal of Personality and Social Psychology, 32,* 69–75.

CANTOR, J., ZILLMANN, R., & EINSIDEL, E. F. (1978). Female responses to provocation after exposure to aggressive and erotic films. *Communication Research, 5,* 395–413.

CARLSON, J. M. (1983). Crime show viewing by preadults: The impact on attitudes toward civil liberties. *Communication Research, 10,* 529–552.

CARROLL, J. S. (1978). The effect of imagining an event on expectations for the event: An interpretation in terms of the availability heuristic. *Journal of Experimental Social Psychology, 14,* 88–96.

CARRUTHERS, M., & TAGGART, P. (1973). Vagotonicity of violence: Biochemical and cardiac responses to violent films and television programmes. *British Medical Journal, 3,* 384–389.

CASH, T. F., CASH, D. N., & BUTTERS, J. W. (1983). "Mirror, mirror, on the wall . . . ?": Contrast effects and self-evaluations of physical attractiveness. *Personality and Social Psychology Bulletin, 9,* 351–358.

CATTELL, R. B., KAWASH, G. F., & DEYOUNG, G. E. (1972). Validation of objective measures of ergic tension: Response of the sex erg to visual stimulation. *Journal of Experimental Research in Personality, 6,* 76–83.

CENITI, J., & MALAMUTH, N. (1984). Effects of repeated exposure to sexually violent or nonviolent stimuli on sexual arousal to rape and nonrape depictions. *Behaviour Research and Therapy, 22,* 535–548.

CERNY, J. A. (1978). Biofeedback and the voluntary control of sexual arousal in women. *Behavior Therapy, 9,* 847–855.

CHAFFEE, S. (1972). Television and adolescent aggressiveness. In G. Comstock & E. A. Rubinstein (Eds.), *Television and social behaviour, Vol. 3: Television and adolescent aggressiveness.* Washington, D.C.: U.S. Government Printing Office.

CHAPIN, M. (1985). *Debriefings for females exposed to film depictions of violence against women.* Unpublished master's thesis, University of Wisconsin, Madison.

Chaplinsky v. *New Hampshire,* 315 U.S. 568 (1942).

CHECK, J. V. P. (1982, August). *Rape attitudes following participation in pornography experiments employing debriefing procedures.* Paper presented at the annual meeting of the American Psychological Association, Washington, D.C.

———— (1984). *The effects of violent and nonviolent pornography* (Department of Supply and Services Contract No. 05SV 19200-3-0899). Ottawa, Ontario: Canadian Department of Justice.

———— (1985a). Hostility toward women: Some theoretical considerations. In G. W. Russell (Ed.), *Violence in intimate relationships.* Jamaica, NY: Spectrum.

———— (1985b). *The Hostility Toward Women Scale.* Unpublished doctoral dissertation. University of Manitoba, Winnipeg, Canada.

CHECK, J. V. P., ELIAS, B., & BARTON, S. A. (1985). Hostility toward men in female victims of male sexual aggression. G. W. Russell (Ed.), *Violence in intimate relationships.* Jamaica, NY: Spectrum.

CHECK, J. V. P., & HEAPY, N. A. (1985, July). *A survey of Canadian's attitudes regarding sexual content in the media.* Report for the LaMarsh Research Programme, York University, Toronto, Canada.

CHECK, J. V. P., & MALAMUTH, N. (1981, August). *Can exposure to pornography have positive effects?* Paper presented at the annual meeting of the American Psychological Association, Los Angeles.

CHECK, J. V. P., & MALAMUTH, N. (1982, May). *Pornography effects and self-reported likelihood of committing acquaintance versus stranger rape.* Paper presented at the meeting of the Midwestern Psychological Association, Minneapolis.

————(1983a). Sex role stereotyping and reactions to depictions of stranger versus acquaintance rape. *Journal of Personality and Social Psychology, 45,* 344–356.

————(1983b). Violent pornography, feminism, and social learning theory. *Aggressive Behavior, 9,* 106–107.

————(1983c, June). *The Hostility Toward Women Scale.* Paper presented at the Western Meetings of the International Society for Research on Aggression, Victoria, Canada.

————(1984a). Can participation in pornography experiments have positive effects? *Journal of Sex Research, 20,* 14–31.

————(1984b). *Ethical considerations in sex and aggression research.* Unpublished manuscript, York University, Toronto, Canada.

————(1986). Pornography and sexual aggression: A social learning theory analysis. In M. L. McLaughlin (Ed.), *Communication yearbook 9.* Beverly Hills, CA: Sage.

CHECK, J. V. P., MALAMUTH, N. M., ELIAS, B., & BARTON, S. (1985). On hostile ground. *Psychology Today, 19,* 56–61.

City County General Ordinance No. 35 (1984). City of Indianapolis, Indiana.

CLARENS, C. (1967). *An illustrated history of the horror film.* New York: Capricorn.

CLARK, L. (1980). Pornography's challenge to liberal ideology. *Canadian Forum, 3,* 9–12.

CLARK, L., & LEWIS, D. (1977). *Rape: The price of coercive sexuality.* Toronto: The Women's Press.

CLINE, V. B. (1970). *Minority report of the U.S. Commission on Obscenity and Pornography.* New York: Bantam.

————(Ed.) (1974a). *Where do you draw the line?* Salt Lake City: Brigham Young University Press.

————(1974b). Another view: Pornography effects, the state of the art. In V. B. Cline (Ed.), *Where do you draw the line?* Provo, UT: Brigham Young University Press.

———— (1976, February). The scientists vs. pornography: An untold story. *Intellect,* pp. 574–576.

CLINE, V. B., CROFT, R. G., & COURRIER, S. (1973). Desensitization of children to television violence. *Journal of Personality and Social Psychology, 27,* 360–365.

CLOR, H. M. (1969). *Obscenity and public morality.* Chicago: University of Chicago Press.

CLORE, G. L., & JEFFREY, K. McM. (1972). Emotional role playing, attitude change, and attraction toward a disabled person. *Journal of Personality and Social Psychology, 23,* 105–111.

COCHRANE, P. (1978). Sex crimes and pornography revisited. *International Journal of Criminology, 6,* 307–317.

Cohen v. *California,* 403 U.S. 15 (1971).

COHEN, M. L., GAROFALO, R., BOUCHER, R., & SEGHORN, T. (1971). The psychology of rapists. *Seminars in Psychiatry, 3,* 307–327.

COLES, C. D., & SHAMP, M. J. (1984). Some sexual, personality, and demographic characteristics of women readers of erotic romances. *Archives of Sexual Behavior, 13*(3), 187–209.

COLKER, R. (1983). Pornography and privacy towards the development of a group based theory for sex based intrusions of privacy. *Law & Inequality, 1,* 191.

COLLINS, W. A., SOBOL, B. L., & WESTBY, S. (1981). Effects of adult commentary on children's comprehension and inferences about a televised aggressive portrayal. *Child Development, 52,* 158–163.

COLSON, C. E. (1974). The evaluation of pornography: Effects of attitude and perceived physiological reaction. *Archives of Sexual Behavior, 3,* 307–323.

Comment (1975). Washington's attempt to view sexual assault as more than a "violation" of the moral woman: The revision of the rape laws. *Gonzaga Law Review, 11,* 145–177.

Comment (1976). Toward a consent standard in the law of rape. *University of Chicago Law Review, 43,* 613–645.

Committee on Obscenity and Film Censorship (1979). *Report of the Committee on Obscenity and Film Censorship.* Cmnd. 772. London: Her Majesty's Stationery Office.

Commission on Obscenity and Pornography. (1970). *The report of the Commission on Obscenity and Pornography.* Washington, D.C.: U.S. Government Printing Office.

Commonwealth v. *Sharpless,* 2 S. & R. (Pa 1815).

COMSTOCK, G. (1978). The impact of television on American institutions. *Journal of Communication, 28,* 12–28.

——— New emphases in research on the effects of television and film violence. In *Children and the faces of television: Teaching, violence, selling.* New York: Academic Press.

COMSTOCK, G., CHAFFEE, S., KATZMAN, N., McCOMBS, M., & ROBERTS, D. (1978). *Television and human behavior.* New York: Columbia University Press.

COOK, R. F., & FOSEN, R. H. (1970). Pornography and the sex offender: Patterns of exposure and immediate arousal effects of pornographic stimuli. *Technical reports of the Commission on Obscenity and Pornography* (Vol. 7). Washington, D.C.: U.S. Government Printing Office.

COOK, R. F., FOSEN, R. H., & PACHT, A. (1971). Pornography and the sex offender: Patterns of previous exposure and arousal effects of pornographic stimuli. *Journal of Applied Psychology, 55,* 503–511.

COOK, T. D., & FLAY, B. R. (1978). The persistence of experimentally induced attitude change. In L. Berkowitz (Ed.), *Advances in experimental social psychology* (Vol. 11). New York: Academic Press.

COOK, T. D., KENDZIERSKI, D. A., & THOMAS, S. V. (1983). The implicit assumptions of television research: An analysis of the 1982 NIMH report on television and behavior. *Public Opinion Quarterly, 47,* 161–201.

COONS, W. H., & McFARLAND, P. A. (1985). Obscenity and community tolerance. *Canadian Psychology, 26*(1), 30–38.

CORDER-BOLZ, C. (1982). Television literacy and critical television viewing skills. In D. Pearl, L. Bouthilet, & J. Lazar (Eds.), *Television and behavior: Ten years of scientific progress and implications for the eighties* (Vol. 2: Technical reviews). Rockville, MD: U.S. Department of Health and Human Services.

CORRY, J. (1983, July 31). The networks shrug off violence. *The New York Times,* Arts and Leisure Section.

COSTIN, F. (1985). Beliefs about rape and women's social roles. *Archives of Sexual Behavior, 14,* 319–325.

COURT, J. H. (1976). Pornography and sex-crimes: A re-evaluation in the light of recent trends around the world. *International Journal of Criminology and Penology, 5,* 129–157.

——— (1979). Rape and pornography in white South Africa. *De Jure, 12,* 236–241.

————(1980). *Pornography and the harm condition.* Adelaide: Flinders University.

————(1981, May). Pornography update. *British Journal of Sexual Medicine,* pp. 28–30.

————(1982). Rape and trends in New South Wales: A discussion of conflicting evidence. *Australian Journal of Social Issues, 17,* 202–206.

————(1984). Sex and violence: A ripple effect. In N. Malamuth & E. Donnerstein (Eds.), *Pornography and sexual aggression.* Orlando, FL: Academic Press.

COWAN, G. (1979). *See no evil: The backstage battle over sex and violence on television.* New York: Simon & Schuster.

Cox, M. (1979). Dynamic psychotherapy with sex-offenders. In I. Rosen (Ed.), *Sexual deviation.* Oxford: Oxford University Press.

CREPAULT, C. (1972). Sexual fantasies and visualization of pornographic scenes. *Journal of Sex Research, 8,* 154–155.

CUNNINGHAM, S. (1985, August). Motives, mission unclear in pornography probe. *American Psychological Association Monitor, 16*(8), 26–27.

CURTIS, L. A. (1976). Sexual combat. *Society, 13,* 69–72.

DAVIDOW, R. P., & O'BOYLE, M. (1977). Obscenity laws in England and the United States: A comparative analysis. *Nebraska Law Review, 56,* 249–288.

DAVIDSON, G. C., & WILSON, G. T. (1973). Processes of fear-reduction in systematic desensitization: Cognitive and social reinforcement factors in humans. *Behavior Therapy, 4,* 1–21.

DAVIS, J., & SMITH, T. (1982). *General social surveys, 1972–1982: Cumulative codebook.* National Opinion Research Center. Chicago: University of Chicago Press.

DAVIS, K. E., & BRAUCHT, G. N. (1970). Exposure to pornography, character and sexual deviance. *Technical reports of the Commission on Obscenity and Pornography*(Vol. 7). Washington, D.C.: U.S. Government Printing Office.

————(1973). Exposure to pornography, character, and sexual deviance: A retrospective survey. *Journal of Social Issues, 29,* 183–196.

Defendants' memorandum in opposition to plantiff's motion for a summary judgment, Cause No. IP 84-761C (S.D. Ind. July 3, 1984), p. 8.

DeGRAZIA, E., & NEWMAN, R. K. (1982). *Banned films: Movies, censors, & the First Amendment.* New York: Bowker.

DEITZ, S. R., BLACKWELL, K. T., & DALEY, P. C. (1982). Measurement of empathy toward rape victims and rapists. *Journal of Personality and Social Psychology, 43,* 372–384.

DEITZ, S. R., & BYRNES, L. E. (1981). Attribution of responsibility for

Sexual Assault: The influence of observer empathy and defendant occupation and attractiveness. *The Journal of Psychology, 108,* 17–29.

DEMARE, D. (1985). *The effects of erotic and sexually violent mass media on attitudes toward women and rape.* Unpublished manuscript, University of Winnipeg, Winnipeg, Manitoba.

DENGERINK, H. A. (1976). Personality variables as mediators of attack-instigated aggression. In R. G. Geen & E. C. O'Neal (Eds.), *Perspectives on aggression.* New York: Academic Press.

DERMER, M., & PYSZCZYNSKI, T. A. (1978). Effects of erotica upon men's loving and liking responses for women they love. *Journal of Personality and Social Psychology, 36,* 1302–1309.

DEROGATIS, L. R. (1977). *SCL-90: Administration, scoring and procedures manual — I, and other instruments of the psychopathology rating scale series.* Johns Hopkins University School of Medicine, Clinical Psychometrics Research Unit, Baltimore.

DIAMOND, I. (1980). Pornography and repression: A reconsideration. *Signs, 5,* 686–701.

DIENSTBIER, R. A. (1977). Sex and violence: Can research have it both ways? *Journal of Communication, 27,* 176–188.

DIETZ, P. E., & EVANS, B. (1982). Pornographic imagery and prevalence of paraphilia. *American Journal of Psychiatry, 139,* 1493–1495.

DIETZ, P. E., HARRY, B., & HAZELWOOD, R. R. (1986). Detective magazines: Pornography for the sexual sadist? *Journal of Forensic Sciences,* JFSCA, *31*(1), 197–211.

DOUGLAS, D. (1966). *Horror!* New York: Macmillan.

DOMINICK, J., & GREENBERG, B. S. (1972). Attitudes toward violence: Interaction of television, social class, and family attitudes. In G. Comstock & E. A. Rubinstein (Eds.), *Television and social behaviour, Vol. 3: Television and adolescent aggressiveness.* Washington, D.C.: U.S. Government Printing Office.

DONNERSTEIN, E. (1979). Pornography and sexual violence. *Medical Aspects of Human Sexuality, 13,* 103.

———(1980a). Aggressive erotica and violence against women. *Journal of Personality and Social Psychology, 39,* 269–277.

———(1980b). Pornography and violence against women. *Annals of the New York Academy of Sciences, 347,* 277–288.

———(1983). Erotica and human aggression. In R. Geen & E. Donnerstein (Eds.), *Aggression: Theoretical and empirical reviews.* New York: Academic Press.

———(1983). Aggressive pornography: Can it influence aggression against women? In G. Albee, S. Gordon, & H. Leitenberg (Eds.), *Promot-*

ing sexual responsibility and preventing sexual problems. Hanover, NH: University of New England Press.

——— (1984). Pornography: Its effect on violence against women. In M. Malamuth and E. Donnerstein (Eds.), *Pornography and sexual aggression.* New York, Academic Press.

DONNERSTEIN, E., & BARRETT, G. (1978). The effects of erotic stimuli on male aggression toward females. *Journal of Personality and Social Psychology, 36,* 180–188.

DONNERSTEIN, E., & BERKOWITZ, L. (1981). Victim reactions in aggressive erotic films as a factor in violence against women. *Journal of Personality and Social Psychology, 41,* 710–724.

DONNERSTEIN, E., & BERKOWITZ, L. (1983). *Effects of film content and victim association on aggressive behavior and attitudes.* Unpublished manuscript, University of Wisconsin, Madison.

DONNERSTEIN, E., BERKOWITZ, L., & LINZ, D. (1986). *Role of aggressive and sexual images in violent pornography.* Unpublished manuscript, University of Wisconsin, Madison.

DONNERSTEIN, E., DONNERSTEIN, M., & BARRETT, G. (1976). Where is the facilitation of media violence: The effects of nonexposure and placement of anger arousal. *Journal of Research in Personality, 10,* 386–398.

DONNERSTEIN, E., DONNERSTEIN, M., & EVANS, R. (1975). Erotic stimuli and aggression: Facilitation or inhibition. *Journal of Personality and Social Psychology, 32,* 237–244.

DONNERSTEIN, E., & HALLAM, J. (1978). Facilitating effects of erotica on aggression against women. *Journal of Personality and Social Psychology, 36,* 1270–1277.

DONNERSTEIN, E., & LINZ, D. (1984, January). Sexual violence in the media, a warning. *Psychology Today,* pp. 14–15.

——— (1986). Mass media sexual violence and male viewers: Current theory and research. *American Behavioral Scientist, 29,* 601–618.

DONNERSTEIN, E., & MALAMUTH, N. (1982a). Pornography: Its consequences on the observer. In L. B. Schlesinger (Ed.), *Sexual dynamics of antisocial behavior.* Springfield, IL: Charles C. Thomas.

DONNERSTEIN, E., MUELLER, C., & HALLAM, J. (1983). *Erotica and aggression toward women: The role of aggressive models.* Unpublished manuscript, University of Wisconsin, Madison.

DONNERSTEIN, E., PENROD, S., & LINZ, D. (1984). *Report to the Human Subjects Committee: Reply to the committee's letter of August 13, 1984.* Unpublished manuscript, University of Wisconsin, Madison.

DONNERSTEIN, E., & WILSON, D. W. (1976). Effects of noise and perceived control on ongoing and subsequent aggressive behavior. *Journal of Personality and Social Psychology, 34,* 774–481.

DOOLITTLE, J. (1976). *Immunizing children against the possible anti-social effects of viewing television violence: A curricular intervention.* Unpublished doctoral dissertation, University of Wisconsin, Madison.

DORR, A. (1981). Television viewing and fear of functioning: Maybe this decade. *Journal of Broadcasting, 25,* 334–345.

DORR, A., GRAVES, S., & PHELPS, E. (1980, Summer). Television literacy for young children. *Journal of Communication, 30,* 71–83.

DORR, A., & KOVARIC, P. (1980). Some of the people some of the time — but which people? Televised violence and its effects. In E. L. Palmer & A. Dorr (Eds.), *Children and the faces of television.* New York: Academic Press.

DRABMAN, R., & THOMAS, M. (1974). Does media violence increase children's toleration of real-life aggression? *Developmental Psychology, 10,* 418–421.

DUGGAN, L. (1984, October 16). Censorship in the name of feminism. *Village Voice,* pp. 11–12; 16–17; 42.

DUNWOODY, V., & PEZDEK, K. (1979). Factors affecting the sexual arousal value of pictures. *Journal of Sex Research, 15,* 276–284.

DUTCHER, L. W. (1975). Scarcity and erotica: An examination of commodity theory dynamics. *Dissertation Abstracts International, 37(6-B),* 3069.

DWORKIN, A. (1979). Pornography: The new terrorism. *New York University Review of Law and Social Change, 8,* 215–218.

——— (1981). *Pornography: Men possessing women.* New York: Perigee.

——— (1984). *Effect of pornography on women and children.* Testimony at the Hearings before the Subcommittee on Juvenile Justice of the Comm. on the Judiciary, 98th Cong., 2nd Sess., 227–255.

——— (1985). Against the male flood: Censorship, pornography, and equality. *Harvard Women's Law Journal, 8,* 1–29.

EGAN, D. (1955). *Testimony before Senate Subcommittee to Investigate Juvenile Delinquency,* Committee on the Judiciary, 84th Congress, 1st Session, Hearings pursuant to S. Res. 62, May 24, 26, 31, June 9, 18; p. 72.

EINSIEDEL, E. (1986). Social and behavior science research analysis. In *Attorney General's Commission on Pornography Final Report.* Washington, D.C.: U.S. Government Printing Office.

EISENMAN, P. (1983). Sexual behavior as related to sex fantasies and experimental manipulation of authoritarianism and creativity. *Journal of Personality and Social Psychology, 48,* 853–860.

ELLIS, L., & BEATTIE, C. (1983). The feminist explanation for rape: An empirical test. *Journal of Sex Research, 19(1),* 74–93.

Elmore v. *American Motors.* 70 578 (*California Reporter,* 1969).

ENGLAR, R. C., & WALKER, C. E. (1973). Male and female reactions to erotic literature. *Psychological Reports, 32,* 481–482.

ERON, L. D. (1980). Prescription for a reduction of aggression. *American Psychologist, 35,* 244–252.

——— (1986). Interventions to mitigate the psychological effects of media violence on aggressive behavior. *Journal of Social Issues, 42*(3).

ERON, L. D., & HUESMANN, L. R. (1980). Adolescent aggression and television. *Annals of the New York Academy of Sciences, 347,* 319–331.

EYSENCK, H. J. (1978). *Sex and personality.* London: Open Books.

——— (1972). The uses and abuses of pornography. In H. J. Eysenck (Ed.), *Psychology is about people.* London: Penguin.

EYSENCK, H. J., & NIAS, H. (1978). *Sex, violence, and the media.* London: Spector.

FALWELL, J. (1980). *Listen America.* Garden City, NY: Doubleday.

FARKAS, G. M. (1979). *Trait and state determinants of male sexual arousal to description of coercive sexuality.* Doctoral dissertation, University of Hawaii.

FARKAS, G. M., SINE, L. F., & EVANS, I. M. (1978). Personality, sexuality, and demographic differences between volunteers and nonvolunteers for a laboratory study of male sexual behavior. *Archives of Sexual Behaviour, 87,* 513.

——— (1979). The effects of distraction, performance demand, stimulus explicitness and personality on objective and subjective measures of male sexual arousal. *Behaviour Research and Therapy, 17*(1), 25–32.

FCC v. *Pacific Foundation,* 438 U.S. 726, 742–748 (1978).

FEHR, F. S., & SCHULMAN, M. (1978). Female self-report and autonomic responses to sexually pleasurable and sexually aversive readings. *Archives of Sexual Behavior, 7*(5), 443–453.

FEILD, H. S. (1978). Attitudes towards rape: A comparative analysis of police, rapists, crisis counsellors and citizens. *Journal of Personality and Social Psychology, 36,* 156–179.

FEINBERG, J. (1979). Pornography and criminal law. In D. Copp & S. Wendell (Eds.), *Pornography and censorship.* New York: Prometheus.

——— (1983). *The moral limits of law.* New York: Oxford University Press.

FESHBACH, S. (1972). Reality and fantasy in filmed violence. In J. Murray, E. Rubinstein, & G. Comstock (Eds.), *Television and social behavior* (Vol. 2). Washington, D.C.: Dept. of Health, Education and Welfare.

Filmgore [Film] (1983). K. Dixon (Director). Filmgore productions.

FINKLEHOR, D. (1984). *Child sexual abuse: New theory and research.* New York: Free Press.

FINKLEHOR, D., & ARAJI, S. (1983). *Explanations of pedophilia: A four factor model.* Durham, NH: University of New Hampshire.

FISHER, J. L., & HARRIS, M. B. (1976). Modeling, arousal, and aggression. *The Journal of Social Psychology, 100,* 219–226.

FISHER, W. A. (1976). *Individual differences in behavioral responsiveness to erotica: Cognitive labeling, transfer of arousal, and disinhibition considerations.* Unpublished master's thesis, Purdue University.

FISHER, W. A., & BYRNE, D. (1976, May). *Individual differences in socialization to sex as mediators of responses to an erotic film: Teach your children well.* Paper presented at the Midwestern Psychological Association, Chicago.

———(1978). Individual differences in affective, evaluative, and behavioral responses to an erotic film. *Journal of Applied Social Psychology, 8,* 355–365.

———(1978). Sex differences in response to erotica? Love versus lust. *Journal of Personality and Social Psychology, 36,* 117–125.

FLAY, B. R. (1985). Psychosocial approaches to smoking prevention: A review of findings. *Health Psychology, 4,* 449–488.

———(1986, May). *Mass media and smoking cessation.* Paper presented at the International Communication Association, Chicago.

FLAY, B. R., & SOBEL, J. L. (1983). The role of mass media in preventing adolescent substance abuse. In T. Glynn, C. Leukfeld, & J. Ludford (Eds.), *Preventing adolescent drug abuse: Intervention strategies.* Washington, D.C.: National Institute on Drug Abuse, Research Monograph 47.

FODDY, W. H. (1981). Obscenity reactions: Toward a symbolic interactionist explanation. *Journal for the Theory of Social Behavior, 11,* 125–146.

Freedman v. *State of Maryland,* 380 U.S. 51, 85 S.Ct. 734 (1965).

FREEDMAN, J. L. (1965). Long-term behavioral effects of cognitive dissonance. *Journal of Experimental Social Psychology, 1,* 145–155.

———(1984). Effect of television violence on aggressiveness. *Psychological Bulletin, 96,* 227–246.

FRIDAY, N. (1980). *Men in love.* New York: Delacorte.

FRIEDMAN, H., & JOHNSON, R. L. (1972). Mass media use and aggression: A pilot study. In G. A. Comstock & E. A. Rubinstein (Eds.), *Television and social behaviour, Vol. 3: Television and adolescent aggressiveness.* Washington, D.C.: U.S. Government Printing Office.

FRODI, A. (1977). Sexual arousal, situational restrictiveness, and aggressive behavior. *Journal of Research in Personality, 11,* 48–58.

FRODI, A., MACAULEY, J., & THOME, P. R. (1977). Are women always less aggressive than men? A review of the experimental literature. *Psychological Bulletin, 84,* 634–660.

FROMKIN, H. L., & BROCK, T. C. (1973). Erotic materials: A commodity theory analysis of the enhanced desirability that may accompany their unavailability. *Journal of Applied Social Psychology, 3,* 219–231.

FURNHAM, A., & GUNTER, B. (1985). Sex, presentation mode and memory for violent and non-violent news. *Journal of Educational Television, 11,* 99–105.

GAERTNER, S. L., & DOVIDIO, J. F. (1977). The subtlety of white racism, arousal, and helping behavior. *Journal of Personality and Social Psychology, 35,* 691–707.

GAGER, N., & SCHURR, C. (1978). *Sexual assault: Confronting rape in America.* New York: Grosset & Dunlap.

GAGNON, J. H., & SIMON, W. (1967). *Sexual deviance.* New York: Harper & Row.

———(1973). *Sexual conduct: The social sources of human sexuality.* Chicago: Aldine.

GAUGHAN, E., & MICHAEL, W. (1973). College student rating of arousal value of pornographic photographs. *Proceedings of the 81st Annual Convention of the American Psychological Association, 8,* 409–410.

GEBHARD, P. H., GAGNON, J. H., POMEROY, W. B., & CHRISTENSON, C. V. (1965). *Sex offenders: An analysis of types.* New York: Harper & Row.

GEEN, R. G. (1975). The meaning of observed violence: Real vs. fictional violence and consequent effects on aggression and emotional arousal. *Journal of Research in Personality, 9,* 270–281.

———(1976). Observing violence in the mass media: Implications of basic research. In R. Geen & E. O'Neal (Eds.), *Perspectives on aggression.* New York: Academic Press.

———(1978). Some effects of observing violence upon the behavior of the observer. In B. Maher (Ed.), *Progress in experimental personality research* (Vol. 8). New York: Academic Press.

———(1981). Behavioral and physiological reactions to observed violence: Effects of prior exposure to aggressive stimuli. *Journal of Personality and Social Psychology, 40,* 868–875.

GEEN, R. G., & BERKOWITZ, L. (1966a). Film violence and the cue properties of available targets. *Journal of Personality and Social Psychology, 3,* 525–530.

———(1966b). Name-mediated aggressive cue properties. *Journal of Personality, 34,* 456–465.

———(1967a). Some conditions facilitating the occurrence of aggression after the observation of violence. *Journal of Personality, 35,* 666–676.

———(1967b). Stimulus qualities of the target of aggression: A further study. *Journal of Personality and Social Psychology, 5,* 364–368.

GEEN, R. G., & QUANTY, M. B. (1977). The catharsis of aggression: An evaluation of a hypothesis. In L. Berkowitz (Ed.), *Advances in experimental social psychology* (Vol. 10), New York: Academic Press.

GEEN, R. G., & RAKOSKY, J. J. (1973). Interpretations of observed violence and their effects on GSR. *Journal of Experimental Research in Personality, 6,* 289–292.

GEEN, R. G., STONNER, C., & SHOPE, G. L. (1975). The facilitation of aggression by aggression: Evidence against the catharsis hypothesis. *Journal of Personality and Social Psychology, 31,* 721–726.

GEEN, R. G., & THOMAS, S. L. (1986). The immediate effects of media violence on behavior. *Journal of Social Issues, 42*(3).

GEER, J. H., & FUHR, R. (1976). Cognitive factors in sexual arousal: The role of distraction. *Journal of Consulting and Clinical Psychology, 44,* 238–243.

GEER, J. H., MOROKOFF, P., & GREENWOOD, P. (1974). Sexual arousal in women: The development of a measurement device for vaginal blood volume. *Archives of Sexual Behavior, 3,* 559–564.

GEIS, G. (1977). Forcible rape: An introduction. In D. Chappell, R. Geis, & G. Geis (Eds.), *Forcible rape: The crime, the victim and the offender.* New York: Columbia University Press.

GEIS, G., & GEIS, R. (1979). Rape in Stockholm: Is permissiveness relevant? *Criminology, 17,* 311–322.

GERBNER, G. (1972). Violence in television drama: Trends and symbolic functions. In G. A. Comstock & E. S. Rubinstein (Eds.), *Television and social behavior, Vol. 1: Media content and control.* Washington, D.C.: U.S. Government Printing Office.

GERETY, T. (1979). Pornography and violence. *University of Pittsburgh Law Review, 40,* 627–651.

GIARRUSSO, R., JOHNSON, P., GOODCHILDS, J. D., & ZELLMAN, G. (1979, April). *Adolescents' cues and signals: Sex and assault.* Symposium presented at the meeting of the Western Psychological Association, San Diego.

GIBBONS, F. X. (1973). Sexual standards and reactions to pornography: Enhancing behavioral consistency through self-focused attention. *Journal of Personality and Social Psychology, 36,* 976–987.

GLASSMAN, M. B. (1979). A uses and gratifications approach to the study of sexual materials. *Dissertation Abstracts International, 40*(-A), 467.

GOLDSTEIN, M. J. (1973). Exposure to erotic stimuli and sexual deviance. *Journal of Social Issues, 29*(3), 197–219.

———(1977). A behavioral scientist looks at obscenity. In B. D. Sales (Ed.), *The criminal justice system.* New York: Plenum.

GOLDSTEIN, M. J., & KANT, H. S. (with Hartman, J. J.) (1973). *Pornography and sexual deviance: A report of the legal and behavioral institute.* Berkeley: University of California Press.

GOLDSTEIN, M., KANT, H., JUDD, L., RICE, C., & GEEN, R. (1970). Exposure to pornography and sexual behavior in deviant and normal groups. *Technical Reports of the Commission on Obscenity and Pornography* (Vol. 7). Washington, D.C.: U.S. Government Printing Office.

————(1971). Experience with pornography: Rapists, pedophiles, homosexuals, transsexuals, and controls. *Archives of Sexual Behavior, 1,* 1–15.

GOODMAN, W. (1984, July 3). Battle on pornography spurred by new tactics. *New York Times.*

GORANSON, R. E. (1970). Media violence and aggressive behavior: A review of experimental research. In L. Berkowitz (Ed.), *Advances in experimental social psychology* (Vol. 5). New York: Academic Press.

GORDON, M., & BELL, R. R. (1969). Medium and hardcore pornography: A comparative analysis. *Journal of Sex Research, 5,* 260–268.

GOSSELIN, C. (1978). Personality attributes of the averse rubber fetishist. In M. Cook & G. D. Wilson (Eds.), *Love and attraction: An international conference.* Oxford: Pergamon.

GOULD, L. (1977). Pornography for women. In T. H. Gagmen (Ed.), *Human sexuality in today's world.* Boston: Little, Brown.

GRAY, C. (1984). Pornography and violent entertainment: Exposing the symptoms. *Canadian Medical Association Journal, 130,* 769–772.

GRAY, S. H. (1982). Exposure to pornography and aggression toward women: The case of the angry male. *Social Problems, 29,* 387–398.

GRIFFIN, S. (1981). *Pornography and silence.* New York: Harper & Row.

GRIFFITT, W. (1973). Response to erotica and the projection of response to erotica in the opposite sex. *Journal of Experimental Research in Personality, 6,* 330–338.

————Sexual experience and sexual responsiveness: Sex differences. *Archives of Sexual Behavior, 4,* 32–235.

————(1979). Sexual stimulation and sociosexual behaviors. In M. Cook & G. Wilson (Eds.), *Love and attraction.* Oxford: Pergamon.

GRIFFITT, W., & KAISER, D. L. (1978). Affect, sex guilt, gender, and the rewarding-punishing effects of erotic stimuli. *Journal of Personality and Social Psychology, 36,* 850–850.

GRIFFITT, W., MAY, J., & VEITCH, R. (1974). Sexual stimulation and interpersonal behavior: Heterosexual evaluative responses, visual behavior, and physical proximity. *Journal of Personality and Social Psychology, 3,* 367–377.

GROSS, L. S. (1983). *Telecommunications: An introduction to radio, television and the developing media.* Dubuque, IA: W. C. Brown.

GROTH, N. A. (1979). *Men who rape: The psychology of the offender.* New York: Plenum.

GROTH, N., & BURGESS, A. W. (1977). Rape: A sexual deviation. *American Journal of Orthopsychiatry, 47,* 400–406.

GROTH, N., BURGESS, A. W., & HOLMSTROM, L. L. (1977). Rape: Power, anger, and sexuality. *American Journal of Psychiatry, 134,* 1239–1243.

GROTH, N. A., & HOBSON, W. F. (1983). The dynamics of sexual assault. In L. B. Schlesinger & E. Revitch (Eds.), *Sexual dynamics of anti-social behavior.* Springfield, IL: Charles C. Thomas.

GRUSEC, J. (1973). Effects of co-observer evaluations on imitation: A developmental study. *Developmental Psychology, 8,* 141.

GUNTER, B. (1983). Personality and perceptions of harmful and harmless TV violence. *Personality and Individual Differences, 4,* 665–670.

GUNTER, B., & FURNHAM, A. (1983). Personality and the perception of TV violence. *Personality and Individual Differences, 4,* 315–321.

——— (1985). Androgyny and the perception of television violence as perpetrated by males and females. *Human Relations, 38,* 535–549.

GUTIERRES, S., KENRICK, D., & GOLDBERG, L. (1983, August). *Adverse effect of popular erotica on judgments of one's mate.* Paper presented at the 91st annual convention of the American Psychological Association, Anaheim, CA.

HALL, E. R., & FLANNERY, P. J. (1984). Prevalence and correlates of sexual assault experiences in adolescents. *Victimology: An International Journal, 9,* 398–406.

HAMMER, E. F. (1954). A comparison of H-T-Ps of rapists and pedophiles. *Journal of Projective Techniques, 18,* 346–354.

HAMRICK, N. D. (1974). Physiological and verbal responses to erotic visual stimuli in a female population. *Behavioral Engineering, 2,* 9–16.

HANS, V. P. (1980, September). *Pornography and feminism: Empirical evidence and directions for research.* Paper presented at the annual meeting of the American Psychological Association, Montreal.

HARLECH, RT. HON. THE LORD (1982, March). *Film censorship in Britain— Past, present and future.* Presentation given at International Conference of Film Regulators, London.

HATFIELD, E., SPRECHER, S., & TRAUPMANN, J. (1978). Men's and women's reactions to sexually explicit films: A serendipitous finding. *Archives of Sexual Behavior, 7,* 583–591.

HAWKINS, R. P., & PINGREE, S. (1982). Television's influence on constructions on social reality. In D. Pearl, L. Bouthilet, & J. Lazar (Eds.), *Television and behavior: Ten years of scientific progress and implications for the eighties, Vol. 2: Technical Reports.* Washington, D.C.: U.S. Government Printing Office.

HAYES, S. C., BROWNELL, K. D., & BARLOW, D. H. (1978). The use of self-administered covert sensitization in the treatment of exhibitionism and sadism. *Behavior Therapy, 9,* 283–289.

HEAROLD, S. L. (1979). *Meta-analysis of the effect of television on social behavior.* Unpublished doctoral dissertation, University of Colorado.

HEFFNER, R. (1984, September). *Film classification.* Presentation to the Film Regulators Second International Conference, Toronto.

HEIMAN, J. A., & HATCH, J. P. (1980). Affective and physiological dimensions of male sexual response to erotica and fantasy. *Basic and Applied Social Psychology, 1,* 315–327.

HEIMAN, J. R. (1975, April). Women's sexual arousal: The physiology of erotica. *Psychology Today,* pp. 90–94.

——— (1977). A psychophysiological exploration of sexual arousal patterns in females and males. *Psychophysiology, 14,* 226–274.

HENLEY, N. M. (1977). *Body politics: Power, sex and nonverbal communication.* Englewood Cliffs, NJ: Prentice-Hall.

HENN, F. A. (1978). The aggressive sexual offender. In I. L. Kutash, S. B. Kutash, & L. B. Schlesinger (Eds.), *Victimology: A new focus.* Lexington, MA: Lexington Books.

HENSON, D., & RUBIN, H. (1971). Voluntary control of eroticism. *Journal of Applied Behavior Analysis, 4,* 37–44.

HERMAN, S. H., BARLOW, D. H., & AGRAS, W. S. (1974). An experimental analysis of exposure to "explicit" heterosexual stimuli as an effective variable in changing arousal patterns of homosexuals. *Behavior Research and Therapy, 12,* 335–345.

HERRELL, J. M. (1975). Sex differences in emotional responses to "erotic literature." *Journal of Consulting and Clinical Psychology, 43,* 921.

HICKS, D. (1968). Effects of co-observer's sanctions and adult presence on imitative aggression. *Child Development, 38,* 303–308.

HIGH, R., RUBIN, H., & HENSON, E. (1979). Color as a variable in making an erotic film more arousing. *Archives of Sexual Behavior, 8,* 263–267.

HILKER, A. K. (1979). Tort liability of the media for audience acts of violence. A constitutional analysis. *Southern California Law Review, 52,* 529–571.

HINDELANG, M. (1981). Variations in sex-race-age specific incidence of offending. *American Sociological Review, 46,* 461–474.

HINTON, J. W., O'NEILL, M. T., & WEBSTER, S. (1980). Psychophysiological assessment of sex offenders in a security hospital. *Archives of Sexual Behavior, 9,* 205–216.

HOLBROOK, D. (1973). *The case against pornography.* New York: Library Press.

HOLMSTROM, L. L., & BURGESS, A. W. (1983). Rape and everyday life. *Society, 6,* 33–40.

HOON, P. W., WINCZE, J. P., & HOON, E. F. (1977). A test of reciprocal

234   *The Question of Pornography*

inhibition: Are anxiety and sexual arousal in women mutually inhibitory. *Journal of Abnormal Psychology, 86,* 65–74.

HOROWITZ, M. J. (1969). Psychic trauma: Return of images after a stress film. *Archives of General Psychiatry, 20,* 552–559.

HOROWITZ, M. J., & BECKER, S. S. (1973). Cognitive response to erotic and stressful films. *Archives of General Psychiatry, 29,* 81–84.

HOUSTON, J. A. (1974). Capturing policies of pornographic pictorial representations by normative judgment analysis. *Dissertation Abstracts International, 34*(9-B), 5713–5714.

HOUSTON, J. A., & HOUSTON, S. (1974). Identifying pornographic materials with judgment analysis. *Journal of Experimental Education, 42,* 18–26.

HOUSTON, J. A., HOUSTON, S., & OHLSON, E. (1974a). On determining pornographic material. *Journal of Psychology, 88,* 277–287.

HOUSTON, J. A., HOUSTON, S., & OHLSON, E. (1974b). The atypicality of pornography and public policy: A pilot investigation. *Psychology, 11*(4), 3–7.

HOWARD, J. L., LIPTZIN, M. B., & REIFLER, C. B. (1973). Is pornography a problem? *Journal of Social Issues, 29,* 133–145.

HOWARD, J. L., REIFLER, C. B., & LIPTZIN, M. B. (1970). Effects of exposure to pornography. In *Technical report of the Commission on Obscenity and Pornography* (Vol. 8). Washington, D.C.: U.S. Government Printing Office.

HOWITT, D. (1982). *Mass media and social problems.* New York: Pergamon.

HUESMANN, L. (1982). Television violence and aggressive behavior. In D. Pearl, L. Bouthilet, & J. Lazar (Eds.), *Television and behavior: Ten years of scientific progress and implications for the eighties.* Rockville, MD: Department of Health and Human Services.

HUESMANN, L. R., ERON, I., KLEIN, R., BRICE, P., & FISCHER, P. (1981). *Mitigating the imitation of aggressive behaviors.* Technical Report, Department of Psychology, University of Illinois at Chicago Circle.

———(1983). Mitigating the imitation of aggressive behavior by changing children's attitudes about media violence. *Journal of Personality and Social Psychology, 44,* 899–910.

HUESMANN, L. R., LAGERSPETZ, K., & ERON, L. D. (1984). Intervening variables in the TV violence-aggression relation: Evidence from two countries. *Developmental Psychology, 20,* 746–755.

HUNT, M. (1974). *Sexual behavior in the 1970s.* New York: Dell.

HYMAN, S. E. (1970). In defense of pornography. In D. A. Hughes (Ed.), *Perspectives on pornography.* New York: St. Martin's Press.

Indianapolis and Marion County, Ind., Ordinance 35, sec. 2, 16-3(q) Proposal No. 298 (June 15, 1984).

IRELAND, J. (1978). Reform rape legislation: A new standard for sexual responsibility. *University of Colorado Law Review, 49,* 185–204.

ISTVAN, J. (1983). Effects of sexual orientation on interpersonal judgment. *Journal of Sex Research, 19,* 178–191.

IWAWAKI, S., & WILSON, G. (1983). Sex fantasies in Japan. *Personality and Individual Differences, 4,* 543–545.

IZARD, C. E., & CAPLAN, S. (1974). Sex differences in emotional responses to erotic literature. *Journal of Consulting and Clinical Psychology, 42,* 468.

Jacobellis v. *Ohio,* 378 U.S. 184 (1964).

JAFFE, Y. (1975). *Sex and aggression: An intimate relationship.* Unpublished doctoral dissertation, University of California, Los Angeles.

JAFFE, Y., & BERGER, A. (1977). Cultural generality of the relationship between sex and aggression. *Psychological Report, 41,* 335–336.

JAFFE, Y., MALAMUTH, N., FEINGOLD, J., & FESHBACH, S. (1974). Sexual arousal and behavioral aggression. *Journal of Personality and Social Psychology, 30,* 759–764.

JAKOBOVITS, L. (1965). Evaluational reactions to erotic literature. *Psychological Reports, 16,* 985–994.

JOHN, P., & GOODCHILDS, J. (1973). Pornography, sexuality and social psychology. *Journal of Social Issues, 29,* 231–238.

JOHNSON, W. T., KUPPERSTEIN, L. R., & PETERS, J. J. (1970). Sex offenders' experience with erotica. In *Technical report of the Commission on Obscenity and Pornography* (Vol. 7). Washington, D.C.: U.S. Government Printing Office.

JONES, R. J., GRUBER, K. J., & FREEMAN, M. H. (1983). Reactions of adolescents to being interviewed about their sexual assault experiences. *Journal of Sex Research, 19,* 160–172.

JONES, R. N., & JOE, V. C. (1980). Pornographic materials and commodity theory. *Journal of Applied Social Psychology, 10,* 311–322.

JULIEN, E., & OVER, R. (1984). Male sexual arousal with repeated exposure to erotic stimuli. *Archives of Sexual Behavior, 13,* 211–222.

KAHNEMANN, D., & TVERSKY, A. (1981). The framing of decisions and the psychology of choice. *Science, 211,* 453–458.

KANIN, E. J. (1957). Male aggression in dating-courtship relations. *American Journal of Sociology, 63,* 197–204.

——— (1965). Male sex aggression and three psychiatric hypotheses. *Journal of Sex Research, 1,* 221–231.

——— (1977). Sexual aggression: A second look at the offended female. *Archives of Sexual Behavior, 6,* 67–76.

——— (1983). Rape as a function of relative sexual frustration. *Psychological Reports, 52,* 133–134.

———(1984). Date rape: Unofficial criminals and victims. *Victimology: An International Journal, 9,* 95–108.

———(1985). Date rapists: Differential sexual socialization and relative deprivation. *Archives of Sexual Behavior, 14,* 219–231.

KANIN, E. J., & PARCELL, S. R. (1977). Sexual aggression: A second look at the offended female. *Archives of Sexual Behavior, 6,* 67–76.

KANT, H. S. (1971). Exposure to pornography and sexual behavior in deviant and normal groups. *Corrective Psychiatry and Journal of Social Therapy, 17,* 5–17.

KANT, H. S., & GOLDSTEIN, M. J. (1978). Pornography and its effects. In D. Savitz & J. Johnson (Eds.), *Crime in society.* New York: Wiley.

KAPLAN, R. (1983). The measurement of human aggression. In R. Kaplan, V. Koenci, & R. Novaco (Eds.), *Aggression in children and youth.* Rijn, Netherlands: Sijthoff & Noordhuff International.

KARACON, I., WILLIAMS, R. L., GUERRARO, M. W., SALIS, P. J., THORNBY, J. I., & HURSCH, C. J. (1974). Nocturnal penile tumescence and sleep of convicted rapists and other prisoners. *Archives of Sexual Behavior, 3,* 19–26.

KARPMAN, J. J. (1954). *The sexual offender and his sex offenses.* New York: The Julian Press.

KATZ, L. (1985). Special alert! *Censorship News, 22,* 1–4.

KAZDIN, A. E., & WILCOXIN, L. A. (1976). Systematic desensitization and nonspecific treatment effects: A methodological evaluation. *Psychological Bulletin, 83,* 729–758.

KELLEY, H. H. (1971). *Attribution in social interaction.* Morristown, NJ: General Learning Corporation.

KELLEY, K. (1985). The effects of sexual and/or aggressive film exposure on helping, hostility, and attitudes about the sexes. *Journal of Research in Personality, 19,* 472–483.

KENRICK, D. T., & GUTIERRES, S. E. (1980). Contrast effects and judgments of physical attractiveness: When beauty becomes a social problem. *Journal of Personality and Social Psychology, 38,* 131–140.

KENRICK, D. T., GUTIERRES, S. E., & GOLDBERG, L. (in press). Influence of popular erotica on interpersonal attraction judgments: The uglier side of pretty pictures. *Journal of Personality and Social Psychology.*

KENRICK, D. T., STRINGFIELD, D. O., WAGENHALS, W. L., DAHL, R. H., & RANDSELL, H. J. (1980). Sex differences, androgyny, and approach responses to erotica: A new variation on the old volunteer problem. *Journal of Personality and Social Psychology, 38,* 517–524.

KENYON, F. E. (1975). Pornography, the law and mental health. *British Journal of Psychiatry, 126,* 225–233.

KERCHER, G. A., & WALKER, C. E. (1973). Reactions of convicted rapists to sexually explicit stimuli. *Journal of Abnormal Psychology, 81,* 46–50.

KILPATRICK, J. J. (1967, April). *Testimony before House of Representatives Select Subcommittee on Education, Committee on Education and Labor, 90th Congress, 1st Session.* Hearing on H. R. 2525, April 20 and 24, 24.

———(1975, January 3). Decriminalization: Pot, yes; but pornography? No! *Lincoln* (Nebraska) *Evening Journal.*

KING, L. (1985). Censorship and law reform: Will changing the laws mean a change for the better? In V. Burstyn (Ed.), *Women against censorship,* Vancouver, B.C.: Douglas McIntyre.

KIRKPATRICK, C., & KANIN, E. (1957). Male sex aggression on a university campus. *American Sociological Review, 22,* 52–58.

KIRKPATRICK, M. (1984). Declaration in Reply Brief of the American Civil Liberties Union and the Indiana Civil Liberties Union as *Amici Curiae. American Booksellers Association* v. *Hudnut,* Cause no. IP 84-791C, (S.D. Ind., 1984).

KIRSCHENER, N. M. (1976). Effect of need for approval and situational variables on the viewing of erotic material. *Journal of Consulting and Clinical Psychology, 44,* 869.

KLEIN, D. (1981). Violence against women: Some considerations regarding its causes and its elimination. *Crime and Delinquency, 27,* 64–80.

KOLARSKY, A., & MADLAFOUSEK, J. (1972). Female behavior and sexual arousal in heterosexual male deviant offenders. *The Journal of Nervous and Mental Disease, 155,* 110–118.

KOLARSKY, A., MADLAFOUSEK, J., & NOVOTNA, V. (1978). Stimuli eliciting sexual arousal in males who offend adult women: An experimental study. *Archives of Sexual Behavior, 7,* 79–87.

KOOP, E. (1983, October). *Presentation to the National Coalition on Television Violence.* Department of Health and Human Services, Washington D.C.

KOSS, M. F., & LEONARD, K. E. (1984). Sexually aggressive men: Empirical findings and theoretical implications. In N. M. Malamuth & E. Donnerstein (Eds.), *Pornography and sexual aggression.* Orlando, FL: Academic Press.

KOSS, M., & OROS, C. (1982). Sexual Experiences Survey: A research instrument investigating aggression and victimization. *Journal of Consulting and Clinical Psychology, 50,* 445–457.

KOSTASH, M. (1985). Second thoughts. In V. Burstyn (Ed.), *Women against censorship.* Vancouver, B.C.: Douglas McIntyre.

KRAFKA, C. L. (1985). *Sexually explicit, sexually violent, and violent media: Effects of multiple naturalistic exposures and debriefing on female viewers.* Unpublished doctoral dissertation, University of Wisconsin, Madison.

KRATTENMAKER, T. G., & POWE, L. A., JR. (1978). Televised violence: First

Amendment principles and social science. *Virginia Law Review, 64,* 1123–1297.

KROGH, I. (1980, November). British report proven wrong on impact of pornography in Denmark. *Newsweekly* (Melbourne), pp. 8–9.

KRUGLANSKI, A. W. (1975). The human subjects in the psychology experiment: Fact and artifact. In L. Berkowitz (Ed.), *Advances in experimental social psychology* (Vol. 8). New York: Academic Press.

KUBIE, L. (1967). *Testimony before House of Representatives Select Subcommittee on Education, Committee on Education and Labor, 90th Congress, 1st Session.* Hearings on H.R. 2525, Washington, D.C., April 20 and 24, p. 69.

KUPPERSTEIN, L., & WILSON, W. C. (1970). Erotica and anti-social behavior: An analysis of selected social indicator statistics. *Technical reports of the Commission on Obscenity and Pornography* (Vol. 7). Washington, D.C.: U.S. Government Printing Office.

KUTCHINSKY, B. (1970a). Pornography in Denmark: Pieces of a jigsaw puzzle collected around New Year 1970. In *Technical reports of the Commission on Obscenity and Pornography* (Vol. 4). Washington, D.C.: U.S. Government Printing Office.

——— (1970b). Sex crimes and pornography in Copenhagen: A survey of attitudes. *Technical reports of the Commission on Obscenity and Pornography* (Vol. 7). Washington, D.C.: U.S. Government Printing Office.

——— (1973a). The effect of easy availability of pornography on the incidence of sex crimes: The Danish experience. *Journal of Social Issues, 29,* 163–181.

——— (1973b). Eroticism without censorship. *International Journal of Criminology and Penology, 1,* 217–225.

——— (1985). Pornography and its effects in Denmark and the United States: A rejoinder and beyond. In *Comparative social research: An annual.*

LABARRE (1955). Obscenity: An anthropological appraisal. *Law and Contemporary Problems, 20,* 533.

LADER, M. H., & MATTHEWS, A. M. (1968). A physiological model of phobic anxiety and desensitization. *Behavioral Research and Therapy, 6,* 411–421.

LANG, A. R., SEARLES, J., LAUERMAN, R., & ADESSO, V. (1980). Expectancy, alcohol, and sex guilt as determinants of interest in and reaction to sexual stimuli. *Journal of Abnormal Psychology, 89,* 644–653.

LANG, P. J. (1977). Imagery in therapy: An information processing analysis of fear. *Behavior Therapy, 8,* 862–886.

——— (1984). Cognition in emotion: Concept and action. In C. E. Izard,

J. Kagan, & R. B. Zajonc (Eds.), *Emotions, cognition, and behavior.* Cambridge: Cambridge University Press.

LANGEVIN, R., PAITICH, D., & RUSSON, A. E. (1985). Are rapists sexually anomalous, aggressive, or both? In R. Langevin (Ed.), *Erotic preference, gender identity, and aggression in men: New research studies.* Hillsdale, NJ: Erlbaum.

LARGEN, M. A. (1976). History of the women's movement in changing attitudes, laws, and treatment toward rape victims. In M. J. Walker & S. L. Brodsky (Eds.), *Sexual assault.* Lexington, MA: D.C. Heath.

Law Reform Commission of Canada. (1977). *Working Paper 10, Limits of the criminal law; Obscenity: A test case.* Ottawa: Minister of Supply and Services Canada.

LAWS, D. R. (1977). A comparison of the measurement characteristics of two circumferential penile transducers. *Archives of Sexual Behavior, 6,* 45–51.

LAWS, D. R., & HOLMEN, M. L. (1978). Sexual response faking by pedophiles. *Criminal Justice and Behavior, 5,* 343–356.

LAZARUS, R. S., & ALFERT, E. (1964). Short-circuiting of threat by experimentally altering cognitive appraisal. *Journal of Abnormal and Social Psychology, 69,* 195–205.

LAZARUS, R. S., SPEISMAN, J. C., MORDKOFF, A. M., & DAVISON, L. A. (1962). A laboratory study of psychological stress produced by a motion picture film. *Psychological Monographs, 76,* (34, Whole No. 533).

LEDERER, L. (1980). *Take back the night: Women on pornography.* New York: William Morrow.

LEFKOWITZ, M. M., ERON, L. D., WALDER, L. O., & HUESMANN, L. R. (1972). Television violence and child aggression: A followup study. In G. A. Comstock and E. A. Rubinstein (Eds.), *Television and social behavior, Vol. 3: Television and adolescent aggressiveness.* Washington, D.C.: U.S. Government Printing Office.

———(1977). *Growing up to be violent: A longitudinal study of the development of aggression.* New York: Pergamon.

LEIFER, A. D., & ROBERTS, D. F. (1972). Children's responses to television violence. In J. P. Murray, E. A. Rubinstein, & G. A. Comstock (Eds.), *Television and social behavior, Vol. 2: Television and social learning.* Washington, D.C.: U.S. Government Printing Office.

LENES, M. S., & HART, E. J. (1975). The influence of pornography and violence on attitudes and guilt. *Journal of School Health, 45,* 447–451.

LEONARD, K. E., & TAYLOR, S. P. (1983). Exposure to pornography, permissive and nonpermissive cues, and male aggression toward females. *Motivation and Emotion, 7,* 291–299.

LEPPER, M. R. (1973). Dissonance, self-perception and honesty in children. *Journal of Personality and Social Psychology, 25,* 65–74.

LERNER, M. J. (1965). The effect of responsibility and choice on a partner's attractiveness following failure. *Journal of Personality, 33,* 178–187.

———(1971). Observer's evaluation of a victim: Justice, guilt, and veridical perception. *Journal of Personality and Social Psychology, 20,* 127–135.

LESTER, D. (1974). Rape and social structure. *Psychological Reports, 35,* 146.

LEVENTHAL, H. (1977). An empirical inquiry into the effect of *Miller v. California* on the control of obscenity. *New York Law Review, 52,* 810–935.

LEVITT, E. E. (1979). Pornography: Some new perspectives on an old problem. *Journal of Sex Research, 5,* 247–259.

LEWITTES, D. J., & SIMMONS, W. L. (1975). Impression management of sexually motivated behavior. *Journal of Social Psychology, 96,* 39–44.

LIBBY, R. W., & STRAUS, M. A. (1980). Make love not war? Sex, sexual meanings, and violence in a sample of university students. *Archives of Sexual Behavior, 9,* 133–148.

LIEBERT, R. M., & SCHWARTZBERG, N. S. (1977). Effects of mass media. *Annual Review of Psychology, 28,* 141–173.

LIEBERT, R. N., SPRAFKIN, J. M., & DAVIDSON, E. S. (1982). *The early window: Effects of television on children and youth* (2nd Ed.). New York: Pergamon.

LINZ, D. (1985). *Sexual violence in the media: Effects on male viewers and implications for society.* Unpublished doctoral dissertation, University of Wisconsin, Madison.

LINZ, D., DONNERSTEIN, E., BROSS, M., & CHAPIN, M. (1986). Mitigating the influence of violence on television and sexual violence in the media. In R. Blanchard (Ed.), *Advances in the study of aggression* (Vol. 2). New York: Academic Press.

LINZ, D., DONNERSTEIN, E., & PENROD, S. (1984). The effects of multiple exposures to filmed violence against women. *Journal of Communication, 34,* 130–147.

———(1986). Sexual violence in mass media: Social psychological implications. In P. Shaver & C. Hendrick (Eds.), *Review of personality and social psychology* (Vol. 7). Beverly Hills: Sage.

LINZ, D., KRAFKA, C., DONNERSTEIN, E., & PENROD, S. (1986). *Combining the results of several studies on the effects of nonviolent pornography on male and female viewers.* Unpublished manuscript, University of Wisconsin, Madison.

LINZ, D., PENROD, S., & DONNERSTEIN, E. (1986). Media violence and antisocial behavior: Alternative legal policies. *Journal of Social Issues, 42*(3).

LINZ, D., TURNER, C. W., HESSE, B. W., & PENROD, S. D. (1984). Bases of liability for injuries produced by portrayals of violent pornography. In N. M. Malamuth & E. Donnerstein (Eds.), *Pornography and sexual aggression* (pp. 277–304). New York: Academic Press.

LIPTON, M. A. (1973). Fact and myth: The work of the Commission on Obscenity and Pornography. In J. Zubin & J. Money (Eds.), *Contemporary sexual behavior: Critical issues in the 1970's*. Baltimore: Johns Hopkins University Press.

LOCKHART, W. B., & McCLURE, R. C. (1954). Literature, the law of obscenity, and the constitution. *Minnesota Law Review, 38,* 295.

LONDON, J. (1977–78). Images of violence against women. *Victimology, 2,* 510–524.

LONGFORD, LORD (1972). *Pornography: The Longford Report*. London: Coronet Books.

LONGINO, H. E. (1980). Pornography, oppression and freedom: A closer look. In L. Lederer (Ed.), *Take back the night: Women on pornography*. New York: William Morrow.

LOVAS, O. I. (1971). Effect of exposure to symbolic aggression on aggressive behavior. *Child Development, 32,* 37–44.

LOVE, R. E., SLOAN, L. R., & SCHMIDT, M. J. (1976). Viewing pornography and sex guilt: The priggish, the prudent, and the profligate. *Journal of Consulting and Clinical Psychology, 44,* 624–629.

LOWRY, D. T., LOVE, G., & KIRBY, M. (1981). Sex on the soap operas: Patterns of intimacy. *Journal of Communication, 31,* 90–96.

LURIA, Z. (1982). Sexual fantasy and pornography: Two cases of girls brought up with pornography. *Archives of Sexual Behavior, 11,* 395–404.

MacDONALD, A. P., JR. (1983, February). A little bit of lavender goes a long way: A critique of research on sexual orientation. *The Journal of Sex Research, 19,* 94–100.

MacKINNON, C. (1984). Not a moral issue. *Yale Law and Policy Review, 2,* 321–345.

———(1985). Pornography, Civil Right, and Speech: Commentary. *Harvard Civil Rights-Civil Liberties Law Review, 20,* 1–70.

MALAMUTH, N. (1978, September). *Erotica, aggression and perceived appropriateness*. Paper presented at the annual meeting of the American Psychological Association, Toronto.

———(1981a). Rape fantasies as a function of exposure to violent sexual stimuli. *Archives of Sexual Behavior, 10,* 33–47.

————(1981b). Rape proclivity among males. *Journal of Social Issues, 37,* 138–157.

————(1982). *Predictors of aggression against female as compared to male targets of aggression.* Paper presented at the annual meeting of the American Psychological Association, Washington, D.C.

————(1983). Factors associated with rape as predictors of laboratory aggression against women. *Journal of Personality and Social Psychology, 45,* 432–442.

MALAMUTH, N. M. (1984). Aggression against women: Cultural and individual causes. In N. M. Malamuth & E. Donnerstein (Eds.), *Pornography and sexual aggression.* Orlando, FL:Academic Press.

————(1985). The mass media and aggression against women. *American Academy of Psychiatry and the Law Newsletter, 10,* 22–24.

————(1986). Predictors of naturalistic sexual aggression. *Journal of Personality and Social Psychology, 50,* 953–962.

————(in press). The mass media and aggression against women: Research findings and prevention. In G. Abel (Ed.), *Rape: Research and prevention.* New York: Brunner-Mazel.

MALAMUTH, N. M., & BILLINGS, V. (1986). The functions and effects of pornography: Sexual communication versus the feminist models in light of research findings. In J. Bryant & D. Zillmann (Eds.), *Perspectives on media effects.* Hillsdale, NJ: Eribaum.

MALAMUTH, N. M., & BRIERE, J. (1986). Sexual violence in the media: Indirect effects on aggression against women. *Journal of Social Issues, 42*(3).

MALAMUTH, N., & CENITI, J. (1986). Repeated exposure to violent and nonviolent pornography: Likelihood of raping ratings and laboratory aggression against women. *Aggressive Behavior, 12,* 129–137.

MALAMUTH, N. M., & CHECK, J. V. P. (1980a). Penile tumescence and perceptual responses to rape as a function of victim's perceived reactions. *Journal of Applied Social Psychology, 10,* 528–547.

————(1980b). Sexual arousal to rape and consenting depictions: The importance of the women's arousal. *Journal of Abnormal Psychology, 89,* 763–766.

————(1981a). The effects of mass media exposure on acceptance of violence against women: A field experiment. *Journal of Research in Personality, 15,* 436–446.

————(1983). Sexual arousal to rape depictions: Individual differences. *Journal of Abnormal Psychology, 92,* 55–67.

————(1984). Debriefing effectiveness following exposure to pornographic rape depictions. *Journal of Sex Research, 20,* 1–13.

————(1985). The effects of aggressive pornography on beliefs of rape myths: Individual differences. *Journal of Research in Personality, 19,* 299–320.

MALAMUTH, N. M., CHECK, J. V. P., & BRIERE, J. (1986). Sexual arousal in response to aggression: Ideological, aggressive and sexual correlates. *Journal of Personality and Social Psychology, 50,* 330–340.

MALAMUTH, N. M., & DONNERSTEIN, E. (1982). The effects of aggressive-pornographic mass media stimuli. In L. Berkowitz (Ed.), *Advances in experimental social psychology* (Vol. 15). New York: Academic Press.

———(Eds.). (1984). *Pornography and sexual aggression.* New York: Academic Press.

MALAMUTH, N., FESHBACH, S., FERA, T., & KUNATH, J. (1976, April). *Aggressivity in erotica.* Paper presented at the annual meeting of the Western Psychological Association, Los Angeles.

MALAMUTH, N., FESHBACH, S., & JAFFE, Y. (1977). Sexual arousal and aggression: Recent experiments and theoretical issues. *Journal of Social Issues, 33,* 110–133.

MALAMUTH, N., HABER, S., & FESHBACH, S. (1980). Testing hypotheses regarding rape: Exposure to sexual violence, sex differences, and the "normality" of rapists. *Journal of Research in Personality, 14,* 121–137.

MALAMUTH, N., HEIM, M., & FESHBACH, S. (1980). Sexual responsiveness of college students to rape depictions: Inhibitory and disinhibitory effects. *Journal of Personality and Social Psychology, 38,* 399–408.

MALAMUTH, N., REISIN, I., & SPINNER, B. (1979, September). *Exposure to pornography and reactions to rape.* Paper presented at the 87th annual convention of the American Psychological Association, New York.

MALAMUTH, N., & SPINNER E. (1980). A longitudinal content analysis of sexual violence in the best-selling erotica magazines. *Journal of Sex Research, 16,* 226–237.

MALLORY, C. H. (1974). An investigation of motor response measure of the approach-avoidance aspects of subjective reactions to filmed erotic stimuli. *Dissertation Abstracts International, 34(9-B),* 4635.

MANN, J., BERKOWITZ, L., SIDMAN, J., STARR, S., & WEST, S. (1974). Satiation of the transient stimulating effect of erotic films. *Journal of Personality and Social Psychology, 30,* 729–735.

MANN, J., SIDMAN, J., & STARR, S. (1970). Effects on erotic films on sexual behavior of married couples. In *Technical report of the Commission on Obscenity and Pornography* (Vol. 8). Washington, D.C.: U.S. Government Printing Office.

———(1973). Evaluating social consequences of erotic and sexual deviance: A retrospective surgery. *Journal of Social Issues, 29,* 133–139.

MANN, L., & JANIS, I. L. (1968). A follow-up study on the long-term effects of emotional role playing. *Journal of Personality and Social Psychology, 8,* 339–342.

Manual Enterprises v. *Day* (370, U.S. 478, 1962).

MARSHALL, W. L. (1979). Satiation therapy: A procedure for reducing deviant sexual arousal. *Journal of Applied Behavior Analysis, 12,* 377–389.

MARSHALL, W. L., & BARABEE, H. E. (1978). The reduction of deviant arousal: Satiation treatment for sexual aggressors. *Criminal Justice and Behavior, 5,* 294–303.

———— (1984). A behavioral view of rape. *International Journal of Law and Psychiatry, 7,* 51–77.

MASLIN, J. (1982, November 11). Bloodbaths debase movies and audiences. *New York Times.*

MASSAM, A. (1985, October 16). 'Nasties' a cause of violence on streets. *The London Standard.*

MAVISSAKALIAN, M., BLANCHARD, E., ABEL, G., BARLOW, D. (1975). Subjective and erectile responses to complex erotic stimuli in homosexual and heterosexual males. *British Journal of Psychology, 126,* 252–257.

McCARTHY, S. J. (1980, Sept/Oct). Pornography, rape, and the cult of macho. *The Humanist,* pp. 11–20.

McCAULEY, C., & SWANN, C. P. (1978). Male-female differences in sexual fantasy. *Journal of Research in Personality, 12,* 76–86.

McCONAHAY, N. (1974). Penile volume responses to moving and still pictures of male and female nudes. *Archives of Sexual Behavior, 3,* 565–570.

McCONAHAY, N., & CHECK, J. (1973). *Explorations in sex and violence.* Unpublished manuscript, Yale University.

McCONAHAY, S. A., & McCONAHAY, J. B. (1977). Sexual permissiveness, sex-role rigidity, and violence across cultures. *Journal of Social Issues, 33,* 134–143.

McCORMACK, T. (1978). Machismo in media research: A critical review of research on violence and pornography. *Social Problems, 25,* 544–555.

McCUTCHEON, B. A., & ADAMS, H. E. (1975). The physiological basis for implosive therapy. *Behaviour Research and Therapy, 13,* 93–100.

McGUIRE, W. J. (1985). The myth of massive media impact: Savagings and salvagings. In G. Comstock (Ed.), *Publication communication and behavior* (Vol. 1). New York: Academic Press.

McINTIRE, J., & TEEVAN, J. (1972). Television violence and deviant behavior. In G. A. Comstock & E. A. Rubinstein (Eds.), *Television and social behaviour, Vol. 3: Television and adolescent aggressiveness.* Washington, D.C.: U.S. Government Printing Office.

McKAY, H. B., & DOLFF, D. J. (1984). The impact of pornography: An analysis of research and summary of findings. In *Working papers on pornography and prostitution: Report 13.* Canada: Department of Justice.

Media and Values. (1985, Fall). Special issue: Violence and sexual violence in the media, *33.*

MERRIT, C. G., GERSTL, J. E., & LoSciuto, L. A. (1975). Age and perceived effects of erotica-pornography: A national sample study. *Archives of Sexual Behavior, 4,* 605–621.

MEYER, T. P. (1972a). The effects of sexually arousing and violent films on aggressive behavior. *Journal of Sex Research, 8,* 324–331.

———(1972b). The effects of viewing justified and unjustified real film violence on aggressive behavior. *Journal of Personality and Social Psychology, 23,* 21–29.

MICHELSON, P. (1975). The pleasures of commodity, or how to make the world safe for pornography. In R. C. Rist (Ed.), *The pornography controversy.* New Brunswick, NJ: Transaction Books.

MILAVSKY, J. R., KESSLER, R., STIPP, H., & RUBENS, W. (1982a). *Television and aggression: The results of a panel study.* New York: Academic Press.

———(1982b). Television and aggression: The results of a panel study. In D. Pearl, L. Bouthilet, & J. Lazar (Eds.), *Television and behavior: Ten years of scientific progress and implications for the 80's, Vol. 2): Technical Review.* Rockville, MD: National Institute of Mental Health.

Miller v. *California,* 413 U.S. 15 (1973).

MILLER, C. T. (1977). *Generalizability of the facilitating effect of anger on sexual arousal.* Unpublished master's thesis, Purdue University.

MILLER, C. T., BYRNE, D., & FISHER, J. D. (1980). Order effects and responses to sexual stimuli by males and females. *Journal of Sex Research, 16,* 131–147.

MILLER, R. (1985). *Bunny.* New York: Holt, Rinehart & Winston.

MILLER, R. L., BRICKMAN, P., & BOLAN, D. (1975). Attribution versus persuasion as for modifying behavior. *Journal of Personality and Social Psychology, 31,* 430–441.

MILLET, K. (1971). *The prostitution papers.* New York: Basic Books.

Mishkin v. *New York,* 383 U.S. 502 (1965).

MITCHELL, F. B. (1978). A preliminary investigation of reported sex attitudes in a sexually deviant group as a function of a stimulus presentation and group interaction. *Dissertation Abstracts International, 38 (7-B),* 3407.

MONEY, J. (1973). Pornography in the home: A topic in medical education. In J. Zubin & J. Money (Eds.), *Contemporary sexual behavior: Critical issues in the 1970's.* Baltimore: Johns Hopkins University Press.

———(1984). Declaration in Reply Brief of the American Civil Liberties Union and the Indiana Civil Liberties Union as *Amici Curiae. Ameri-*

can Booksellers Association v. *Hudnut,* Cause no. IP 84-791C, (S. D. Ind., 1984).

———(1985). Gender: History, theory and usage of the term in sexology and its relationship to nature/nurture. *Journal of Sex and Marital Therapy, 11,* 71–79.

MONEY, J., & LEHNE, G. K. (1983). Biomedical and criminal-justice concepts of paraphilia: Developing convergence. *Medicine and Law, 2,* 257–261.

MOREAULT, D. M. (1978). Women's sexual fantasies: As a function of sex guilt and experimental sexual stimulation. *Dissertation Abstracts International, 38 (9-B),* 4989.

MOREAULT, D. M., & FOLLINGSTAD, D. R. (1978). Sexual fantasies of females as a function of sex guilt and experimental response cues. *Journal of Clinical and Consulting Psychology, 46,* 1385–1393.

MORGAN, R. (1978a, November). How to run the pornographers out of town (and preserve the First Amendment). *Ms, 8,* 55; 78–80.

———(1978b). *Going too far.* New York: Vintage Books.

———(1980). Theory and practice: Pornography and rape. In L. Lederer (Ed.), *Take back the night: Women on pornography.* New York: William Morrow.

MOROKAFF, P. J., & HEIMAN, J. R. (1980). Effects of erotic stimuli on sexually functional and dysfunctional women: Multiple measures before and after sex therapy. *Behaviour Research and Therapy, 18,* 127–137.

MOSHER, D. L. (1970).Sex callousness toward women. In *Technical report of the Commission on Obscenity and Pornography,* (Vol. 7): Washington, D.C.: U.S. Government Printing Office.

———(1973). Sex differences, sex experience, sex guilt, and explicitly sexual films. *Journal of Social Issues, 29,* 95–112.

———(1979). Sex guilt and sex myths in college men and women. *The Journal of Sex Research, 15,* 224–234.

MOSHER, D. L., & ABRAMSON, P. R. (1972). Subjective sexual arousal to films of masturbation. *Journal of Consulting and Clinical Psychology, 45,* 796–807.

MOSHER, D. L., & ANDERSON, R. D. (1986). Macho personality, sexual aggression, and reactions to guided imagery of realistic rape. *Journal of Research in Personality, 20,* 77–94.

MOSHER, D. L., & KATZ, H. (1971). Pornographic films, male verbal aggression against women, and guilt. *Technical report of the Commission on Obscenity and Pornography*(Vol. 8). Washington, D.C.: U.S. Government Printing Office.

MOSHER, D. L., & O'GRADY, K. E. (1979). Homosexual threat, negative attitudes toward masturbation, sex guilt, and males' sexual and affective reactions to explicit sexual films. *Journal of Consulting and Clinical Psychology, 47,* 860–873.

———(1979). Sex guilt, trait anxiety, and females' subjective sexual arousal to erotica. *Motivation and Emotion, 3,* 235–250.

MOSHER, D. L., & WHITE, B. B. (1980). Effects of committed or casual erotic guided imagery on females' subjective sexual arousal and emotional response. *Journal of Sex Research, 16,* 273–733.

MUELLER, C. W., & DONNERSTEIN, E. (1977). The effects of humor-induced arousal upon aggressive behavior. *Journal of Research in Personality, 11,* 73–82.

———(1981). Film-facilitated arousal and prosocial behavior. *Journal of Experimental Social Psychology, 17,* 31–41.

MUELLER, C. W., NELSON, R., & DONNERSTEIN, E. (1977). Facilitative effects of media violence on helping. *Psychological Reports, 40,* 775–778.

MULVEY, E. P., & HAUGAARD, J. L. (1986). *Report of the Surgeon General's workshop on pornography and public health.* U.S. Public Health Service, Washington, DC.

MURDOCK, G. (1982). Mass communication and sexual violence: A critical review of recent research trends. In P. Marsh & A. Campbell (Eds.), *Aggression and violence.* Oxford: Basil Blackwell.

NATIONAL ASSOCIATION OF BROADCASTERS. (1973). Code Authority. *Television Code* (19th edition). In F. J. Kahn (Ed.), *Documents of American broadcasting* (2nd ed.). New York: Appleton-Crofts.

NATIONAL COMMISSION ON THE CAUSES AND PREVENTION OF VIOLENCE. (1969). *Report.* Washington, D.C.: U.S. Government Printing Office.

NAWY, H. (1971). The San Francisco erotic market place. In *Technical report of the Commission on Obscenity and Pornography* (Vol. 9). Washington, D.C.; U. S. Government Printing Office.

———(1973). In the pursuit of happiness? Consumers of erotica in San Francisco. *Journal of Social Issues, 29,* 147–161.

NELSON, E. C. (1982). Pornography and sexual aggression. In M. Yaffe & E. C. Nelson (Eds.), *The influence of pornography on behavior.* New York: Academic Press.

NELSON, G. K. (1985). The findings of the National Viewers' Survey. In G. Barlow & A. Hill (Eds.), *Video violence and children.* New York: St. Martin's Press.

New York Times (1973, October 4). Six youths burn woman to death in Boston attack.

New York v. *Ferber,* 458 U.S. 747 (1982).

NOTE. (1984). *Harvard Law Review, 98,* pp. 460–481.

NOBILE, P., & NADLER, E. (1986). *United States of America vs. Sex: How the Meese Commission lied about pornography.* New York: Minotaur.

Oakland Tribune (1983, August 6). Two accused of murder in snuff film.

O'GRADY, K. E. (1982). Affect, sex guilt, gender, and the rewarding-punishing effects of erotic stimuli: A reanalysis and reinterpretation. *Journal of Personality and Social Psychology, 43,* 618–622.

Olivia v. *National Broadcasting Co., Inc.* (1978). *California Reporter, 141,* 511–515.

ORNE, M. T. (1969). Demand characteristics and quasi-controls. In R. Rosenthal & R. L. Rosnow (Eds.), *Artifact in behavior research.* New York: Academic Press.

OSBORN, C. A., & POLLACK, R. H. (1977). The effects of two types of erotic literature on physiological and verbal measures of female sexual arousal. *Journal of Sex Research, 13,* 250–256.

PALLY, M. (1985). Ban sexism, not pornography. *The Nation, 240,* 784–813.

PALMER, C. E. (1979). Pornographic comics: A content analysis. *Journal of Sex Research, 15,* 285–297.

PALYS, T. S. (1984). A content analysis of sexually explicit videos in British Columbia. *Working Papers on Pornography and Prostitution, Report No. 15.* Department of Justice, Ottawa, Ontario.

———(1986). Testing the common wisdom: The social content of video pornography. *Canadian Psychology, 27,* 22–35.

PALYS, T. S., & LOWMAN, J. (1984). *A study of the definition and contents of pornographic media.* Application for Research Grant from the Social Science and Humanities Research Council of Canada.

Paris Adult Theatre I. v. *Slaton,* 413 U.S. 49 (1973).

PARKE, R. D., BERKOWITZ, L., LEVINE, J. P., WEST, S. G., & SEBASTIAN, R. J. (1977). Some effects of violent and non-violent movies on the behavior of juvenile delinquents. In L. Berkowitz (Ed.), *Advances in experimental social psychology* (Vol. 10). New York: Academic Press.

PARSONS, J. E. (1982, March). *Sex differences in achievement patterns.* Paper presented at the meetings of the American Psychological Association, Washington, D.C.

PAUL, G. L., & BERNSTEIN, D. A. (1973). *Anxiety and clinical problems: Systematic desensitization and related techniques.* Morristown, NY: General Learning Press.

PENROD, S., & LINZ, D. (1984). Using psychological research on violent pornography to inform legal change. In N. M. Malamuth & E. Donnerstein (Eds.), *Pornography and sexual aggression.* Orlando, FL: Academic Press.

People v. *Winters*, 63 N.E. 2d 98 (1945).

PERDUE, W. C., & LESTER, D. (1972). Personality characteristics of rapists. *Perceptual and Motor Skills, 35,* 514.

PERLMAN, B. J., & WEBER, S. J. (1979). The effects of pre-information on reactions to a violent passage and an erotic passage. *Journal of Social Psychology, 109,* 127–138.

PILIAVIN, J. A., PILIAVIN, I. M., & TRUDELL, B. (1974). *Incidental arousal, helping, and diffusion of responsibility.* Unpublished data, University of Wisconsin, Madison.

PINCUS, S., & WATERS, L. K. (1976). Effect of age restrictions and pornographic content on desirability of reading material. *Psychological Reports, 38,* 943–947.

PIRKE, K., KOCKOTT, G., & DITTMAR, F. (1974). Psychosexual stimulation and plasma testosterone in man. *Archives of Sexual Behavior, 3,* 577–584.

POMEROY, W. (1984). Declaration in Reply Brief of the American Civil Liberties Union and the Indiana Civil Liberties Union as *Amici Curiae. American Booksellers Association* v. *Hudnut,* Cause no. IP 84-791C, (S.D. Ind., 1984).

Pornography and Prostitution in Canada. (1985). Report of the Special Committee on Pornography and Prostitution (Vol. 1). Ottawa, Canada: Canadian Government Publishing Centre.

PRESCOTT, J. W. (1975, March-April). Body pleasure and the origins of violence. *Futurist,* pp. 64–80.

PROPPER, M. M. (1971). Exposure to sexually oriented materials among young male prisoners. *Technical report of the Commission on Obscenity and Pornography* (Vol. 8). Washington, D.C.: U.S. Government Printing Office.

PROSSER, W., & WADE, J. W. (1971). *Cases and materials on torts* (5th ed.). Mineola, NY: Foundation Press.

PRZYBYLA, D. P. J., & BYRNE, D. (1984). The mediating role of cognitive processes in self-reported sexual arousal. *Journal of Research in Personality, 18,* 54–63.

Public Hearings on Ordinances to Add Pornography as Discrimination Against Women: Before the Minneapolis City Council Gov't Operations Comm. 1st Sess. 4-12 (Dec. 12, 1983).

QUANTY, M. (1976). Aggression catharsis. In R. G. Geen & E. C. O'Neal (Eds.), *Perspectives on aggression.* New York: Academic Press.

Queen v. *Fred Wagner* (1985, January 16). In the Court of Queen's Bench of Alberta: Judicial District of Calgary.

QUINSEY, V. L., & CARRIGAN, W. F. (1978). Penile responses to visual stimuli. *Criminal Justice and Behavior, 5,* 333–341.

QUINSEY, V. L., CHAPLIN, T. C., & CARRIGAN, W. F. (1981). Biofeedback and signaled punishment in the modification of inappropriate sexual age preferences. *Behavior Therapy, 11,* 567–576.

QUINSEY, V., CHAPLIN, T., & VARNEY, G. (1981). A comparison of rapists' and non-sex offenders' sexual preferences for mutually consenting sex, rape and physical abuse of women. *Behavioral Assessment, 3,* 127–135.

QUINSEY, V. L., & CHAPLIN, T. C. (1982). Penile responses to non-sexual violence among rapists. *Criminal Justice and Behavior, 9,* 372–381.

R. v. *Red Hot Video Ltd.* (1985). 45 *Criminal Reports* (3d). 36.

R. v. *Wagner* (1985). 43 *Criminal Reports* (3d). 318.

RACHMAN, S. (1966). Sexual fetishism: An experimental analogue. *Psychological Record, 16,* 293–296.

RACHMAN, S., & HODGSON, R. J. (1968). Experimentally induced 'sexual fetishism': Replication and development. *Psychological Record, 18,* 25–27.

RADA, R. T. (1977). MMPI profiles of exposers, rapists, and assaulters in a court services population. *Journal of Consulting and Clinical Psychology, 45,* 61–69.

———(1978). *Clinical aspects of the rapist.* New York: Grune & Stratton.

———(1978). Social factors in rapist behaviour. In R. T. Rada, (Ed.), *Clinical aspects of the rapist.* New York: Grune & Stratton.

RADA, R. T., LAWS, D., & KELLNER, R. (1976). Plasma testosterone levels in the rapist. *Psychosomatic Medicine, 38,* 257–268.

RADAR, C. M. (1977). MMPI profile types of exposers, rapists, and assaulters in a court services population. *Journal of Consulting and Clinical Psychology, 45,* 61–69.

RAMIREZ, J., BRYANT, J., & ZILLMANN, D. (1982). Effects of erotica on retaliatory behavior as a function of level of prior provocation. *Journal of Personality and Social Psychology, 43,* 971–978.

RAPAPORT, K., & BURKHART, B. R. (1984). Personality and attitudinal characteristics of sexually coercive college males. *Journal of Abnormal Psychology, 93,* 216–221.

RAY, R. E., & THOMPSON, W. D. (1974). Autonomic correlates of female guilt responses to erotic visual stimuli. *Psychological Reports, 34,* 1299–1306.

RAY, R. E., & WALKER, E. (1973). Biographical and self-report correlates of female guilt responses to visual erotic stimuli. *Journal of Consulting and Clinical Psychology, 41,* 93–96.

REAGE, P. (1965). *The story of O.* New York: Grove Press.

REED, J. P., & REED, R. S. (1972). P.R.U.D.E.S. (Pornography research using direct erotic stimuli). *Journal of Sex Research, 8,* 237–246.

———(1973). Consensus and dissensus in pornography definitions: A content analysis. *International Behavioural Scientist, 5,* 1–12.

REID, L. D. (1973). Processes of fear reduction in systematic desensitization: An addendum to Wilson and Davidson (1971). *Psychological Bulletin, 79,* 107–109.

REIFLER, C. B., HOWARD, J., LIPTON, M. A., LIPTZIN, M. B., & WIDMANN, D. E. (1971). Pornography: An experimental study of effects. *American Journal of Psychiatry, 128,* 575–582.

REISMAN, J. A. (1985, June 18). About my study of 'Dirty Pictures'. *Washington Post.*

———(1985, November 21). *A content analysis of "Playboy", "Penthouse", and "Hustler" magazines with special attention to the portrayal of children, crime, and violence.* Testimony before the United States Attorney General's Commission on Pornography, Miami, Florida.

REPORT TO THE SURGEON GENERAL. (1972). *Television and growing up: Impact of televised violence.* Washington, D.C.: U.S. Government Printing Office.

RICHARDS, D. A. J. (1974-1975). Free speech and obscenity law: Toward a moral theory of the First Amendment. *University of Pennsylvania Law Review, 123,* 45–91.

RIGER, S., & GORDON, M. T. (1981). The fear of rape: A study in social control. *Journal of Social Issues, 37,* 71–92.

RIGGS, R. E. (1981). *Miller v. California* revisited: An empirical note. *Brigham Young University Law Review, 2,* 247–273.

RIST, R. C. (1975). *The pornography controversy: Changing moral standards in American life.* New Brunswick, NJ: Transaction Books.

ROPER ORGANIZATION, INC. (1981, July). *Sex, profanity, and violence: An opinion survey about seventeen television programs.* Conducted for the National Broadcasting Company and presented to The New York Advertising Company.

ROSE, V. M. (1977a). Rape as a social problem: A by-product of the feminist movement. *Social Problems, 25,* 75–89.

———(1977b). The rise of the rape problem. In A. Mauss & J. Wolfe (Eds.), *Our land of promises: The rise and fall of social problems in America.* Philadelphia: Lippincott.

ROSEN, L., & TURNER, S. (1969). Exposure to pornography: An exploratory study. *Journal of Sex Research, 5,* 235–246.

ROSEN, R. C., & KEEFE, F. J. (1978). The measure of human penile tumescence. *Psychophysiology, 15,* 366–376.

ROSENE, J. M. (1971). *The effects of violent and sexually arousing film content: An experimental study.* Unpublished doctoral dissertation, Ohio University.

ROSENTHAL, R. (1976). The "file drawer problem" and tolerance for null results. *Psychological Bulletin, 86,* 638–641.

——— (1986). The social consequences of small effects of media on anti-social behavior. *Journal of Social Issues, 42*(3).

ROSENTHAL, R., & ROSNOW, R. L. (1975). *The volunteer subject.* New York: Wiley.

Roth v. *United States,* 354 U.S. 476 (1957).

ROWLAND, W. D. (ED.). (1983). *The politics of TV violence: Policy uses of communication research.* Beverly Hills: Sage.

RUBIN, Z. (1970). Measurement of romantic love. *Journal of Personality and Social Psychology, 16,* 265–273.

RULE, B. G., & FERGUSON, T. J. (1986). The immediate effects of media violence on attitudes, emotions and cognitions. *Journal of Social Issues, 42*(3).

RUSSELL, D. E. H. (1975). *The politics of rape.* New York: Stein & Day.

——— (1977). *Pornography: A feminist perspective.* Presentation at the Symposium " Women against violence and pornography in the media," San Francisco.

——— (1980a). Pornography and the women's liberation movement. In L. Lederer (Ed.), *Take back the night: Women on pornography. New York: William Morrow.*

——— (1980b). Pornography and violence: What does the new research say? In L. Lederer (Ed.), *Take back the night: Women on pornography.* New York: William Morrow.

——— (1980c). Testimony against pornography: Witness from Denmark. In L. Lederer (Ed.), *Take back the night: Women on pornography.* New York: William Morrow.

——— (1983). The prevalence and incidence of forcible rape and attempted rape of females. *Victimology: An International Journal, 7,* 1–4.

——— (1984). *Sexual exploitation: Rape, child sexual abuse and workplace harassment.* Beverly Hills: Sage.

SANDFORD, D. A. (1974). Patterns of sexual arousal in heterosexual males. *Journal of Sex Research, 10,* 150–155.

SAPOLSKY, B. S. (1977). The effect of erotica on annoyance and hostile behavior in provoked and unprovoked males. *Dissertation Abstracts International, 38*(8-A), 4433.

——— (1984). Arousal, affect, and the aggression-moderating effect of erotica. In N. M. Malamuth and E. Donnerstein (Eds.), *Pornography and sexual aggression.* Orlando, FL: Academic Press.

SAPOLSKY, B. S., & ZILLMANN, D. (1981). The effect of soft-core and hard-core erotica on provoked and unprovoked hostile behavior. *Journal of Sex Research, 17,* 319–343.

SAUNDERS, D. G., LYNCH, A., GRAYSON, M, & LINZ, D. (1986). *The inventory of beliefs about wife-beating: The development and initial validation of an attitude measure.* Unpublished manuscript, University of Wisconsin, Madison.

SCHAEFER, H. H., & COLGAN, A. H. (1977). The effect of pornography on penile tumescence as a function of reinforcement and novelty. *Behavior Therapy, 8,* 938–946.

SCHAUER, F. (1979). Speech and "speech" — Obscenity and "obscenity": An exercise in the interpretation of constitutional language. *Georgia Law Journal, 67,* 899.

Schenck v. United States, 249 U.S. 47 (1919).

SCHILL, T., & CHAPIN, J. (1972). Sex guilt and males' preference for reading erotic magazines. *Journal of Consulting and Clinical Psychology, 39,* 516.

SCHILL, T., VAN TUINEN, M., & DOTY, D. (1980). Repeated exposure to pornography and arousal levels of subjects varying in guilt. *Psychological Reports, 46,* 467–471.

SCHMIDT, G. (1975). Male-female differences in sexual arousal and behavior during and after exposure to sexually explicit stimuli. *Archives of Sexual Behavior, 4,* 353–364.

SCHMIDT, G., & SIGUSCH, V. (1970). Sex differences in responses to psychosexual stimulation by films and slides. *Journal of Sex Research, 6,* 268–283.

———(1973). Women' sexual arousal. In J. Zubin and J. Money (Eds.), *Contemporary sexual behavior: Critical issues in the 1970's.* Baltimore: Johns Hopkins University Press.

———(1980, September 3). Comment: The effects of pornography. *British Journal of Sexual Medicine, 7,* 3–6.

SCHMIDT, G., SIGUSCH, V., & SCHAFER, S. (1973). Responses to reading erotic stories: Male-female differences. *Archives of Sexual Behavior, 2,* 181–199.

SCHOETTLE, U. C. (1980). Treatment of the child pornography patient. *American Journal of Psychiatry, 137,* 1109–1115.

SCHWARTZ, T. (1982, May 23). Do the networks need violence? *New York Times.*

SCHWARZ, N., & BRAND, J. F. (1983). Effects of salience of rape on sex role attitudes, trust, and self-esteem in non-raped women. *European Journal of Social Psychology, 13,* 71–76.

SCHWENDINGER, J., & SCHWENDINGER, H. (1983). *Rape and inequality.* Beverly Hills: Sage.

SCOTT, D. A. (1985, March). Pornography and its effects on family, community, and culture. *Family Policy Insights, 4*(2), entire issue.

SCOTT, J. E. (1985, May). *Violence and erotic material: The relationship between adult entertainment and rape.* Paper presented at the annual meeting for the American Association for the Advancement of Science, Los Angeles, California.

—————(in press). An updated longitudinal content analysis of sex references in mass circulation magazines. *Journal of Sex Research.*

SEARS, D. O. (1986). College sophomores in the laboratory: Influence of a narrow data base on social psychology's view of human nature. *Journal of Personality and Social Psychology, 51,* 515–530.

SEGAL, Z. V., & MARSHALL, W. L. (1985). Heterosexual social skills in a population of rapists and child molesters. *Journal of Consulting and Clinical Psychology, 53,* 55–63.

SEGAL, Z. V., & STERMAC, L. (1984). A measure of rapists' attitudes towards women. *International Journal of Law and Psychiatry, 7,* 437–440.

SHERIF, C. W. (1980). Comment on ethical issues in Malamuth, Heim, & Feshbach's "Sexual responsiveness of college students to rape depictions: Inhibitory and disinhibitory effects." *Journal of Personality and Social Psychology, 38,* 409–412.

SHIPP, E. R. (1984, May 15). Civil rights law against pornography is challenged. *New York Times.*

SHOHAM, S. G. (1982). The interdisciplinary study of sexual violence. *Deviant Behavior: An Interdisciplinary Journal, 3,* 245–274.

SHULMAN, C. (1986, July 21). Pornography: A poll. *Time, 128,* 22.

SIGUSCH, V., SCHMIDT, G., REINFELD, A., & WIEDEMANN-SUTOR, I. (1970). Psychosexual stimulation: Sex differences. *Journal of Sex Research, 6,* 10–24.

SILBERT, M. H., & PINES, A. M. (1984). Pornography and sexual abuse of women. *Sex roles, 10,* 857–868.

SLADE, J. (1984). Violence in the hard-core pornographic film: An historical survey. *Journal of Communication, 34,* 148–163.

SMITH, D. D. (1976a). *Sexual aggression in American pornography: The stereotype of rape.* Paper presented at the annual meeting of the American Sociological Association, New York.

—————(1976b). The social content of pornography. *Journal of Communication, 26,* 16–33.

SMITH, M. A., CHECK, J. V. P., & HENRY, M. J. (1984, May-June). *Sexual violence in the mass media: A content analysis of feature-length films.* Paper presented at the meeting of the Canadian Psychological Association, Ottawa, Ontario.

SOBEL, L. A. (ED.). (1979). *Pornography, obscenity, and the law.* New York: Facts on File.

Sonenschein, D. (1972). Dynamics in the uses of erotics. *Adolescence, 7,* 233–244.

Soothill, K., & Jack, A. (1975). How rape is reported. *New Society, 32,* 702–703.

Sorenson, R. (1972). *Adolescent sexuality in contemporary America.* New York: World.

Spak, M. (1981). Predictable harm: Should the media be liable? *Ohio State Law Journal, 42,* 671–687.

Sparks, G. G. (1986). Developing a scale to assess cognitive responses to frightening films. *Journal of Broadcasting and Electronic Media, 30,* 65–73.

Spence, J. T., & Helmreich, R. L. (1978). *Masculinity and femininity.* Austin, TX: University of Texas Press.

Sprafkin, J. N., & Silverman, L. T. (1981). Update: Physically intimate and sexual behaviour on prime time television: 1978–1979. *Journal of Communication, 31,* 34–40.

Sprafkin, J. N., Silverman, L. T., & Rubinstein, E. A. (1980). Reactions to sex on television: An exploratory study. *Public Opinion Quarterly, 44,* 303–315.

Stanley v. *Georgia.* 394 U.S. 557 (1969).

Stanmeyer, W. A. (1977–78). Obscene evils v. obscure truths: Some notes on first principles. *Capital University Law Review, 7,* 647–682.

Stauffer, J., & Frost, R. (1976). Explicit sex: Liberation or exploitation? Male and female interest in sexually-oriented magazines. *Journal of Communications, 26,* 25–30.

Steele, D. G. (1973). *Female responsiveness to erotic films and its relation to attitudes, sexual knowledge, and selected demographic variables.* Unpublished doctoral dissertation, Baylor University.

Steele, D. G., & Walker, C. E. (1974). Male and female differences in reaction to erotic stimuli as related to sexual adjustment. *Archives of Sexual Behavior, 3,* 459–470.

——— (1976). Female responsiveness to erotic films and the "ideal" erotic film from a feminine perspective. *Journal of Nervous and Mental Disease, 162,* 266–273.

Steinem, G. (1980). Erotica and pornography: A clear and present difference. In L. Lederer (Ed.), *Take back the night: Women on pornography.* New York: William Morrow.

Steinman, D. L., Wincze, J. P., Sakheim, Barlow, D. H., & Mavissakalian, M. (1981). A comparison of male and female patterns of sexual arousal. *Archives of Sexual Behavior, 10,* 529–547.

Sterling, B. (1977). The effects of anger, amibiguity, and arousal on helping behavior. *Dissertation Abstracts International, 38,* 1962.

STERN, M. L. (1978). The effect of erotic film-induced of exercise-induced physiological arousal on an instrumental measure of altruistic behavior. *Dissertation Abstracts International, 39(3-B),* 1463.

STOCK, W. E. (1982, November). *The effect of violent pornography on women.* Paper presented at the Society for the Scientific Study of Sex (SSSS), San Francisco.

———(1983). *The effects of violent pornography on the sexual responsiveness and attitudes of women.* Unpublished doctoral dissertation, State University of New York at Stony Brook.

———(1984). *Women's affective responses and subjective reactions to exposure to violent pornography.* Unpublished manuscript, Texas A & M University, Department of Psychology, College Station.

———(1985). Male power, hostility, and sexual coercion. In E. Allgeier, R. Allgeier, T. Perper, & W. Stock, (Eds.), *Sexual coercion.* New York: SUNY Press.

STOLLER, R. J. (1979). Centerfold. *Archives of General Psychiatry, 36,* 1019–1024.

STONE, G. R. (1986). Antipornography legislation as viewpoint discrimination. *Harvard Journal of Law & Public Policy, 9,* 701.

STONE, L. E. (1985). *Child pornography literature: A content analysis.* Unpublished doctoral dissertation. International College, San Diego, CA.

STRAUS, M. (1973). A general systems theory approach to a theory of violence between family members. *Social Science Information, 12,* 105–125.

STUART, I. R., & GREER, J. G. (1984). *Victims of sexual aggression. Treatment of children, women, and men.* New York: Van Nostrand Reinhold.

SUE, D. (1979). Erotic fantasies of college students during coitus. *Journal of Sex Research, 15,* 299–305.

SUNSTEIN, C. (in press). Pornography and the First Amendment. *Duke Law Journal.*

SURGEON GENERAL'S SCIENTIFIC ADVISORY COMMITTEE ON TELEVISION AND SOCIAL BEHAVIOR (1972). *Television and growing up: The impact of televised violence.* Washington, D.C.: U.S. Government Printing Office.

SURGEON GENERAL'S SCIENTIFIC ADVISORY COMMITTEE. (1972). *Television and growing up: The impact of televised violence: Report to the Surgeon General.* U.S. Public Health Service, Dept. of Health, Education, and Welfare Publication N. HSM 72–9090. Rockville, MD: National Institute of Mental Health.

Swearingen v. *United States,* 161 U.S. 446 (1896).

SYMPOSIUM ON MEDIA VIOLENCE AND PORNOGRAPHY (1984, February 5). Symposium at the Ontario Institute for Studies in Education, Toronto, Ontario.

TANNENBAUM, P. H. (1970). Emotional arousal as a mediator of erotic communication effects. *Technical report of the Commission on Obscenity and Pornography* (Vol. 8). Washington, D.C.: U.S. Government Printing Office.

TANNENBAUM, P. H., & ZILLMANN, D. (1975). Emotional arousal in the facilitation of aggression through communication. In L. Berkowitz (Ed.), *Advances in experimental social psychology* (Vol. 8). New York: Academic Press.

TAYLOR, S. P. (1967). Aggressive behavior and physiological arousal as a function of provocation and the tendency to inhibit aggression. *Journal of Personality, 35,* 297–310.

TAYLOR, S. P., & EPSTEIN, S. (1967). Aggression as a function of the interaction of the sex of the victim. *Journal of Personality, 35,* 474–486.

THISTLE, F. (1980). Hollywood goes ape over rape. *Game, 7,* pp. 23–25; 84.

THOMAS, M. H. (1982). Physiological arousal, exposure to a relatively lengthy aggressive film, and aggressive behavior. *Journal of Research in Personality, 16,* 72–81.

THOMAS, M. H., & DRABMAN, R. S. (1975). Toleration of real life aggression as a function of exposure to televised violence and age of subject. *Merrill-Palmer Quarterly, 21,* 227–232.

THOMAS, M. H., HORTON, R. W., LIPPENCOTT, E. C., & DRABMAN, R. S. (1977). Desensitization to portrayals of real-life aggression as a function of exposure to television violence. *Journal of Personality and Social Psychology, 35,* 450–458.

THOMAS, M. H., & TELL, P. M. (1974). Effects of viewing real versus fantasy violence upon interpersonal aggression. *Journal of Research in Personality, 8,* 153–160.

THOMPSON, J. J., & DIXON, P. W. (1974). A power function between ratings of pornographic stimuli and psychophysical responses in young normal adult women. *Perceptual and Motor Skills, 38,* 1236–1238.

TIEGER, T. (1981). Self-reported likelihood of raping and the social perception of rape. *Journal of Research in Personality, 15,* 147–158.

TIEGER, T., & ARONSTAM, J. (1981, August). *"Brutality Chic" images and endoresement of rape myths.* Presented at 1981 Annual Convention of the American Psychological Association, Los Angeles.

Time (1978, April 5). *The Porno Plague,* pp. 58–63.

TJADEN, P. G. (1985, November). *Pornography and sex education.* Paper presented at the Annual Meetings of the American Society of Criminology, San Diego, California.

TURNER, C. W., & SIMONS, L. S. (1974). Effects of subjects sophistication and evaluation apprehension on aggressive responses to weapons. *Journal of Personality and Social Psychology, 30,* 341–348.

TVERSKY, A., & KAHNEMAN, D. (1973). Availability: A heuristic for judging frequency and probability. *Cognitive Psychology, 5,* 207–232.

——— (1982). Availability: A heuristic for judging frequency and probability. In D. Kahneman, P. Slovic, A. Tversky (Eds.), *Judgment under uncertainty: Heuristics and biases.* New York: Cambridge University Press.

UNITED STATES DEPARTMENT OF JUSTICE (1982, April). Violent crime by strangers. *Bureau of Justice Statistics: Bulletin.* Washington, D.C.: U.S. Department of Justice.

——— (1983, May). New state laws and the system's response: Victim and witness assistance. *Bureau of Justice Statistics: Bulletin.* Washington, D.C.: U.S. Department of Justice.

——— (1983, December). An overview of criminal justice systems: The American response to crime. *Bureau of Justice Statistics: Bulletin.* Washington, D.C.: U.S. Department of Justice.

——— (1984, April). Family violence. *Bureau of Justice Statistics: Special Report.* Washington, D.C.: U.S. Department of Justice.

——— (1984, June). Criminal victimization 1983. *Bureau of Justice Statistics: Bulletin.* Washington, D.C.: U.S. Department of Justice.

United States v. *Harriss,* 347 U.S. 612, 617 (1954).

United States v. *One Book Called "Ulysses."* 5 F. Supp. 182 (S.D. N.Y., 1933).

VANCE, C. S. (1985, April). What does the research prove? *Ms., 8,* 40.

VAN DEN HAAG, E. (1967). Is pornography a crime? *Encounter, 29,* p. 53.

Village Voice (1977, May 9). Pretty poison: The selling of sexual warfare, pp. 18–23.

WADE, J. W. (1973). On the nature of strict tort liability for products. *Mississippi Law Journal, 44,* 825–851.

WAKSHLAG, J., VIAL, V., & TAMBORI, R. (1983). Selecting crime drama and apprehension about crime. *Human Communication, 10,* 227–242.

WALKER, C. E. (1970). Erotic stimuli and the aggressive sexual offender. In *Technical reports of the Commission on Obscenity and Pornography* (Vol. 7). Washington, D.C.: U.S. Government Printing Office.

WALLACE, D. H. (1973). Obscenity and contemporary community standards: A survey. *Journal of Social Issues, 29,* 53–68.

WALLACE, D. H., & WEHMER, G. (1971). Pornography and attitude change. *Journal of Sex Research, 7,* 116–125.

——— (1972). Evaluations of visual erotica by sexual liberals and conservatives. *Journal of Sex Research, 8,* 147–153.

WALSCHE-BRENNAN, K. S. (1976). Psychodynamics of pornography. *Nursing Mirror and Midwives Journal, 142,* 58–60.

WALSTER, E. (1966). Assignment of responsibility for an accident. *Journal of Personality and Social Psychology, 3,* 73–79.

WARE, E., BROWN, M., AMOROSO, D., PILKEY, W., & PRUESSE, M. (1972). The semantic meaning of pornographic stimuli for college males. *Canadian Journal of Behavioral Science, 4,* 204–209.

WARING, E. M., & JEFFERIES, J. J. (1974). The conscience of a pornographer. *Journal of Sex Research, 10,* 40–46.

WARREN, E. J. (1975). Obscenity laws — A shift to reality. In R. C. Rist (Ed.), *The pornography controversy,* New Brunswick, NJ: Transaction.

WATHEN, P. W. (1981, September 12). Schiro's sexual behavior linked to pornography. *The Evansville (Indiana) Courier.*

WATTS, W. A. (1967). Relative persistence to opinion change induced by active compared to passive participation. *Journal of Personality and Social Psychology, 5,* 4–15.

WEBER, S. J., & COOK, D. T. (1972). Subject effects in laboratory research: An examination of subject roles, demand characteristics, and valid inference. *Psychological Bulletin, 77,* 273–295.

Webster's Third New International Dictionary (1965). Springfield, MA: G. & C. Merriam.

WEIDNER, G., & GRIFFITT, W. (1983). Rape: A sexual stigma? *Journal of Personality, 51,* 152–166.

WEIS, K., & BORGES, S. S. (1973). Victimology and rape: The case of the legitimate victim. *Issues in Criminology, 8,* 71–115.

WERTHAM, F. (1948, May 24). The comics . . . very funny! *Saturday Review of Literature,* p. 19.

WHITE, L. A. (1978). Affective response to erotic stimulation and human aggression. *Dissertation Abstracts International. 39(2-B),* 965.

———— (1979). Erotica and aggression: The influence of sexual arousal, positive affect, and negative affect on aggressive behavior. *Journal of Personality and Social Psychology, 37,* 591–601.

WHITE, L., FISHER, W., BYRNE, D., & KINGMEN, R. (1977, May). *Development and validation of a measure of affective orientation to erotic stimuli.* Paper presented at the Midwestern Psychological Association, Chicago.

Whitney v. *California,* 274 U.S. 357 (1927).

WILKINS, W. (1971). Desensitization: Social and cognitive factors underlying the effectiveness of Wolpe's procedure. *Psychological Bulletin, 76,* 311–317.

WILLIAMS, J., & HOLMES, R. A. (1981). *The second assault: Rape and public attitudes.* Westport, CT: Greenwood Press.

WILLIS, E. (1981, July 12). Nature's revenge: Review of *Pornography and Silence* and *Pornography. New York Times.*

WILLS, G. (1977, August). Measuring the impact of erotica. *Psychology Today, 11,* pp. 30–34; 74–76.

WILSON, G. T., LAWSON, D. M., & BRAMS, D. B. (1978). Effects of alcohol on sexual arousal in male alcoholics. *Journal of Abnormal Psychology, 87,* 609–616.

WILSON, J. Q. (1974). Violence, pornography and social science. In V. B. Cline (Ed.), *Where do we draw the line?* Provo, UT: Brigham Young University Press.

———(1975). Violence, pornography and social science. In R. C. Rist (Ed.), *The pornography controversy.* New Brunswick: Transaction Books.

WILSON, W. C. (1973). Law enforcement officers' perceptions of pornography as a social issue. *Journal of Social Issues, 29,* 41–51.

———(1978). Can pornography contribute to the prevention of sexual problems? In C. B. Qualls, J. P. Wincze, & D. H. Barlow (Eds.), *The prevention of sexual disorders: Issues and approaches.* New York: Plenum.

WILSON, W. C., & ABELSON, H. I. (1972). Experience with and attitudes toward explicit sexual materials. *Journal of Social Issues, 29,* 19–39.

WILSON, W., & LIEDTKE, V. (1984). Movie-inspired sexual practices. *Psychological Reports, 54,* 328.

WINCZE, J., HOON, P., & HOON, E. (1977). Sexual arousal in women: A comparison of cognitive and physiological responses by continuous measurement. *Archives of Sexual Behavior, 6,* 121–133.

WINICK, C. (1971). Some observations on characteristics of patrons of adult theatres and bookstores. In *Technical reports of the Commission on Obscenity and Pornography* (Vol. 9). Washington, D.C.: U.S. Government Printing Office.

———(1985). A content analysis of sexuality explicit magazines sold in adult bookstores. *Journal of Sex Research, 21,* 206–210.

Winters v. *New York,* 333 U.S. 507 (1948).

WISHNOFF, R. (1978). Modeling effects of explicit and nonexplicit sexual stimuli on the sexual anxiety and behavior of women. *Archives of Sexual Behavior, 7,* 455–461.

WOBER, M. (1984). See as you would be seen by: 'Video Nasty'antagonists in a personality mirror. *Psychology News & In Mind, 37,* 7.

WOLCHIK, S. A., BRAVER, S. L., & JENSEN, K. (1985). Volunteer bias in erotica research: Effects in intrusiveness of measure and sexual background. *Archives of Sexual Behavior, 14,* 93–107.

WOLCHIK, S. A., SPENCER, S. L., & LISI, I. S. (1983). Volunteer bias in research employing vaginal measures of sexual arousal: Demographic, sexual and personality characteristics. *Archives of Sexual Behavior, 12,* 339–408.

WOLFE, J., & BAKER, V. (1980). Characteristics of imprisoned rapists and circumstances of the rape. In C. G. Warner (Ed.), *Rape and sexual assault.* Germantown, MD: Aspen Systems Co.

WOLPE, J. (1958). *Psychotherapy by reciprocal inhibition.* Stanford, CA: Stanford University Press.

WOLPE, J., & LANG, F. J. (1964). A fear survey schedule for use in behavior therapy. *Behavior Research and Therapy, 2,* 27–30.

WYER, R., BODENHAUSEN, G. V., & GORMAN, T. F. (1985). Cognitive mediators of reactions to rape. *Journal of Personality and Social Psychology, 48,* 324–338.

WYER, R. S., & SRULL, T. K. (1980). The processing of social stimulus information: A conceptual integration. In R. Hastie, T. M. Ostrom, E. B. Ebbesen, R. S. Wyer, D. L. Hamilton, & D. E. Carlston (Eds.), *Person memory: The cognitive basis of social perception.* Hillsdale, NJ: Erlbaum.

YAFFE, M. (1974, January 24). Letter to the editor. *New Society,* p. 211.

YAFFE, M., & NELSON, E. C. (EDS.) (1982). *The influence of pornography on behaviour.* New York: Academic Press.

Young v. American Mini Theatres, 427 U.S. 50, 66 (1976).

ZELLINGER, D. A., FROMKIN, H. L., SPESLER, D. E., & KOHN, D. A. (1975). A commodity theory analysis of the effects of age restrictions on pornographic materials. *Journal of Applied Psychology, 60,* 94–99.

ZELLMAN, G. L., GOODCHILDS, J. D., JOHNSON, P. B., & GIARRUSSO, R. (1981, August). *Teenagers' application of the label "rape" to nonconsensual sex between acquaintances.* Symposium presented at the meeting of the American Psychological Association, Los Angeles.

ZILLMANN, D. (1971). Excitation transfer in communication-mediated aggressive behavior. *Journal of Experimental Social Psychology, 7,* 419–434.

———(1979). *Hostility and aggression.* Hillsdale, NJ: Erlbaum.

———(1980). Anatomy of suspense. In P. H. Tannenbaum (Ed.), *The entertainment function of television.* Hillsdale, NJ: Erlbaum.

———(1984). *Victimization of women through pornography.* Proposal to the National Science Foundation, Indiana University, Bloomington.

———(1986). Coition as emotion. In D. Byrne & K. Kelley (Eds.), *Approaches to human sexuality.* Albany, NY: SUNY Press.

ZILLMANN, D., & BRYANT, J. (1982). Pornography, sexual callousness, and the trivialization of rape. *Journal of Communication, 32,* 10–21.

———(1984). Effects of massive exposure to pornography. In N. Malamuth & E. Donnerstein (Eds.), *Pornography and Sexual Aggression.* New York: Academic Press.

———(1986). *Pornography's impact on sexual satisfaction.* Unpublished manuscript, Indiana University, Bloomington.

ZILLMANN, D., BRYANT, J., & CARVETH, R. A. (1981). The effect of erotica featuring sadomasochism and bestiality on motivated intermale aggression. *Personality and Social Psychology Bulletin, 7,* 153–159.

ZILLMANN, D., BRYANT, J., COMISKY, P. W., & MEDOFF, N. J. (1981). Excitation and hedonic valence in the effect of erotica on motivated intermale aggression. *European Journal of Social Psychology, 11,* 233–252.

ZILLMANN, D., HOYT, J. L., & DAY, K. D. (1974). Strength and duration of the effect of aggressive, violent, and erotic communications on subsequent aggressive behavior. *Communication Research, 1,* 286–306.

ZILLMANN, D., & JOHNSON, R. C. (1973). Motivated aggressiveness perpetuated by exposure to aggressive films and reduced by exposure to nonaggressive films. *Journal of Research in Personality, 7,* 261–276.

ZILLMANN, D., KATCHER, A. H., & MILAVSKY, B. (1972). Excitation transfer from physical exercise to subsequent aggressive behavior. *Journal of Experimental Social Psychology, 8,* 247–259.

ZILLMANN, D., & MUNDORF, N. (1986, April). *Effects of sexual and violent images in rock-music videos on music appreciation.* First-place paper of the BEA Faculty Paper Competition presented at the 31st Annual Convention of the Broadcast Education Association, Dallas.

ZILLMANN, D., & SAPOLSKY, B. (1977). What mediates the effect of mild erotica on annoyance and hostile behavior in males.? *Journal of Personality and Social Psychology, 35,* 587–596.

ZILLMANN, D., & WAKSHLAG, J. (1985). Fear of victimization and the appeal of crime drama. In D. Zillmann & J. Bryant (Eds.), *Selective Exposure to Communication,* Hillsdale, NJ: Erlbaum.

ZILLMANN, D., WEAVER, J. B., MUNDORF, N. & AUST, C. F. (1986). Effects of an opposite-gender companion's affect to horror on distress, delight, and attraction. *Journal of Personality and Social Psychology, 51,* 586–594.

ZUCKERMAN, M. (1971). Physiological measures of sexual arousal in the human. *Psychological Bulletin, 75,* 297–329.

———(1976). *Research on pornography: Sex and the life cycle.* New York: Grune & Stratton.

ZUCKERMAN, M., & LUBIN, B. (1965). *Manual for the Multiple Affect Adjective Check List.* San Diego, CA: Educational and Industrial Testing Service.

APPENDIX 1

Annotated Bibliography: Research Conducted for the 1970 Commission on Obscenity and Pornography

Volume 6

1. *Public attitudes towards and experience with erotic materials,* H. Abelson, R. Cohen, E. Heaton, & C. Suder. *Aims:* National survey of adults and young people in the United States to determine (1) the amount and type of exposure individuals have had to pornography; (2) their attitudes toward the control of sexually explicit materials; and (3) the relationship between certain demographic characteristics and exposure to erotica. *Results:* A majority of respondents (more than 90 percent of men and more than 80 percent of women) have had experience with sexual materials, although they differ in what they consider pornographic. Respondents considered the effects of viewing erotica to be harmless. However, there was some indication that, if scientists were to find negative effects, respondents might favor some form of censorship.

2. *Public attitudes towards and experience with erotic materials: methodological report,* L. LoSciuto, A. Spector, E. Michels, & C. Jenne. *Aims:* A report on the method used to conduct the national survey. Complete questionnaires are provided along with sampling plan.

Volume 7

1. *Exposure to pornography and sexual behavior in deviant and normal groups,* M. J. Goldstein, H. S. Kant, L. L. Judd, C. J. Rice, & R. Green. *Aims*: Use of pornography and subsequent behavior by sexual offenders. *Types of subjects*: Institutionalized sex offenders, noninstitutionalized sexual deviants (homosexuals, transsexuals), users of pornography, and controls. *Results*: Rapists report less exposure to sexual materials during adolescence compared to the control group. In addition, they report less exposure during the last year to sexual materials.

2. *Erotic stimuli and the aggressive sexual offender,* C. E. Walker. *Aims*: Do sexual and nonsexual offenders differ in their rate of exposure to pornography, and do they differ in their thoughts, fantasies, and ideas following exposure to pornography? *Subjects*: Rapists; convicted nonsexual offenders; and a control group. *Results*: No differences in amount of exposure, with controls having had first exposure at a younger age. Some indication that rapists have exposure to different types of materials, but the author does not tell us what types. Rapist group, more than nonsexual offenders, indicated that pornography led them to commit their crime and had something to do with their being in prison. They also believed that their sexual activity increased more after exposure than controls believed.

3. *Pornography and the sex offender: Patterns of exposure and immediate arousal effects of pornographic stimuli,* R. F. Cook and R. H. Fosen. *Aims*: Differences in exposure patterns and arousal levels of sex offenders versus nonsexual offenders. The type and frequency of exposure during childhood and the effect the material had on their current crime. *Subjects*: Sexual and nonsexual offenders. *Measures of arousal*: Self-report. *Materials*: 26 slides. No pictures of violence or aggressive images. *Results*: The two groups did not differ in arousal to the sexual materials or in self-reported exposure to pornography in the year before going to prison. There was no evidence that pornography was viewed by the sexual offenders during a 24-hour period before their crime. Sex offenders reported less exposure during childhood and adolescence. Finally sex offenders indicated more masturbation after exposure to pornography while nonsex offenders engaged in more sexual relations after exposure.

4. *Sex offenders' experience with erotica,* W. T. Johnson, L. R. Kupperstein, & J. J. Peters. *Aims*: Sex offenders' experience with sexual materials. *Subjects*: Offenders of sex crimes versus males surveyed in national study by Abelson et al. for the commission. *Results*: Sex offenders and

nonsex offenders first viewed pornography at a similar age. Sex offenders report more exposure to pornography after age 21 than do nonoffenders. The sex offenders tended to have more contact with written materials that had violent themes (e.g., involving whips, belts, spanking). When discussing their most recent exposure to pornography, sex offenders reported that the material had less overall impact (either positive or negative) on them than nonsex offenders reported.

5. *Exposure to pornography, character, and sexual deviance,* K. E. Davis & G. N. Braucht. *Aims:* Study the impact of pornography on moral development and deviant behavior. Is it possible that people at lower stages of moral development are more likely to seek out pornographic material than are those at higher stages of development? *Subjects:* Males between 18 and 30. No sexual offenders. College students, seminary students, and county jail inmates. *Results:* Early exposure to pornography was found to be correlated with sexual deviance and moral development. Stronger effects after age 17. The authors suggest that low moral character may contribute to a deviant lifestyle in which searching out pornography plays a part.

6. *Pornography and sex crimes: the Danish experience,* R. Ben Veniste. *Aim:* Examination of sex crimes in Copenhagen since pornography has been available. *Results:* From 1967 (year of enactment of law) through 1969 the number of sex crimes decreased. The author indicates that violent pornography, if available, may increase sex crimes, but no data on the effects of violent pornography are available at this time.

7. *Towards an explanation of the decrease in registered sex crimes in Copenhagen,* B. Kutchinsky. *Aim:* What may account for the decrease in sex crimes in Copenhagen? Is it due to a change in attitudes? *Subjects:* Interviews of 400 people in Copenhagen. *Results:* The data suggest that, for the crimes of peeping and physical indecency toward girls, attitude change is not the reason for the decreases; the availability of pornography best accounts for these reductions.

8. *Erotica and antisocial behavior: an analysis of selected social indicator statistics,* L. R. Kupperstein & W. C. Wilson. *Aim:* Is there a relationship between crime statistics and availability of pornography in the United States? *Results:* The availability of sexually explicit materials increased two- to fivefold between 1960 and 1969. Although the number of sex offenses increased during this time, they did not increase as much as nonsexual crimes.

9. *A pilot comparison of two research instruments measuring exposure to pornography,* H. S. Kant, M. J. Goldstein, & D. J. Lepper. *Aim:* The comparison of two interview instruments to measure attitudes and

experience with pornography. *Results:* The two instruments received similar responses, but there were some differences which researchers should note when using these questionnaires.

Volume 8

1. *An investigation of behavioral, psychological, and physiological reactions to pornographic stimuli,* D. M. Amoroso, M. Brown, M. Pruesse, E. E. Ware, & D. W. Pilkey. *Aim:* How long would individuals expose themselves to pornography as a function of sexual arousal and being alone or with others? Also, would there be changes in sexual activity after exposure to pornography? *Subjects:* College students. *Materials:* 27 slides. No aggressive materials. *Results:* Subjects spent less time looking at the slides if they were with other subjects. The only reported changes in activity were in masturbation and dreams, with no reported change in sexual activity with another person.

2. *The effect of erotic stimuli on sex arousal, evaluative responses, and subsequent behavior,* D. Byrne & J. Lamberth. *Aim:* Effects of exposure to sexual stimuli on arousal, evaluations, and later behavior. *Subjects:* 42 married couples. *Results:* Little difference between male and female subjects in reported arousal after exposure to pornography, and little change in actual sexual behavior after exposure.

3. *Reactions to viewing films of erotically realistic heterosexual behavior,* K. E. Davis & G. N. Braucht. *Aim:* Various reactions to sexual films. Look at arousal, thoughts, and behavior as a function of demographics and prior exposure to such materials. *Results:* Individuals with established heterosexual relationships were more likely to engage in sexual activity after viewing sexually explicit films. Those without an established relationship were more sexually aroused and indicated increased masturbation following film exposure.

4. *Effects of exposure to pornography,* J. L. Howard, C. B. Reifler, & M. B. Liptzin. *Aim:* The effects of long-term exposure to pornography. Look at effects on sexual arousal, attitudes, and behavior. *Design:* Subjects first saw a pornographic movie, then for the following three weeks were exposed to various pornographic stimuli. They then saw a second pornographic movie, waited eight weeks, and returned to see a third movie. *Results:* Subjects showed decreased responsiveness (moods, interest, sexual arousal) with repeated exposure to pornography. However, they became more liberal in their attitudes toward pornography.

5. *The effect of pornography: A pilot experiment on perception, behavior, and*

attitudes, B. Kutchinsky. *Aim*: Effect of one hour of exposure to pornography on attitudes immediately after exposure and two weeks later. *Results*: There were no changes in attitudes about sex crimes, nor a desire to see more pornography. Subjects tended to find the material more boring and less interesting after the one hour of exposure. Sexual activity during the first 24 hours after exposure was reported if subjects were in the experiment with their spouse.

6. *Effects of erotic films on sexual behavior of married couples*, J. Mann, J. Sidman, & S. Starr. *Aim*: Effects of exposure to pornography on married couples over a 12-week period. *Design*: View one film a week (about 25 min) for four weeks. *Results*: Subjects reported increases in their sexual activity on film-viewing nights.

7. *Psychological reactions to pornographic films*, D. L. Mosher. *Aim*: To assess the immediate impact of viewing two pornographic films. *Results*: Both males and females did not report increased sexual behavior within 24 hours after film exposure, although subjects talked more about sex and had more sexual fantasies during this time. There was a decrease in sex-calloused attitudes for males, and high-sex-guilt subjects (people who feel anxious about sexual matters) found the films more pornographic.

8. *Sex callousness toward women*, D. L. Mosher. *Aim*: Development of sex-callousness survey. *Results*: The scale that measured sex-calloused attitudes was correlated with sexual aggression in men.

9. *Emotional arousal as a mediator of erotic communication effects*, P. H. Tannenbaum. *Aim*: To demonstrate that emotional arousal from film exposure is a more important determinant of aggressive behavior than actual content (e.g., aggressive depictions). *Results*: A highly arousing sexual film led to more aggressive behavior than a less arousing aggressive film. A sexual film was found, however, to increase rewarding behavior if subjects were in a positive mood. The addition of aggressive images and content to a sexual film also increased aggression, as did the censoring of explicit portions of a pornographic film.

10. *Pornographic films, verbal aggression against women, and guilt*, D. L. Mosher & H. Katz. *Aim*: Does viewing a pornographic film increase verbal aggression against a women. *Subjects*: College students. *Results*: Sexual arousal from viewing a sexually explicit film was not related to aggression. Male subjects did increase their verbal aggression against a woman if they were informed that doing this would result in their being able to view another pornographic film.

Author Index

Subject Index